WINNING AT IT:
Grant Writing for Technology Grants

Corporate & Government Tech Grants
With Winning Proposals & Projects for
Individuals - Libraries & Museums - Non-Profits
Health - K-12 Schools - Colleges & Universities -
National Science Foundation Eligible Organizations

A Technology Grant News Publication

[Winning At Information Technology:
Grant Writing for Technology Grants]

Winning At IT:
Grant Writing for Technology Grants

Corporate & Government Tech Grants
With Winning Proposals & Projects for
Individuals - Libraries & Museums - Non-Profits
Health - K-12 Schools - Colleges & Universities
- National Science Foundation Eligible Organizations

(c) 2009 Technology Grant News
A Technology Grant News Publication
561 Hudson Street #23
New York, N.Y. 10014

ISBN: 1-933639-56-3
978-1-933639-56-7

Library of Congress Cataloguing-in-Publication Data Pending

PREFACE

"TECHNOLOGY GRANT NEWS HAS GRANTED YOUR WISH FOR A SOURCE THAT COVERS TECHNOLOGY GRANTS IN ONE PLACE," SAYS AMERICAN LIBRARY ASSOCIATION'S AMERICAN LIBRARIES

If you are writing a grant application for a technology grant, Winning at IT has done the leg work for you. Winning at IT shows you winning proposals and projects, with models of thinking and examples you can use to write your grant applications. It shows you - how it is done, who has gone before you, and how they have done it. Winning at IT also shows over 75 ongoing current technology grant award programs available for your sector - for Individuals, Libraries & Museums, Non-Profits, Health, K-12 Schools, Colleges & Universities, or all organizations eligible for National Science Foundation grants.. We have done the research for you.

The goal in this approach is to:
- Allow you to see "what" funders are funding
- Allow you to "get ideas" from other people's winning projects
- Allow you to see "how" a winning proposal is framed and put forward
- Give you "real" examples of actual winning proposals
- Show you by example "how" to construct a winning proposal

This reader:

- Shows over 75 ongoing current technology grant opportunities – awarded and to be awarded in the future. Our companion publication, Everything Technology, Directory of Technology Grants-Awards-Contests-Fellowships ISBN: 1-933639-45-8 covers over 700 technology grant and award programs for Non-Profits, Libraries & Museums, K-20 Schools, Colleges & Universities, Health, and Individuals.
- Covers winning grants and recent awards made under these technology grant programs
- Covers over 75 grant award programs available across the different sectors, showing the unique and specialized applications chosen and funded
- Covers winning grants made to Non-Profits, Libraries & Museums, K-12 Schools, Colleges & Universities, Health and Individuals
- Shows actual proposals

We are providing you "models" of thinking, based on real winning projects that you can use in developing your own thoughts and in constructing your applications.

You are in for a treat in our section on writing K-12 Tech Grants. Bryan Feci, Fourth-Grade Teacher in California, shares his enthusiastic saavy writing winning grants. His articles, with actual grant proposals winning over $28,000 in technology equipment for his classroom, model how to go about developing a tech grant program for your classroom or school.

TABLE OF CONTENTS

COLLEGES & UNIVERSITIES 168

Category: Individuals-Awards-Contests-Competitions-Scholarships-Fellowships

AAUW Fellowships and Grants

AAUW Educational Foundation
Dept. 60
301 ACT Drive
Iowa City, IA 52243-4030
319/337-1716 ext. 60
http://www.aauw.org/education/fga//fellowships_grants/index.cfm
http://tiny.cc/UbXov

Description

One of the world's largest sources of funding exclusively for graduate women, the AAUW Educational Foundation supports aspiring scholars around the globe, teachers and activists in local communities, women at critical stages of their careers, and those pursuing professions where women are underrepresented.

Recent Awards, Winning Projects & Award Winners

Career Development Grants
http://tiny.cc/AQyjx
Name Felicia E. Battle
Degree and Field M.I.S.M., Information security
Institution DeVry University
Location Charlotte, North Carolina
Award Year 2007-08
After receiving a bachelor's degree in information systems management, Felicia Battle served as a senior reporting specialist for one of the top five U.S. banks. She recently become a corporate information security officer and will pursue Certified Information Security Systems Professional accreditation. She plans to diversify the largely male-dominated field and serve as a role model for minorities and women.

Name Marilyn A. Hines
Degree and Field M.L.I.S., Library science
Institution University of Rhode Island
Location Greene, Rhode Island
Award Year 2007-08
Marilyn Hines' academic interests include an exploration of the influence of gender—or cultural conceptions of gender—on a child's educational experience. She's looking particularly at interventions that successfully minimize the observed gender gap in technology. She plans to work as a school library specialist, teaching information literacy and bridging gender gaps in the use of technology.

Name Stephanie L. Sapienza
Degree and Field M.A., Moving image archive studies
Institution University of California, Los Angeles
Location West Hollywood, California
Award Year 2007-08
Stephanie has worked as a researcher and associate producer for documentaries and television shows for more than six years. With a master's degree, she aims to broaden access for documentary filmmakers and help public-access news archives digitize their collections and program experimental film series.

Name Lisa E. Smith
Degree and Field M.S., Forensic sciences
Institution George Washington University
Location Arlington, Virginia
Award Year 2007-08
A career and a longtime passion for forensic science prompted Lisa Smith to study computer forensics. She plans to conduct computer investigations of high-tech crimes, such as computer virus attacks, identity theft, fraud, and child pornography to ensure that the Internet is a safe place for individuals, consumers, and children.

Name Faith G. Cole
Degree and Field M.A., City and regional planning
Institution University of Pennsylvania
Location Philadelphia, Pennsylvania
Award Year 2007-08
With a master's degree, Faith Cole plans to work as a local planner, helping create healthy and sustainable urban environments that are accessible to all residents. She received a bachelor's degree from Carnegie Mellon University, where she majored in history-anthropology and German and minored in international relations.

Name Cheri E. Johnson
Degree and Field A.A., Interior design
Institution Art Institute of New York City
Location New York, New York
Award Year 2007-08
After teaching and working for a number of nonprofit organizations, Cheri Johnson has seen a need for organizations to have efficient, uplifting spaces. She aims to own her own design company and employ women who share her dream of doing pro bono work for needy organizations and low-income individuals.

Selected Professions Fellowships
http://tiny.cc/DJr5s

Name Melissa A. Straw
Degree and Field M.S.I.S., Conservation
Institution University of Texas, Austin
Location Albuquerque, New Mexico
Award Year 2007-08
Melissa Straw plans to repair books as a collections care conservator at an academic research library. She sees the dissemination of information as crucial and believes that if bindings are too weak for books and papers to be handled, research materials cannot serve their original purpose.

Name Robyn D. Wilmouth
Degree and Field M.S.E., Civil and environmental engineering
Institution University of Washington
Location Seattle, Washington
Award Year 2007-08
Robyn Wilmouth focuses on water and sanitation systems, their appropriate design and use, and their implications for public health. She plans to work with small communities in Latin America, India, or China to establish potable water systems, safe drinking water standards, and an appropriate sanitation infrastructure.

Name Jessica J. Braun
Degree and Field M.Arch., Architecture
Institution University of Texas, Austin
Location Austin, Texas
Award Year 2007-08
Jessica Braun has always been interested in the ways in which humans creatively affect their daily living environment. Her dedication to social relevance and community service brought her to architecture as a graduate degree. She will use design as a vehicle for community service and a means to reconcile the human environment and the health of the larger natural environment.

Name Zoé Edgecomb
Degree and Field M.Arch., Architecture
Institution University of Virginia
Location Charlottesville, Virginia
Award Year 2007-08
The convergence of art and science into design has characterized the trajectory of Zoé Edgecomb's career. Beginning with painting and sculpture, she has experimented in many media to explore the structure of human life. Architecture has provided a way of contextualizing the human within the natural. She continues to seek ways of harmonizing and understanding these intertwined systems.

Name Katherine E. Scott
Degree and Field M.Arch., Urban planning
Institution Columbia University
Location Brooklyn, New York
Award Year 2007-08
Kate Scott believes that design has a role in addressing critical challenges facing today's cities. Using short-term installations, she aims to enact change at an individual, a neighborhood, and, over time, a city scale. She is interested in adaptive reuse projects and the use of fabrication technologies to develop customizable designs that respond to an individual's needs.

Name Alyson B.R. Tanguay
Degree and Field M.Arch., Architecture
Institution Harvard University
Location Cambridge, Massachusetts
Award Year 2007-08
Project Name A Revalorization of Modernist Utopia, From the Ground Up
Alyson Tanguay's academic career has been characterized by the pursuit of a broader understanding of architecture. Beyond the classroom, she works to promote the inclusion of voices that have been underrepresented in the field. She aims to contribute to civic and public projects that establish her as a thoughtful designer and productive citizen.

<u>**American Fellowships**</u>
http://tiny.cc/GpCWr
Name M. Maille Lyons
Degree and Field Ph.D., Oceanography
Institution University of Connecticut
Location Swansea, Massachusetts
Award Year 2007-08
Project Name The Role of Marine Aggregates in the Ecology of Aquatic Pathogens Associated With Bivalve Mollusks
Maille Lyons focuses on diseases associated with filter-feeding bivalve mollusks (e.g., clams and oysters), including bivalve pathogens and human pathogens acquired via the consumption of contaminated bivalves. Her discovery of pathogens in marine snow opens a new area of research in marine disease ecology.

ACLS Digital Innovation Fellowships

American Council of Learned Societies
633 Third Avenue, 8th floor
(40th - 41st Streets)
New York, NY 10017-6795
212-697-1505 x124
Saul Fisher (Director of Fellowship Programs)
http://www.acls.org/grants/Default.aspx?id=508
http://tiny.cc/jXWbJ

Description

This program supports digitally based research projects in all disciplines of the humanities and humanities-related social sciences. It is hoped that projects of successful applicants will help advance digital humanistic scholarship by broadening understanding of its nature and exemplifying the robust infrastructure necessary for creating further such works.

ACLS Digital Innovation Fellowships are intended to support an academic year dedicated to work on a major scholarly project that takes a digital form.

The aim of this program is to provide scholars the means to pursue intellectually significant projects that deploy digital technologies intensively and innovatively.

Recent Awards, Winning Projects & Award Winners

Flower, John M., Director, Chinese Studies and Global Initiatives, Sidwell Friends School (Dr. Flower was Associate Professor, History, University of North Carolina, Charlotte at the time of the award.)
Moral Landscape in a Sichuan Mountain Village: A Digital Ethnography of Place

This project explores the histories, beliefs, livelihoods, and local identities in Xiakou Village, China, in order to understand Xiakou as an evolving cultural landscape, defined as the interwoven field of physical environment, historical memory, and moral agency. The project comprises an online monograph, media archive, and information structures integrating essays, multimedia artifacts, and GIS maps. The project's digital form vividly reveals the interconnected dimensions of village life, highlights the relationship between source and interpretation, opens up non-linear paths through the ethnography, and pioneers digital ethnography as a widely applicable model for the presentation of humanities research.

Rubin, Anne Sarah, Associate Professor, History, University of Maryland, Baltimore County
Through the Heart of Dixie: Sherman's March and America Mapping Memory

This project explores the myriad ways Americans have remembered William Tecumseh Sherman's 1864-65 march through Georgia, South Carolina, and North Carolina. It uses memories of the march to examine Americans' thoughts on war in general and the American Civil War in particular. It shows different ways of presenting layers of information, primarily through maps and images, but also through sound and text, and incorporates census data, fiction, film, and photographs. This is the digital component of a larger project exploring the impact of the march on the landscape of Georgia, South Carolina, and North Carolina.

Seed, Patricia, Professor, History, University of California, Irvine
The Development of Mapping on the West and South Coasts of Africa by Portuguese Navigators and Cartographers from 1434-1504

The project digitally analyzes the earliest nautical charts of western and southern Africa both to discover their method of construction and to locate African communities and landscapes on the eve of contact with Europeans.

Tsivian, Yuri, Professor, Film, University of Chicago
Cinemetrics: An Open-Access Interactive Website Designed to Collect, Store, and Process Scholarly Data about Film Editing Across the History of Cinema

This project involves the completion of the online application Cinemetrics, an extensive, multifaceted collection of digital data related to film editing. Currently programmed to handle the aspect of editing known in film studies as cutting rates, cinemetrics is expanding into a site that provides a comprehensive multifaceted picture of the factors that effected film editing in the span of its 100-year long-history. Users will view the correlations that exist between the film's dynamic profile, its genre, and its type of story; access the way in which cultural factors define the tempo of film editing; and get a sense of interdependency between cutting rates, on the one hand, and shot scales, staging practices, acting styles, and camera movements on the other.

Adobe® Design Achievement Awards

http://www.adaaentry.com/contact.php
http://tiny.cc/qDKWc

http://www.adobe.com/education/adaa/
http://tiny.cc/dSMJ4

Description

The Adobe® Design Achievement Awards celebrate student achievement reflecting the powerful convergence of technology and the creative arts. The competition — which showcases individual and group projects created with industry-leading Adobe creative software — honors the most talented and promising student graphic designers, photographers, illustrators, animators, digital filmmakers, developers, and computer artists from the world's top institutions of higher education.

The ADAA competition is open to full-time higher education students in the United States, Canada, the United Kingdom, Australia, Austria, Belgium, China, Croatia, the Czech Republic, Denmark, Finland, France, Germany, Hungary, India, Ireland, Italy, Japan, Korea, Mexico, The Netherlands, New Zealand, Norway, Portugal, Singapore, South Africa, Spain, Sweden, Switzerland, Taiwan, Thailand, Malaysia, Brazil, and Turkey. Projects must be original works completed 50% or more with Adobe software after May 1, 2007.

Recent Awards, Winning Projects & Award Winners

Animation

Winner
Axel Broetje
Braunschweig University of Art
Fische und Schiffe (http://tiny.cc/ZDZ3J)

Finalist:
Johnny Kelly
Royal College of Art
Shelly (http://tiny.cc/2r1xh)

Finalist:

Sean Monahan
Minneapolis College of Art & Design
Rebirth (http://tiny.cc/w30Vv)
Honorable Mentions (http://tiny.cc/fBLIC)

Motion Graphics

Winner:
Benjamin Stephan, Lutz Vogel
University of Applied Sciences Augsburg
Trusted Computing (http://tiny.cc/47qyc)

Finalist:
Jarratt Moody
Savannah College of Art & Design
Meshwork Cinema (http://tiny.cc/gLJlY)

Finalist:
Justin Schrader
Rochester Institute of Technology
Fuse Audio (http://tiny.cc/kTxRs)
Honorable Mentions (http://tiny.cc/RmPPr)

Digital Illustration

Winner:
Jörg Block
Hamburg University of Applied Sciences
Research calendar of the Hamburg University of Applied Sciences 2008 (http://tiny.cc/h8Wyd)

Finalist:
Aaron Kapor, Ricardo Beltran, Yuri Chung,
Kevin Wong
Art Center College of Design
YAY! GPK! (http://tiny.cc/g1Csx)

Finalist:
Cristian Zuzunaga, Peter Smith
Royal College of Art
QUADRAT menswear collection (http://tiny.cc/DpNdj)
Honorable Mentions (http://tiny.cc/PCGw7)

Digital Photography

Winner:
Sean Teegarden
Art Center College of Design
True Character (http://tiny.cc/qQRkt)

Finalist:
Michael Kai
Dortmund University of Applied Science
This Side Up (http://tiny.cc/siw9E)

Finalist:
Julia Bruns
Fachhochschule Würzburg-Schweinfurt
Künstliche Menschlichkeit (http://tiny.cc/uyVxo)
Honorable Mentions (http://tiny.cc/eoz3g)

Environmental Graphics and Packaging

Winner:
Po-Yun Jack Wang
California College of the Arts
You think therefore I am (http://tiny.cc/pjhFD)

Finalist:
Julie Tinker
School of Visual Arts
Our Bodies Our Shelves: A Souvenir Stand for the Sexual Revolution
http://tiny.cc/akdDr

Finalist:
Gertrude Wong
George Brown College
Designing for Dyslexics (http://tiny.cc/CnCpu)
Honorable Mentions (http://tiny.cc/xvdh5)

Interactive and Web Design

Winner:
Kyle Phillips
Minneapolis College of Art & Design
Generative Engine (http://tiny.cc/TA0CJ)

Finalist:
William Ismael
Art Center College of Design
williamismael.com (http://tiny.cc/4WjpX)

Finalist:
Carolin Horn
Massachusetts College of Art
Florian Jenett
Academy of Art and Design Offenbach am Main
Anymails (http://tiny.cc/BKkKj)
Honorable Mentions (http://tiny.cc/hO40q)

Live Action

Winner:
Sean Dekkers
Rochester Institute of Technology
Vulnerant Omnes Ultima Necat (http://tiny.cc/t3zzi)

Finalist:
James Sutton
Coventry U. School of Art & Design
Space Cowboy ft. Nadia Oh - Something 4 The Weekend Music Video (http://tiny.cc/xmjiF)

Finalist:
Marcos Ceravolo
Vancouver Film School
Drop (http://tiny.cc/VPT4t)
Honorable Mentions (http://tiny.cc/BGfUb)

Print Design Multi-page

Winner:
Aaron Kapor
Art Center College of Design
Car Color Timeline (http://tiny.cc/6M4xF)

Finalist:
Sung-Ho Bae
Keimyung university
Nine inverse proportion problems we have (http://tiny.cc/P3ucR)

Finalist:
Sarah Cooper, Nina Gorfer
HDK School of Design and Crafts at Göteborg University
SEEK Volume 01: Iceland (http://tiny.cc/N5TIg)
Honorable Mentions (http://tiny.cc/2zV3l)

Print Design Single page

Winner:
Soo Jin An
Kookmin University
Part of my life (http://tiny.cc/L5Kkf)

Finalist:
Tyler Lang
Ringling School of Art and Design
Ringling Admissions Poster (http://tiny.cc/CYIyp)

Finalist:
Christian Eggenberger
University of the Applied Sciences and Arts in Zurich
How to apply for a Non-immigrant visa to enter the U.S (http://tiny.cc/jPmtx)

The ALISE Award for Teaching Excellence in the Field of Library and Information Science Education

65 East Wacker Place, Suite 1900
Chicago, IL 60601-7246 USA
1 312 795 0996
Dr. Suzanne Stauffer
http://www.alise.org/mc/page.do?sitePageId=55537
http://tiny.cc/q0pdm

Description

ALISE (Association for Library and Information Science Education) is a non-profit organization that serves as the intellectual home of university faculty in graduate programs in library and information science in North America. Its mission is to promote excellence in research, teaching, and service and to provide an understanding of the values and ethos of library and information science. ALISE serves 500 individual members and more than 60 institutional members, primarily in the United States and Canada.

Recent Awards, Winning Projects & Award Winners

Brooke E. Sheldon

Amgen Award for Science Teaching Excellence (AASTE)

One Amgen Center Drive
Thousand Oaks, CA
91320-1799
805-447-4056
http://wwwext.amgen.com/citizenship/aaste_aaste_faq.html
http://tiny.cc/kmn5d

Description

Amgen, a biotechnology pioneer, discovers, develops, manufactures and markets important human therapeutics for serious illnesses. Amgen is committed to dramatically improving people's lives – not only through the therapeutics we deliver to patients but also through supporting programs that advance science literacy throughout North America.

The Amgen Award for Science Teaching Excellence (AASTE) is an annual awards program that recognizes extraordinary contributions by educators across the United States, Puerto Rico and Canada who are elevating the level of science literacy through creativity in the classroom and motivation of students. An independent panel of judges selects the winners based on the following criteria: creativity of teaching methods; effectiveness in the classroom; the plan for the use of grant money to improve science education resources in their schools; an innovative science lesson plan showcasing innovative methods in the classroom; and a plan for dissemination/sharing the lesson plan with other teachers.

Recent Awards, Winning Projects & Award Winners

Jeffrey "Jeff" Adkins
Deer Valley High School
Antioch, CA
"Everything I teach is over your head," Jeff Adkins likes to tell his high school students. With 35 years of experience studying and teaching astronomy and physics — including the use of the Spitzer Infrared Space Telescope and telescopes at Kitt Peak National Observatory, as well as participating in Space Camp for Teachers — Adkins guides his students as they work independently on advanced projects. Adkins established the Earth, Space and Astronomy Center for Education at his school after winning a California Department of Education grant. He was the Antioch Unified School District's Teacher of the Year for 2004-2005, California's Computer-Using Educators' Teacher of the Year in 2006, and he received the Astronomical Association of Northern California's Special Award in 2006. As a child, Adkins loved to copy star charts on poster boards at the library and take them home to study. He earned is astronomy degree from the University of Arizona.

Mike Fischer
Granite Bay High School
Granite Bay, CA

Mike Fischer firmly believes that discovery and application of science are the best ways to make a positive impact on high school students. His physics, applied physics and technology classrooms are filled with creative student projects. Most days call for demonstrations, activities or laboratory experiments that actively involve, excite and challenge his students — whether it's cooking hot dogs with electricity, dropping bowling balls from football stadium bleachers or detonating hydrogen balloons. What's not always obvious, though, is the deeper understanding of science concepts and techniques that follow the action-packed lessons. "It's so much more effective to teach students once they're enthusiastic about the subject," says Fischer, who has taught science for more than 15 years. "But we really do cover the standards thoroughly. It's much more than just the fun you see."

Steve Latshaw
Westlake Hills Elementary School
Westlake Village, CA

Steve Latshaw's passion for science transcends grade levels. In his various capacities, this award-winning fourth-, fifth- and sixth-grade teacher challenges students to think creatively, evaluate conventional wisdom, look for patterns in chaos and discover solutions for the abstract needs — not just the obvious needs — of our society. In his more than 36 years of teaching, Latshaw has encouraged students to respect the scientific method, continuously analyze data, conduct meaningful research and, for years, use the Internet. While a glimpse into his classroom reveals whiteboards filled with mathematical equations, bulletin boards covered with grids, planets hanging from the ceilings, microscopes and computers competing for counter space and robots following pre-programmed courses, you can't overlook the buzz of students' voices interacting with, presenting to and encouraging each other. Field trips to science museums and observatories compete with student science fairs and invention conventions.

Mark Mayo
Los Alamitos High School
Los Alamitos, CA

Mark Mayo has taught science for 32 years at the high school and college levels. In the early 1980s, he created a science lecture series — with support from American Honda and the University of Southern California (USC) — that served thousands of students. In 1993, Mayo and a local doctor began a Mentors for Medicine program featuring lectures and demonstrations by local health professionals. More recently, Mayo performed research at the USC School of Dentistry's Center for Craniofacial Molecular Biology where he published numerous papers and presented his research at various international scientific meetings. As part of that work, he secured funding to train students in research methods at the USC Health Science campus. Mayo's students have received awards of excellence at numerous county and state science fairs. Mayo has received numerous grants and teacher of the year awards, including a national award from the National Institute of Dental & Craniofacial Research in 2000.

Dave Menshew
James C. Enochs High School
Modesto, CA

When a local juvenile detention center employee challenged successful businessman Dave Menshew to volunteer with the students there, Menshew had no idea that the experience would change his life. "What I found," he says, "was that the chance to teach was far more important than financial success." Menshew continued working as president of a multimillion-dollar retail corporation while he returned to school to earn his teaching credential. Upon graduation, he sold his business and began teaching middle school. He soon earned his National Board Certification, an MA in Education and numerous awards including Teacher of the Year from the 21st Century Learning Centers. He went on to create "Fun With Science," a public program enjoyed by hundreds of local students and parents. He recently originated, co-developed and is now lead teacher of the first four-year high school Forensic Biotechnology Career Pathway Program. Today he teaches forensic biology and general biology to ninth and tenth graders.

Jay S. Vavra, Ph.D.
High Tech High
San Diego, CA

When facing tough challenges, Dr. Jay Vavra routinely asks himself, "What would Jane do?" The Jane he refers to is Jane Goodall. Her historical accomplishments inspire Dr. Vavra to encourage students to achieve great things in biology and make the world a better place. Dr. Vavra began his biology research at Stanford University and later earned his marine biology doctorate from the University of Southern California. He brings his diverse life experiences into the classroom from a range of fields: zoo-archaeology, protein chemistry, comparative physiology and environmental assessment. In 2006, Dr. Vavra and his eleventh graders received an Environmental Excellence Award. He recently began a novel collaborative study in conservation forensics with the Department of Conservation and Research for Endangered Species at San Diego's Zoological Society. The project involves developing and testing DNA bar coding for the identification of African bush meat. Dr. Vavra was invited by the Smithsonian to present his students' discoveries at the 2006 American Zoo and Aquarium meeting.

Carolyn Denise Evans Crapo
Grandview High School
Aurora, CO

Carolyn Crapo will go to most any lengths to help students experience real-life applications of the science they're studying. In Crapo's six years of teaching high school physics, her students have used blow guns to analyze projectile motion, Hot Wheels cars to study energy conservation and life-sized cardboard and duct tape boats that they design and row across a swimming pool to study fluids. Crapo takes her students indoor skydiving so they can experience terminal velocity and to amusement parks to analyze the physics of the rides. One summer she volunteered to teach science and math at a rural secondary school in Tanzania. There, she added simple labs using everyday materials to their previously lecture-only curriculum. Her enthusiasm and commitment continue to inspire students to see physics in the world around them.

Pam Schmidt
Thunder Ridge Middle School
Aurora, CO

You might find Pam Schmidt's sixth, seventh and eighth graders digging for fossils in the badlands, building model roller coasters high up in a rainforest canopy or happily surrounded by snakes of all sizes and colors. One thing is for certain: No matter where they are, Schmidt and her students will be engaged in learning and engrossed in the adventure of discovery. Schmidt has amassed a substantial record of fostering student achievement and excitement for exploring the world. While modeling a passion for lifelong learning, Schmidt nurtures positive relationships with her students and creates opportunities for them to achieve their goals and dreams. She has been Colorado Teacher of the Year and a National Milken Educator. She and her students — and their 47 classroom snakes — were recently featured on Animal Planet's "Emergency Vets."

Gary Wilkinson
Monte Vista High School
Monte Vista, CO

"To discover science is to enrich one's life with wonder, amazement and understanding," says Gary Wilkinson, who has dedicated his entire teaching career to the Monte Vista School District. Wilkinson's Science Seminar, which he designed, gives high school students the chance to create high-quality science fair projects. So far, 39 students from that program have participated in the International Science and Engineering Fair. Wilkinson has been the Science, Math, Computer and PE department chair since 1989.

Charles "Charlie" R. Warren, Ph.D., NBCT
The Crestone Charter School
Crestone, CO

Charlie Warren's fascination with science began when he was a small child catching butterflies with his mom. By the 1990s, he was helping to develop the first science curriculum and tests for the state of Ohio. He then developed The Crestone Charter School's outdoor education center in the San Juan Mountains. "It's all about creating memorable learning experiences and observing and reflecting on what happened," says Warren, who teaches sixth, seventh and eight grades. Living in the Sange de Cristo Mountain of southern Colorado, Warren and his students scour the environment for answers to their questions on everything from water purity to local geology. His class camps and hikes all over the area and frequently travels around the country to extend their studies. "Half of the curriculum comes from me," he says. "The rest comes from my students' sense of wonder." Warren is a National Board Certified Science Teacher and a Colorado Master Teacher.

Millie Blandford
Washington County High School
Springfield, KY

When Millie Blandford saw how much her daughter disliked her middle school science class — taught solely through textbook instruction — she knew there had to be a better way. So Blandford became a science teacher herself, determined to teach the subject in a more lively manner to leave students with lasting impressions of lessons and experiences that would help shape their futures and illuminate the world around them. Today her ninth graders shoot rubber bands to visualize Newton's Laws, camouflage butterflies all over the school for other students to find and collaborate with the chemistry class to "adopt an element." It's these strategies that excite, motivate and challenge her students. In 2004, she was named Who's Who Among America's Teachers, and Incentive Publications published her science resource guide. In 2005, she made the Who's Who list twice, received Campbellsville University's Teacher of Excellence award and celebrated when Science Kit produced two science activities she designed.

Andrea Broyles
South Elementary
Corbin, KY

Fourth-grade teacher Andrea Broyles was inspired to teach elementary science because of the lack of quality, hands-on science instruction at the lower grade levels — especially in the rural Appalachian area of Eastern Kentucky. She believes that the love of science must be instilled early in the lives of her students. For the past 10 years, she has provided a variety of engaging activities including the use of real-life lab equipment and exposure to relative science situations. Her summer science camp sessions include dissection, among other activities. Broyles has conducted science workshops for fellow teachers. In 2002, she traveled to Puerto Rico to conduct environmental research on behalf of Kentucky's Murray State University

Joshua Underwood
Deming School
Mt. Olivet, KY

"Science is learning how the world works around you," says high school physical sciences teacher Joshua Underwood. "The world is exciting and so should science be when taught." Since 2000, Underwood's students have learned by investigating the world through a variety of labs. They've tested everything from concrete strength to the percentage of water in popcorn in attempts to better understand the materials they are exposed to every day. Underwood traces his love of science back to his childhood when he would arrive at his family's milk barn with armloads of rocks instead of the cows. This love has taken him across the United States, Costa Rica and Iceland to engage in educational opportunities that he now shares with his students.

Fred Whittaker
St. Francis of Assisi
Louisville, KY

Growing up in a household headed by a professor of parasitology, Fred Whittaker spent family vacations collecting research data, including gathering parasites from road kill. Whittaker uses his deep-rooted knowledge of science, passion for teaching and a love for children to fulfill his personal mission to make the world a more peaceful place. Whittaker weaves social justice awareness into his science curriculum. He and mentors from several science fields help sixth, seventh and eighth graders pursue rigorous science fair projects on environmental, health and social issues. In 2005, the Anne Frank Foundation honored him with the Educator's Spirit of Anne Frank Award. In 2006, the Discovery Channel Young Scientist Challenge recognized him for Outstanding Science Mentoring when one of his students won the national Discovery Commerce "Sights to See" award. In fact, of the five semifinalists in Kentucky, three were Whittaker's students.

Angela Cardono Cunard
Seekonk High School
Seekonk, MA

Thanks to the inspiration of a high school teacher, Angela Cunard developed a love of science and enjoyed a career in scientific research. In 2001, she received a Massachusetts Institute for New Teachers signing bonus and became a teacher, herself. She's been with Seekonk High School for six years now, and has received several environmental and biotechnology awards. Cunard's classroom has no desks. Instead, her juniors and seniors gather around tables to work on cooperative learning activities. She teaches concepts with hands-on labs and activities, along with Socratic questioning and problem-solving challenges. She often uses current news and real-life application to engage students. Her students can be found discussing exploding frogs in Germany, wading in a river to measure dissolved oxygen, taking their pictures with pineapples at Stop & Shop as part of a plant life scavenger hunt, dissecting Gummi bears, investigating a "crime" scene or selling investors on their startup biology company.

Ellen Graham
Marlborough High School
Marlborough, MA

Ellen Graham always knew she wanted to teach school. She became interested in biology after losing both of her parents to cancer when she was young. "I was determined to know more about diseases and how to save myself," she says. As a life sciences teacher and researcher, Graham works hard to provide a differentiated learning curriculum that allows students of all learning styles to achieve. "There is no student who doesn't have the ability if taught in a learning style that fits his or her need," says Graham, the seventh great-granddaughter of Sir Isaac Newton. Graham's ninth and tenth graders have initiated a School-Wide Recycling Project, turning cans and bottles into cash. They used the proceeds to purchase Pervian Rainforest acreage. All the students were involved, and they celebrated their land ownership at their Earth Day Celebration.

Theresa Piazza
Wilmington Middle School
Wilmington, MA

Theresa Piazza's career as a math and science teacher began in high school, where she spent her free time tutoring elementary students. Her passion has grown ever since. Not only does she love teaching science, she especially loves teaching middle school students. They're the perfect age, she says, for exploring details, and they're still excited to win prizes and share a laugh. "Often, kids lose interest in science when they're in middle school," Piazza says. "I want to change that." Her students count a weathering photo book as one of their favorite projects. A trip to New Hampshire's Polar Caves and an Essex River boat cruise both provide photo opportunities and field experience. Piazza recently earned her Master of Education Degree in Middle School Science with a 4.0 GPA.

James Schliefke
Horace Mann Middle School
Franklin, MA

James Schliefke's passion for science began at a young age when he experienced 1985's Hurricane Gloria. Today, he is known as "The Horace Mann Weatherman," providing weather forecasts for his anxiously awaiting colleagues, especially during the winter months. Schliefke combines his interest in science with his passion for fun and engaging hands-on activities for his seventh-grade students. His lessons include interdisciplinary connections to mathematics and social studies so that students can understand the importance of science in their world. He integrates technology into his students' science experience, as well, when they take to the SmartBoard to deliver their own weather forecasts.

Aurea Berrios Saez
Escuela Francisco Morales
Naranjito, PR
Aristotle's declaration that "moral excellence comes about as a result of habit" helps guide Aurea Berrios Saez as she interacts with her students. Saez has devoted almost 30 years to teaching biology and science research, with 20 of those years working on various local, district and regional science fair committees. Her students enjoy a variety of projects including the Luquillo Schoolyard LTER, the Secondary School Forest and the GLOBE Project, where they share scientific information via the Internet. Saez holds a Master of Science Education degree from the University of Puerto Rico and an Environmental Management degree from the Metropolitan University. Among her publications, the most relevant are "El estudio de la Prestoea Montana en el Bosque Pluvial Tropical" and the thesis "Evaluación de los Recursos Naturales del Bosque Estatal de Cambalache, Puerto Rico, y el desarrollo de un Plan Estratégico para su manejo sostenible" (1988).

Julio de Jesús Aponte
Colegio Radians
Cayey, PR
Julio de Jesús Aponte's interest in science began when he was 8 years old, collecting rocks and snails. Today, the scholar community admires his commitment to educating students as well as further educating his colleagues through developing professional courses. Last year, Aponte was one of 25 teachers chosen by the Foundation for Teaching Economics to participate in an environment and economy program. He also was one of 25 teachers selected for Gillette's Leadership Program. Aponte has participated in University of Georgia's Proteomics and Genomics Workshop and was one of 20 teachers accepted to The Maury Project on oceanography at the United States Naval Academy in Annapolis, MD.

Zugeily Marcano Irizarry
Colegio Angeles Custodios
Río Piedras, PR
In her short four years as teacher, Zugeily Marcano Irizarry has learned the importance of communicating with her students and ensuring that they recognize opportunities to reach their full potential. Last year, she started the successful "Chemistry in the Environment" program where students take on projects and present their work to the rest of the school. Irizarry plans to expand the concept this year. "My students are already leaving prints that are part of my journey as a teacher," she says. "They see me as a role model and that, even though I'm young, I have a lot of knowledge and determination. I believe this motivates students to build bridges toward discovering a new tomorrow in the science world."

José A. Rivera
Escuela Dr. Carlos Gonzalez
Aguada, PR

His inquisitive mind led José A. Rivera to the field of science. He calls himself a self-specialist, finding answers to questions on his own — and he encourages his students to do the same. During his 23 years of teaching physics, Rivera has his students search for answers on a variety of nature- and life-related questions. His "The Universe at the Reach of Your Hands" program, for example, show students how astronomy can answer many questions about the world's creation. His "Star Night" activity prompts further questions and answers regarding the universe. Rivera won a Teacher of Excellence award from Aguada in 2005

Robert Williams "Otter" Brown
The Wheeler School
Providence, RI

A product of the Massachusetts Audubon Society Education Department, Otter Brown has taught elementary, middle and high school students at the Wheeler School for 35 years. In the 1990s, his student stream teams won more than $200,000 in awards and competitions. Brown coached six different five-student Envirothon teams to the Rhode Island State Championships. Last year, he was honored as the Siemens AP Math Science Teacher of the Year in Rhode Island. He plans to use his Amgen award to support teams of CoyoteKids in his next endeavor of researching urban coyotes through the use of tracking telemetry and GPS radio collars. Brown wants his students to feel the wild within and share his sense of wonder.

Doris E. Lawson
Potter Burns Elementary School
Pawtucket, RI

"Tell me, I forget. Show me, I remember. Involve me, I understand." This ancient proverb has been Doris Lawson's philosophy of education for 28 years. She involves her third-grade students in a science adventure that makes them wonder and discover the marvels of the world in which they live. You never know what you'll find when you walk in her classroom. Lawson could be standing on a desk preparing to let a rock crash into a pile of flour-sprinkled dirt to simulate the creation of a moon crater. You might find her students in the cafeteria flying airplanes to determine how many paper clips will minimize the drag. Or they're likely at the river investigating animal habitats. Lawson is a National Board Certified Teacher and a grant writer for the Potter Burns School.

Dr. Joel Gluck
NEL/CPS Construction Career Academy
Cranston, RI

Dr. Joel Gluck believes that all students have the ability to learn and reach high standards. As a teacher, he says it's his responsibility to monitor and adjust his science instruction based on their individual needs. He has been developing a curriculum that teaches the wonder of scientific inquiry in such a way as to encourage, challenge and nurture students. Classroom visitors will see students engaged in active learning, prompted to solve problems by brainstorming, troubleshooting, researching and experimenting. Dr. Gluck's attraction to science education stems from his training as a physician. "The real challenge is getting my students to believe in themselves," he says. "I love seeing the look of astonishment on their faces when they finally 'get it.' They are learning not to please me as much as they are learning to please themselves." Dr. Gluck won the 2006 EDS Technology Grant for innovation and bringing technology to the forefront of the science classroom.

Daniel J. Potts
Chariho Regional Middle School
Wood River Junction, RI
After 16 years teaching middle school students, the only thing Daniel Potts is certain of is the uncertainty of each day. "That is why our science experience is a full-year adventure outside of the classroom walls as well as inside," Potts says. He and his seventh and eighth graders kayak down the Wood River, research and track the fish population in a nearby stream, participate in a winter night hike at the W. Alton Jones Campus of the University of Rhode Island and pull weeds in the hot summer sun from the Kid's Grow garden. The idea: Keep students actively engaged in their education. With the help of science professionals, Potts ensures that his students participate in real science inquiry so they can make informed decisions about issues that impact their lives today and tomorrow. "My students work diligently in rigorous activities, and they have fun while learning valuable skills," Potts says.

Mario Alberto Godoy-Gonzalez
Royal High School
Royal City, WA

Royal High School teacher Mario Godoy-Gonzalez has shared his renewed passion for science with his students since 1994 and has received state and national recognition for his work. As a language teacher, the offer to teach science was somewhat unexpected. But when the Royal School District asked Godoy-Gonzalez, originally from Chile, to develop a program to support the academic improvement of migrant and Hispanic students, he willingly returned to college to better prepare himself for his new teaching challenge. Today, Godoy-Gonzalez uses science across the curriculum to help students acquire or develop reading and writing skills as well as science knowledge and lab competence. This Golden Apple Award recipient takes pride in the increasing number of minority students he helps to graduate from Royal High School so they can pursue their American dream as college undergraduates

Sheila Guard
Canyon Park Junior High
Bothell, WA
"I am driven every day to provide students with opportunities to do science," says Sheila Guard, who has taught science for the past 15 years. One of her greatest accomplishments is her ability to connect with junior high students and inspire and train them to become better scientists. Guard is a 2003 Washington Initiative Award winner. She earned her National Board Certification in the fall of 2005, and takes pride in her efforts to share knowledge with her peers. Perhaps most important is what she has led her students to accomplish. During the past 12 years, she has helped hundreds of Canyon Park Junior High students win awards and team trophies in multiple state and national Science Olympiad and Science Decathlon championships.

Misty Nikula
Whatcom Day Academy
Bellingham, WA

Misty Nikula always dreamed of being a teacher. As a child, she "played school" for hours at her small toy desk. Her high school science teachers inspired her deep and enduring love for learning about how things work — a curiosity that prompts her to seek out programs such as Teachers and Researchers – Exploring and Collaborating, where she works in the field with real scientists and brings those experiences back to her school and community. She kindles the natural curiosity in her middle school students through engaging lessons and projects that let them become archaeologists, oceanographers, chemists and biologists in their classroom. By considering herself a scientist first, then a teacher, Nikula is a role model for students to see themselves as scientists, as well.

Eleanor "Ellie" J. Peterson
Seattle County Day School
Seattle, WA

Ellie Peterson became passionate about science while in high school, working as a tutor for the younger students. These days, she finds herself in a classroom full of inquisitive sixth and seventh graders and up to her elbows in inquiry-based curriculum. Her class activities include building edible cell models, solving staged "crimes" with forensics and identifying mystery sand samples. She has participated in the University of Washington's Physics Education Group Summer Institute three times and recently completed her MA with a focus on Science Curriculum and Instruction.

Change Agent Awards

Anita Borg Institute for Women and Technology 1501 Page Mill Road, MS 1105
Palo Alto, CA 94304
(650) 236-4756
Amy Clark
http://www.anitaborg.org/initiatives/awards/change-agent-awards/
http://tiny.cc/V3Puq

Description

The Anita Borg Change Agent Awards celebrate the accomplishments of technical women from emerging countries. These awards are designed to recognize up-and-coming leaders that impact or advance women's participation in technology, while also internationally expanding the reach of the Grace Hopper Celebration of Women in Computing conference.

Recent Awards, Winning Projects & Award Winners

Wafa AlMansoori (Bahrain) (http://tiny.cc/I44pH)
Zeinab Safar (Egypt) (http://tiny.cc/U2Kwk)

Irina Khomeriki (Georgia). (http://tiny.cc/yZs6l)

Christine Mirzayan Science & Technology Policy Graduate Fellowship Program

500 5th Street, NW, Room 508
Washington, DC 20001
202-334-2455
http://www7.nationalacademies.org/policyfellows/Application.html
http://tiny.cc/GnhAC

Description

The Christine Mirzayan Science & Technology Policy Graduate Fellowship Program within the Policy and Global Affairs Division (http://tiny.cc/7SjcZ) of the National Academies is designed to engage graduate science, engineering, medical, veterinary, business, public policy, and law students in the analytical process that informs the creation of national policy-making with a science/ technology element. As a result, students develop basic skills essential to working in the world of science policy.

Recent Awards, Winning Projects & Award Winners

Boonchai Boonyaratanakornkit (BCST/DELS) graduated from the University of California, Berkeley with a PhD in Chemical Engineering in June 2006. Boonchai hails from a Thai-Chinese background hence the long last name. His doctoral research focused on the cultivation of extremophiles from deep-sea hydrothermal vents and the elucidation of genes that allow for survival in such extreme environments. Boonchai received his B.S. in Biochemical/Chemical Engineering at the University of California, Davis where he got to enjoy the rural life, biking around campus, and research in air quality and viticulture. He recently worked as a post-doctoral fellow at Lawrence Berkeley National Lab and explored enzymatic and electrochemical means to convert carbon dioxide into dense, carbon-neutral liquid fuels. He is excited to be living on the East Coast and learning about the interrelationship between policy and research instead of doing bench science. During his time at BCST, he hopes to apply and expand his speaking and writing skills in order to pursue possible careers in scientific writing and patent law. In his free time, he enjoys working out, reading, learning new languages, writing chorales, and playing tennis, basketball, and softball.

Sarah Case (BEES & DEPS EO/DEPS) defended her PhD thesis in soft condensed matter physics at the University of Chicago in September of 2007, just before starting her fellowship at the NAS. Her graduate research focused on experimental fluid dynamics, and in particular, her thesis work involved the development of an electrical method to study the earliest stages of the coalescence of two droplets of salt water. While in graduate school, she worked with non-profit organizations serving sustainable development and the environment, and traveled to Rwanda and rural Costa Rica to learn about environmental concerns in the developing world and their human impact. She also worked part-time with an environmental engineering laboratory at the Illinois Institute of Technology, helping to develop technology for solar concentrators. She is looking forward to working with BEES, where she will likely focus on the "America's Energy Future" project. She hopes that this fellowship will help her to learn about energy and environmental policy, and about the world outside academia.

Jennifer Flexman (GUIRR/PGA) completed her PhD in Bioengineering at the University of Washington in August 2007, where she used molecular imaging techniques to study cellular and molecular processes. Specifically, she studied neural stem cell migration in the brain using non-invasive magnetic resonance imaging. She completed a B.Eng. in Electrical Engineering at McGill University and working in the field for two years in Boston, MA. While in graduate school, she was a Co-Director of the Forum on Science Ethics and Policy (FOSEP), a student and post-doctoral fellow group devoted to promoting dialogue among scholars, policy experts, and the public about the role of science in society. Jennifer also represents over 3,500 students as Student Representative to the IEEE Engineering in Medicine and Biology Society. She completed the Program on Technology Commercialization at the University of Washington, where she developed a business plan for an emerging bioengineering technology. Because of her interests in science policy, commercialization and the translational aspect of her discipline, Jennifer hopes to learn more about university-industry relationships through working with GUIRR. A native of Vancouver, Canada, she enjoys just about any sport involving snow, reading, jogging and traveling to new places.

Mark Fleury (CASEE/NAE) recently completed his PhD in biomedical engineering at the École Polytechnique Fédérale de Lausanne (EPFL) in Switzerland where he studied the role of small convective flows in the promotion of cancer metastases and new blood vessel formation. He received an M.S. from Northwestern University in chemical engineering as well as a B.S. in the same field from Kansas State University. Mark is a licensed professional engineer and prior to graduate school he worked for Cargill Incorporated as a process engineer in the corn sweetener industry and as a project engineer with experience in wastewater treatment design. Mark plans on continuing his research career with a post-doc studying the misregulation of cellular signaling pathways in cancer, but would like to use the fellowship opportunity to explore ways to become more involved in bringing the needs of researchers and the public together. In his free time Mark enjoys travel, cooking, black and white photography, reading, and mountain sports.

Shikha Gupta (NMAB/DEPS) is currently finishing a Ph.D in the Applied Science and Technology Program at the University of California, Berkeley. Her interdisciplinary doctoral work focuses on the development of experimental and numerical microscale materials characterization methods for both natural and synthetic orthopaedic biomaterials, particularly for biological tissues from small animal models. During her time as a graduate student, Shikha has also been involved in engineering education research that focuses on the assessment and evaluation of cognitive sophistication in project-based engineering instruction. Prior to joining graduate school, Shikha spent a year working, volunteering, and traveling in Bangalore, India. She received her B.S. in Materials Science & Engineering from MIT. Shikha is quite fond of research, and hopes to continue her scientific endeavors in the future in a national lab setting or in academia. Shikha is excited about her tenure with the National Materials Advisory Board at the National Academies--she is eager to apply her technical expertise outside the laboratory setting and to add a new, enriching dimension to her education by interfacing with both lawmakers and scientists in a policy-making capacity. In addition to her left-brained work, Shikha engages herself in a variety of right-brained athletic and musical pursuits, including tennis, hiking, salsa dancing and singing.

Rae Benedict (COSEPUP/PGA) is currently completing her Ph.D. in aquatic toxicology at the University of Maryland-Baltimore where she has been educated through the National Institute of Environmental Health Sciences (NIEHS) training grant. Her research examines the metabolism of brominated flame retardants. Specifically, she focused on polybrominated diphenyl ethers and enzymes involved in thyroid hormone metabolism. Rae earned a M.S. in Environmental Health Management and a B.S. in Marine Biology and Marine Fisheries. Her educational and career pursuits have provided her the opportunity to live on every coast of the U.S., including Alaska's Inside Passage. Rae hopes her fellowship will further develop her skills and provide an understanding on science policy creation to advance her efforts of becoming an effective leader. She plans to continue working in science policy after completion of the fellowship. In her free time, she works on domestic violence issues and the mentoring of students and scientists. She also enjoys hiking with her dog, riding her motorcycle and participating in day-long volunteer events. Contact by email (bene_rae@hotmail.com).

Josh Braun (Koshland/NAS) is a masters student at Cornell University, working toward a Ph.D. in communication. Currently, his research examines the nature of debate in online political communities, with the ultimate goal of understanding the rich context in which discussions of health and science unfold within these forums. Josh holds a masters in bioethics from the University of Pennsylvania, and a bachelors in "science in the media" from UC Santa Barbara's individual studies program. His studies have focused on the effective communication of science and health information in both the mass media and interpersonal settings. He hopes to further this project through work in either policy or academia, and is excited to be working at the Koshland Museum, which provides excellent opportunities to gain experience and insight into the process of communicating about science. Josh has worked as a science journalist for NPR and Seed Magazine, where he covered diverse topics ranging from nuclear security to deep-sea oceanography to prison reform. He has previously visited Washington as an intern for ABC News' Nightline and This Week programs. Josh is a tortured Phillies fan, and in his free time, enjoys hiking, documentary films, and photography. Contact by email (Joshua.A.Braun@gmail.com).

Jay Cole (BHEW/PGA) is currently completing his Ph.D. in Education and Public Policy at the University of Michigan. His dissertation is a study of the factors affecting the diffusion of science and technology policy innovations among states. He has a M.A. in the history and philosophy of education from The Ohio State University, where he held a Foreign Language and Area Studies fellowship, and a B.A. in Political Science and History from West Virginia University, where he was selected as a Truman Scholar. For the last six and a half years, Jay has served as the Governor's education policy advisor and Deputy Secretary of Education and the Arts in his home state of West Virginia. In these positions, he works on a wide variety of K-12 and postsecondary education policy issues, including the promotion of education and research in STEM fields. During his fellowship, Jay looks forward to exploring the state-level policy implications of BHEW's work on graduate education. In his free time, Jay enjoys following college football and all of the professional Pittsburgh sports teams, learning about Ancient Egypt, reading about politics, and listening to country music. Jay is married to Lisa DeFrank-Cole and they have one cat, Buffett (named for Jimmy, not Warren). Contact by email (colejay@earthlink.net).

Patrick Cunningham (CASEE/NAE) completed his Ph.D. in mechanical engineering at Purdue University in the fall of 2006. His doctoral research focused on monitoring diesel particulate filters. Specifically, he investigated experimental and theoretical correlations between dynamic pressure signal features and the amount of diesel particulate stored in a filter. Part of his graduate work was funded by an NSF fellowship. Patrick's MSME and BSME were also from Purdue University. Since November 2006 Patrick has been following his passion teaching at Rose-Hulman Institute of Technology as an assistant professor in the mechanical engineering department. He is particularly interested in how we teach engineers to handle the often competing forces of social, cultural, political, economic, and environmental responsibilities. As a fellow with CASEE, he is excited about seeing the broader landscape of scholarly engineering education research and participating in it. His career goals in academia include teaching mechanical engineering courses, improving ethical and social acuity of students and the pedagogy behind it, and conducting research promoting efficient energy conversion and reduced emissions. Patrick enjoys running, hiking, reading, roasting and drinking coffee, and spending time with his wife, Jennie, in his personal time. Currently he and Jennie are pursuing the adoption of a Guatemalan child. Contact by email (cunning@rose-hulman.edu).

Chantel F. Fuqua (BCYF/DBASSE) recently completed her Ph.D. in Cancer Biology at Meharry Medical College in Nashville, TN. Her doctoral research focused on the signaling mechanisms of IL-21, an immunoregulatory cytokine that is currently being considered as a possible treatment for the regulation of the immune system in asthma and cancer patients. She received her B.S. in Chemistry from Saint Louis University, and conducted research focused on size-dependent diffusion of organic compounds. Her interest in being a policy fellow stems from a personal goal of hers to gain additional training in ethics and policy, and learn how to facilitate active dialogue between researchers, educators, and policymakers to improve health and society in minority populations. This experience will also enable her to transition from training as a student to a productive professional. She hopes to one day to be able to reduce health disparities through education, research, and designing community outreach programs that can ultimately influence policy making. In her free time, she enjoys playing the piano, going out to see live music and theater performances, spending time with friends and family, reading, and traveling. Contact by email (fuquacf@msn.com).

Yeimy Garcia (COSEPUP/PGA) is currently completing her Ph.D. in chemistry at the University of California, Los Angeles. Her research, funded by the National Institutes of Health, uses computational chemistry to explore mechanisms of reactions catalyzed by organic catalysts and to examine sources of regioselectivity for reactions catalyzed by transition metal complexes. She received a B.S. in chemistry from Seton Hall University in 2005, where she was actively involved in the Martin Luther King Scholarship Association. Yeimy hopes to pursue a career in science policy, and she is excited that this internship will help define her interest. She looks forward to working with COSEPUP on issues related to underrepresented minorities in science and engineering. Yeimy enjoys cooking, reading, running, and biking—especially in beautiful Southern California. She is eager to explore DC this summer. Contact by email (yeimy.garcia@gmail.com).

Noah Giansiracusa (CISAC/PGA) is currently pursuing a Ph.D. in pure mathematics at Brown University, focusing on algebraic geometry. During his undergraduate education at the University of Washington he spent a summer as a cryptological intern at the National Security Agency and immediately afterward lived in Moscow, Russia as part of a mathematical study abroad program.

Working at the NSA helped him to develop an interest in applying the mathematical sciences to international security -- and studying in Russia made it clear that the best way to strive toward global peace is by encouraging international collaboration and open communication between scientists, not just politicians, throughout the world. Noah would like to stay in academia after graduation, but he wants to be actively involved the development of programs designed to enable students and scientists at all levels of their studies to cross international cultural barriers with the hope of building a more collaborative and amicable global environment for research. While working at the National Academies, Noah hopes to gain a first-hand perspective of the policy side of research necessary to establish such programs. Whenever possible, Noah plays the piano and tries to surround himself with classical music, in all ways ranging from the opera house to an MP3 player. Contact by email (noahgian@gmail.com).

Nathaniel "Nate" Hafer (CISAC & DSC/PGA) completed his Ph.D. in Molecular Biology at Princeton University in May 2007. His doctoral research focused on understanding a novel gene in the fruit fly that regulates RNA localization and expression in the germline and nervous system. Prior to graduate school Nate received a B.S. in Biology from Penn State with a minor in Science, Technology, and Society. He believes it is important for scientists to be actively engaged in policy making, and looks forward to working on science policy first hand. In particular, Nate wants to ensure that science and technology are used responsibly without sacrificing scientific inquiry and freedom. He hopes to combine his knowledge of the life sciences with his interest in international relations and apply these skills to biological weapons control. In his spare time Nate enjoys cooking and eating good food, listening to music, and participating in a variety of sports. Contact by email (nathanielhafer@gmail.com).

Alicia Jackson (COSEPUP/PGA) recently earned her Ph.D. in Materials Science and Engineering from the Massachusetts Institute of Technology in June 2007. Her dissertation focused on the phase separation and nanostructuring in the ligand shell of nanoparticles. This discovery has a number of interesting biotechnological applications, as well as having wide reaching implications for the environmental health and safety implications of nanoparticles. She received a B.S. in Materials Science and Engineering from MIT as well. Alicia's interest in science policy grew out of her desire to have a broader impact on scientific advancement than that afforded to her through basic research. While at MIT, she co-created a new science policy course for science and engineering graduate students and post-docs. The aim of the course is to develop a new generation of policy versed and active scientists. During her time at the National Academies, she is looking forward to working with the Committee on Science, Engineering, and Public Policy on the project of Ensuring the Utility and Integrity of Research Data in a Digital Era. After completing her fellowship, Alicia will serve as the 2007 MRS/OSA Congressional Fellow, where she looks forward to developing policies that will encourage the critical scientific developments and technology transfers necessary to solve the many environmental, health, and defense challenges facing us today and that encourage the link between technological and economic development and contribute to human progress. Contact by email (alicianano@gmail.com).

Vikas Khanna (NMAB/DEPS) is currently completing his Ph.D in Chemical Engineering at The Ohio State University, Columbus. His doctoral research is part of an EPA STAR grant and focuses on addressing the environmental implications of nanotechnology using life cycle assessment and systems analysis. Vikas received his undergraduate degree in Chemical Engineering from Panjab University, India. He recently also received his Masters in Applied Statistics from The Ohio State University. Before coming to Graduate School, Vikas worked as a Senior Process Engineer with Technip KT India Ltd. He believes that systems view coupled with technology and policy perspective can be very beneficial for guiding decision making and ensuring that the expected benefits of technology manifests themselves in real form. Vikas hopes that the fellowship experience at the Academies will facilitate him to broaden his scientific perspective and expand its reach into the public policy arena. In the long-term, Vikas would like to pursue a research oriented career either in academia or industry. In his free time, Vikas enjoys reading, playing racquet ball, and running. Contact by email (khanna.105@osu.edu).

Puneet Kishor (BESR/DELS & BISO/PGA) is working on his Ph.D. in Land Resources at the Nelson Institute for Environmental Studies, University of Wisconsin-Madison, and is also the Chair of the Education Committee of the Open Source GeoSpatial Foundation (OSGeo). His research interests are in open source computing as "appropriate technology" for rural development and the role of public policy in open data access. Puneet returned to academia in 2006 after a 13 years detour, first via international development at the World Bank, then at a geographic information systems (GIS) consulting company. After completing his undergraduate in engineering from the Indian Institute of Technology, New Delhi, Puneet started his career working for a non-governmental rural development agency designing better hand-looms. Puneet believes that his open source work is bringing him back full- circle to where he started — applying high technology to solving problems that beset the least fortunate. Since the government looks after those overlooked by the free-market, Puneet is looking forward to NAS giving him an insider's view of the process of informing the government. In the unlikely event that he is able to find any free time this summer, he will seek out live jazz, the original open source movement, and hand-crafted espressos, hopefully being served concurrently. Contact by email (punkish@eidesis.org).

Lawrence Lin (BEES & DEPS EO/DEPS) completed his Ph.D. in physics at the University of California, Santa Barbara in June of 2006. His graduate research involved the use of simplified models of biological membranes as a means for studying various biophysical processes. Working with these models, he did theoretical calculations and performed simulations to quantitatively analyze different systems containing biological membranes. His undergraduate studies were done at Brown University where he wrote a thesis in the area of cosmology and large scale structure of the universe. Lawrence is looking forward to his fellowship and hopes to learn more about energy technology and policy while working with the Executive Office of the Division on Engineering and Physical Sciences as well as with the Board on Energy and Environmental Systems. After the fellowship, he would like to work in either government or the nonprofit sector on science policy issues related to his interests in energy, climate, and sustainable development. Contact by email (Lawrence4@gmail.com).

Anne Murdaugh (GUIRR/PGA) is currently completing her Ph.D. in experimental condensed matter physics at the University of Arizona (UA). Her research uses atomic force microscopy to explore the principles governing the growth of crystalline monolayers at the nanoscale. A warm weather enthusiast, she originally hails from Atlanta where she received her B.S. in physics from Georgia Tech in 2002. Anne's interest in science policy began with her election to the UA Graduate and Professional Student Council in 2005, and recently she has become involved with the National Association of Graduate and Professional Students, with a special interest in legislative affairs. Through these associations, she witnessed the intricate relationship between policy and research and became inspired to pursue a career in science policy and advocacy. She hopes her time at the Academies will help her explore the complicated realm of science policy and further define her career goals. Anne is excited to be a part of GUIRR and working to better enable collaborations between universities and industry. For relaxation, she practices Shotokan Karate and enjoys good movies, books, and jazz. Contact by email (amurdaugh@gmail.com).

Jamie Skipper (EBM RT/IOM) graduated from the University of Glasgow, Scotland with a Ph.D. in cardiac physiology in December 2002. During her graduate research, Jamie examined the biophysics of cardiac muscle under the stress of a failing heart. Her research in cardiac basic science and her years as a registered nurse in adult and pediatric cardiology lead her to the NIH (National Institutes of Health) where she worked for the NHLBI (National Heart Lung and Blood Institute). Here Jamie managed and directed millions of dollars worth of national research efforts in heart failure. In 2006, she led a national initiative to leverage clinical trial funds to co-invest in national heart, lung and blood basic science research. During her time at the NIH, Jamie began to aspire toward a future in health science policy and hopes this fellowship will give her further insight into the relationship between health science research and national policies. Jamie hopes to have a promising career in national health policy and make a positive impact on US national healthcare. In her free time Jamie enjoys her family, traveling, competitive sports, and cooking. She also admits to being addicted to Scrabble and finding the next best kitchen gadget. Contact by email (drjskipper@hotmail.com).

Susan Su (DEW/NAE) graduated from the University of California, San Diego with a Ph.D. in Bioengineering in January 2007. Her graduate research focused on the mechanotransducing behavior of human leukocytes in the context of inflammation. More specifically, Susan used numerical methods to characterize the membrane stress of leukocytes under blood flow and recorded the translocation of membrane molecules in these cells that resulted from fluid shear. She graduated magna cum laude from Binghamton University with a B.S. in Mechanical Engineering and a minor in Spanish. Throughout her graduate years, Susan had been very active with volunteer work, devoting more than 500 hours at various public educational activities of the Birch Aquarium at Scripps. She is very excited to be doing her fellowship with DEW where she will assist in the launching of a new initiative that encourages young women to pursue a career in engineering. Susan hopes to eventually become involved in scientific project management for an international organization/company. In her spare time, Susan enjoys indoor rock climbing, Argentine tango, day-tripping, and when time and finance permitting, traveling. Contact by email (sususan79@gmail.com)

Jennifer Weisman (Koshland/NAS) received her Ph.D. in Physical Chemistry from the University of California, Berkeley in 2003. Her doctoral research focused on the identification and study of compounds responsible for the diffuse interstellar bands using quantum computational chemistry. Jenni received her B.S. in Chemistry from the College of William and Mary and has just finished a Giannini Family Foundation postdoctoral fellowship at the University of California, San Francisco, where she worked on the discovery of new therapeutics to treat malaria. She will be a AAAS Science & Technology Policy Fellow at the NIH this fall. Jenni believes that her fellowship with the Academies will be an excellent introduction to science policy and education, and hopes that the experience will guide her career path as she transitions out of bench science. She is thrilled to be working at the Koshland Science Museum this summer, and looks forward to the opportunity to further her experience in non-traditional science education, which she has begun to explore through volunteering at the Exploratorium science museum and teaching partnerships in public schools in San Francisco. In her free time, she enjoys practicing ashtanga yoga, throwing pottery, learning Korean, playing the flute, running, and cooking. Contact by email (jlweisman@gmail.com).

Boonchai Boonyaratanakornkit (BCST/DELS) graduated from the University of California, Berkeley with a PhD in Chemical Engineering in June 2006. Boonchai hails from a Thai-Chinese background hence the long last name. His doctoral research focused on the cultivation of extremophiles from deep-sea hydrothermal vents and the elucidation of genes that allow for survival in such extreme environments. Boonchai received his B.S. in Biochemical/Chemical Engineering at the University of California, Davis where he got to enjoy the rural life, biking around campus, and research in air quality and viticulture. He recently worked as a post-doctoral fellow at Lawrence Berkeley National Lab and explored enzymatic and electrochemical means to convert carbon dioxide into dense, carbon-neutral liquid fuels. He is excited to be living on the East Coast and learning about the interrelationship between policy and research instead of doing bench science. During his time at BCST, he hopes to apply and expand his speaking and writing skills in order to pursue possible careers in scientific writing and patent law. In his free time, he enjoys working out, reading, learning new languages, writing chorales, and playing tennis, basketball, and softball.

Sarah Case (BEES & DEPS EO/DEPS) defended her PhD thesis in soft condensed matter physics at the University of Chicago in September of 2007, just before starting her fellowship at the NAS. Her graduate research focused on experimental fluid dynamics, and in particular, her thesis work involved the development of an electrical method to study the earliest stages of the coalescence of two droplets of salt water. While in graduate school, she worked with non-profit organizations serving sustainable development and the environment, and traveled to Rwanda and rural Costa Rica to learn about environmental concerns in the developing world and their human impact. She also worked part-time with an environmental engineering laboratory at the Illinois Institute of Technology, helping to develop technology for solar concentrators. She is looking forward to working with BEES, where she will likely focus on the "America's Energy Future" project. She hopes that this fellowship will help her to learn about energy and environmental policy, and about the world outside academia. Ultimately, she hopes to use her training to facilitate the interaction between scientists and engineers and decision makers in Washington. In her free time, she enjoys singing, playing guitar, bicycling, and cooking.

Jennifer Flexman (GUIRR/PGA) completed her PhD in Bioengineering at the University of Washington in August 2007, where she used molecular imaging techniques to study cellular and molecular processes. Specifically, she studied neural stem cell migration in the brain using non-invasive magnetic resonance imaging. She completed a B.Eng. in Electrical Engineering at McGill University and working in the field for two years in Boston, MA. While in graduate school, she was a Co-Director of the Forum on Science Ethics and Policy (FOSEP), a student and post-doctoral fellow group devoted to promoting dialogue among scholars, policy experts, and the public about the role of science in society. Jennifer also represents over 3,500 students as Student Representative to the IEEE Engineering in Medicine and Biology Society. She completed the Program on Technology Commercialization at the University of Washington, where she developed a business plan for an emerging bioengineering technology. Because of her interests in science policy, commercialization and the translational aspect of her discipline, Jennifer hopes to learn more about university-industry relationships through working with GUIRR. A native of Vancouver, Canada, she enjoys just about any sport involving snow, reading, jogging and traveling to new places.

Mark Fleury (CASEE/NAE) recently completed his PhD in biomedical engineering at the École Polytechnique Fédérale de Lausanne (EPFL) in Switzerland where he studied the role of small convective flows in the promotion of cancer metastases and new blood vessel formation. He received an M.S. from Northwestern University in chemical engineering as well as a B.S. in the same field from Kansas State University. Mark is a licensed professional engineer and prior to graduate school he worked for Cargill Incorporated as a process engineer in the corn sweetener industry and as a project engineer with experience in wastewater treatment design. Mark plans on continuing his research career with a post-doc studying the misregulation of cellular signaling pathways in cancer, but would like to use the fellowship opportunity to explore ways to become more involved in bringing the needs of researchers and the public together. In his free time Mark enjoys travel, cooking, black and white photography, reading, and mountain sports.

Shikha Gupta (NMAB/DEPS) is currently finishing a Ph.D in the Applied Science and Technology Program at the University of California, Berkeley. Her interdisciplinary doctoral work focuses on the development of experimental and numerical microscale materials characterization methods for both natural and synthetic orthopaedic biomaterials, particularly for biological tissues from small animal models. During her time as a graduate student, Shikha has also been involved in engineering education research that focuses on the assessment and evaluation of cognitive sophistication in project-based engineering instruction. Prior to joining graduate school, Shikha spent a year working, volunteering, and traveling in Bangalore, India. She received her B.S. in Materials Science & Engineering from MIT. Shikha is quite fond of research, and hopes to continue her scientific endeavors in the future in a national lab setting or in academia. Shikha is excited about her tenure with the National Materials Advisory Board at the National Academies--she is eager to apply her technical expertise outside the laboratory setting and to add a new, enriching dimension to her education by interfacing with both lawmakers and scientists in a policy-making capacity. In addition to her left-brained work, Shikha engages herself in a variety of right-brained athletic and musical pursuits, including tennis, hiking, salsa dancing and singing.

Kofi Inkabi (BICE/DEPS) is currently completing his PhD in Civil and Environmental Engineering at the University of California, Berkeley. His doctoral research examines human and organizational influences on engineered water resource systems like dams and reservoirs. Kofi received his B.S. in Civil Engineering from UC Davis in 1999 and his M.S. in Structural Engineering from UC Berkeley in 2000. He then worked as a structural designer and assistant project manager for Parsons Brinckerhoff Quade & Douglas before returning Berkeley where he participated on the forensic investigation of the New Orleans flood defense failure following Hurricane Katrina with the generous support of the National Science Foundation. Kofi hopes the fellowship will broaden his perspective and knowledge of infrastructure risk analysis and methodology and the implications it has for national and state policy. In his free time, Kofi enjoys hiking, tennis, sailing, swimming, and discussing politics.

Bridget Kelly (BCYF/DBASSE) recently completed an MD and a PhD in Neurobiology as part of the Medical Scientist Training Program at Duke University. She is looking forward to this fellowship with the Board on Children, Youth and Families as an ideal opportunity to learn more about the policy process and to continue to integrate her combined background in basic science and clinical medicine, with a particular interest in the fields of neuroscience and mental health. Bridget received her BA in Biology and Neuroscience from Williams College, where she was also the recipient of the Hubbard Hutchinson Fellowship in fine arts. She is a modern dancer and choreographer and volunteers with Choreo Collective and the North Carolina Dance Alliance, two nonprofit organizations that serve dance artists in North Carolina.

Julia Kregenow (STS/PGA) completed her PhD in astrophysics at UC Berkeley, finishing in May 2007. Her stated mission in life is to bring science and math to the masses. Phase one is complete: Julia brought science and math to herself. Wittenberg University (in Ohio) hosted her happy undergraduate exploration of the space between math teacher and neurosurgeon via things like internships in atmospheric sciences and mechanical engineering. In her thesis, Julia studied how the gas in the Galaxy recycles itself through successive generations of stars, providing the raw materials for stars, planets, and ultimately life. This is how the Universe sustains itself. Julia hopes that humans can follow that example. Still reeling from her triumphant grad school finish, Julia was thrilled to be selected to work in the Science and Technology for Sustainability unit at the NAS. Here she looks forward to finding how she can put her science background to practical use helping humanity and the planet. Following this fellowship, she may continue in policy, or may pursue science education research, outreach, or teaching. She is an easygoing gal who likes cheese, gardening, science phenomena as metaphors, and sweatshirts with pockets.

Divine Kumah (BISO/PGA) completed his Masters of Science in Electrical Engineering from the University of Michigan and a Bachelor in Physics from Southern University. He is currently working on his PhD in Applied Physics also at Michigan where he is investigating the internal structure of novel ferroelectric and semiconductor materials using x-rays. During the National Academies' fellowship, he looks forward to gaining a different perspective on how scientific research can be applied in developing policy on a global scale for energy sustainability. After this fellowship, he plans to complete his PhD and work in academia. He also plans to help less-developed countries develop sound policies in the areas of energy, science and technology. Divine loves to travel, read and play soccer and chess.

Frank Hiroshi Ling (Koshland/NAS) is currently a postdoctoral fellow in the Energy and Resources Group at the University of California at Berkeley where he is studying energy scenarios for a lower carbon future. In his models, Frank is evaluating various options for energy efficiency, renewable energy systems, nuclear power, alternative engine technology, biofuels, and vehicle standards. He holds a PhD in Chemistry from UC Berkeley and a B.S. in Chemical Engineering from Caltech. Frank also produces the Berkeley Groks science radio show and podcast from the campus radio station. He was previously a AAAS Science Media Fellow in which he interned at the Voice of America. For his future goals, he plans to study and promote sustainable development through academia and the media. Frank speaks Japanese and Chinese and he hopes to engage these issues at the international level. In his spare time, Frank enjoys playing the piano, gardening, and tennis.

Beth Masimore (BPA/DEPS) is currently completing her PhD in physics at the University of Minnesota. Her doctoral research focuses on adapting theories and techniques developed for condensed matter physics for use with neurological data obtained from behaving animals. She has been involved with an interdisciplinary Neuro-Physical-Computational Sciences group at the University of Minnesota including receiving an NSF-IGERT fellowship for interdisciplinary research. Prior to graduate school, Beth completed her B.S. at Juniata College during which she spent a year abroad at the University of Leeds, Leeds, UK. Beth is excited about the opportunity to learn the process of policy analysis by working on a project identifying research forefronts at the intersection of the physical and life sciences. She also hopes that the fellowship will help her identify post-PhD opportunities beyond academic research.

John McMurdy (CASEE/NAE) is currently working towards his Ph.D in Biomedical Engineering at Brown University. The scope of his research has been in biomedical optics, applications in noninvasive characterization of tissue and biofluids, and implementation of ultra-compact optical sensors fabricated using liquid crystalline materials in these applications. He also acts as the chief technology officer for Corum Medical, a start-up company developing a noninvasive anemia-screening device for hospital triage and blood banking markets. John's graduate studies are supported by a NASA GSRP fellowship focused on compact medical sensors in crew healthcare. He previously completed his B.S. and M.S. in Optics at the University of Rochester. John hopes his experience with the Mirzayan program and CASEE will be both an exposition to technology education policy and a forum in which he can speak about his own unique educational experiences in entrepreneurship, working with start-up companies as a student, and innovation management. In the short term, he intends to find a career in technology consulting for a biotech investment house, R&D institution, or government agency, but eventually hopes to find his way back into academia. John spends free time playing as much golf as possible interspersed with the occasional bicycle ride and Steelers football game.

Cesar Perez-Gonzalez (COSEPUP/PGA) is currently completing his postdoctoral work at the National Institutes of Health. He holds a PhD in evolutionary biology from the University of Rochester and a B.S. in genetics from Iowa State University. His research work has focused on the dynamics of retrotransposable elements in both Drosophila and humans. Thanks to his work on the NIH Fellows Committee and the National Postdoctoral Association's Diversity Committee, Cesar has realized the need for scientists to become more engaged in policy, which has motivated him to come to the National Academies. He hopes to eventually have a career in science policy, focusing on diversity issues, with the goal of increasing the number of Latinos and other underrepresented groups in academic and government research positions. He hopes his work at the Academies will help him develop the skills to achieve this goal. In his spare time Cesar usually enjoys listening to music of all genres, writing, and making his way through his Netflix queue. He is currently though busy planning his April wedding with his fiancée.

Julia Skapik (PHPHP/IOM) is in the last year of her M.D. at the Johns Hopkins School of Medicine, having recently completed her M.P.H. at the Johns Hopkins Bloomberg School of Public Health. Originally from Licking County, Ohio, she attended New College of Florida, graduating with dual B.A.s in Biology and Psychology in 2001. Subsequently, she spent a year at the FDA in Bethesda performing viral and vaccine neurovirulence research. Since then, she has worked on many research projects at the Johns Hopkins Medical Institutions, primarily examining medical errors and the junction of mental and medical illness. She is also the author of the chapter "Psychotic Disorders, Severe Mental Illness, and HIV Infection" in the Comprehensive Textbook of AIDS Psychiatry and was an editor and author of the sixth edition of the review book First Aid for Step 2 CK She also serves as the 2007-8 Health Policy Action Committee chair for the American Medical Student Association, where she works on national projects, promoting legislation and education about universal health care, medical quality improvement, smoke-free indoor air, student activism, nutrition policy, and climate change.

Albert Swiston (COSEPUP/PGA) is currently pursuing a PhD in Polymer Science and Technology at the Massachusetts Institute of Technology. He holds a BS and MSE in Materials Science and Engineering from Johns Hopkins University in Baltimore Maryland, his hometown. Albert's graduate research focuses on the application of ultra-thin polymer films in biological applications, such as immune system engineering. With the generous support of an NSF Fellowship, Albert has had the opportunity to pursue several different projects, including the surface modification of custom-made ocular devices in conjunction with the local non-profit Boston Foundation for Sight. On campus, Albert co-founded the MIT Science Policy Initiative, which seeks to educate graduate students in the US innovation system; as part of the Initiative, students travel to Washington DC to participate in the legislative process by speaking with their elected representatives and their staff. During this Fellowship, he hopes to learn more about how science and government interact. Albert is an avid outdoorsman, and always eager to go cycling, backpacking, canoeing, or rock climbing.

Rima Adler (DELS/BLS) completed her PhD in Genetics at The George Washington University, in Washington DC in December 2006. Her dissertation research was conducted at the National Institutes of Health. She evaluated adult blood stem cell contributions, via retroviral gene insertion site analysis, to better understand hematopoiesis and gene-therapy. She worked in labs at the New York State Department of Health and also on clinical guidelines projects for NY State. Volunteer activities during graduate school (including work with the Student Society for Stem Cell Research, the International Society of Stem Cell Research, and instructor at various levels of education: OASIS, FAES, and Hands on Science) have given her a unique perspective on communicating science, to both scientific peers and lay audiences. During the National Academies' fellowship, she looks forward to continuing to use her scientific expertise to bridge the research-bench to the voting-public to promote sound public policies that are based upon facts rather than fiction. After this fellowship, she plans to do a traditional post-doctoral research fellowship, in a gene-therapy focused lab, before returning to a policy career. Rima is a hobby-linguist, loves to travel, likes to learn about people/cultures, is interested in playing the violin again, and enjoys exploring DC on warm sunny days! Contact by email (rima_ar@yahoo.com).

Kristin Agopian (PGA/GUIRR) graduated from Harvard University with a Ph.D. in Virology in June 2006. Her doctoral research focused on the Nef protein of the Human Immunodeficiency Virus (HIV). Nef is important for the development of AIDS in HIV-infected individuals. Her project had two areas of focus: 1) the interaction of HIV Nef with Pak2, a human serine/threonine kinase which may coordinate the cellular stress response and is involved in T cell activation; 2) the evolution of HIV Nef sequences and functions in viruses within the brain versus lymphoid tissues of AIDS patients. Kristin received an A.B. in Molecular Biology from Princeton University. For her undergraduate thesis, she studied speciation by observing defects in egg development in interspecific hybrid fruit flies. During her graduate work, she developed a growing interest in the commercialization of science and technology as a way to bridge lab discoveries with societal need. She hopes that during her time with GUIRR she will learn more about ways to improve collaboration between industry and academia. Kristin is excited about her fellowship at the National Academies. She hopes to learn as much as possible about the world of science policy and looks forward to exploring Washington, DC. In her spare time she enjoys music of all types, crossword puzzles, cooking, art museums, movies, tennis and outdoor walks. Contact by email (kristin_boston@yahoo.com).

Tylisha Baber (NAE/CASEE) graduated from Michigan State University with a PhD in chemical engineering in December 2005. Her doctoral research was Phase I of a USDA-SBIR funded project focused on the product development and characterization of a novel ozone-mediated treatment of biodiesel derived from soybean oil for fuel quality improvement. During her graduate tenure at Michigan State University, Tylisha received certification in college teaching as a participant in the College Teaching Certification (CTC) program. Teaching and mentoring activities included being a chemistry faculty member at Lansing Community College, a guest lecturer for an undergraduate thermodynamics course, a research mentor for undergraduate students, and a participant in the Future Faculty Career Exploration Program at Rochester Institute of Technology. She also holds a B.S. in chemical engineering from North Carolina State University. Tylisha is looking forward to her fellowship at the Academies and hopes to gain a greater understanding of the analysis tools and resources used to strategically create and implement policies relating to scientific and technical issues. In her free time, Tylisha enjoys reading, exercising, attending performing arts events, and watching professional sports. Contact by email (babertyl@gmail.com).

Tiffani Bailey (NAE/CASEE) completed her PhD in Chemistry from North Carolina State University in December 2006. Her interdisciplinary research focus was on modifying chemical and physical properties at the liquid/solid interface to address optimizing surface chemistry applications. T his research was a collaborative effort in both chemistry and chemical engineering departments. While in graduate school, Tiffani was selected as a Southern Regional Education Board Doctoral Scholar (AGEP), a NASA Harriet Jenkins Predoctoral Fellow and was a recipient of the American Chemical Society YCC Leadership Development Award. Her undergraduate studies were conducted at Hampton University, where she earned her BS in chemistry. During her time as a fellow at the National Academies, Tiffani is interested in enhancing her knowledge on the impact of science and technology policy in higher education. She also hopes to gain insight on assessing and evaluating grants or funds disseminated for research and development. Tiffani has been involved in science and technology research since the age of 7 and is passionate about the importance of educational programs to keep students in the S&T pipeline. In her leisure time she enjoys volunteering in the community, traveling, and being a mentor to students. Contact by email (phd4tiffani@gmail.com).

Pamela Bradley (IOM/IOM EO) received her Ph.D. from The Johns Hopkins School of Medicine in 2001. Her doctoral research, supported by a Howard Hughes Medical Institute Predoctoral Fellowship, investigated how organs adopt a particular shape and position using the fruit fly model system. Her postdoctoral research, at Harvard Medical School and the National Institutes of Health, is aimed at elucidating the molecular mechanisms that control how cells change shape during development. Pam is interested in the translation and application of basic science research to medicine and is looking forward to being a fellow with the Institute of Medicine, where she will support the Roundtable on Evidence-Based Medicine. She hopes to learn how advances in science and clinical medicine are integrated into health policy for the benefit of public health. Whenever possible, she enjoys traveling, especially when it involves sailing, hiking or SCUBA diving. Contact by email (pamelabradley@gmail.com).

Susan Burke (PGA/COSEPUP) is currently completing her Ph.D. in physics at the University of Arizona. Her doctoral research was conducted at the Fermi National Accelerator Laboratory in Batavia, IL, where she studied the top quark—the heaviest known elementary particle. Susan received her B.S. in physics from Miami University, and spent her junior year as an exchange student at the University of Helsinki, Finland. While in graduate school, Susan developed interests in both science communication and science policy. She was a 2002 AAAS Mass Media Fellow, writing and delivering radio stories on a broad range of scientific topics for a NPR-member station in Columbus, OH. Later, she served as the principal investigator of a study assessing the climate for women in her physics department. Susan is excited to be a fellow with COSEPUP where she may continue to research issues that affect the participation of women and minorities in science. She is also considering a career in science policy and sees this fellowship as an opportunity to explore this possibility. In her spare time, Susan enjoys visiting museums, taking walks, and scouring used bookstores. She currently chairs the Fermilab International Film Society. Contact by email (sburke@physics.arizona.edu).

Albert Epshteyn (BCST/DELS) graduated from the University of Maryland, College Park with a PhD in Chemistry in December 2006. In his graduate research Albert explored the fundamental reactivity of early transition metals as pertaining to small molecule activation and catalyst development. In particular, his work enabled the identification of a new class of stable Ta(IV) alkyl complexes. Albert's undergraduate studies were also at UMD where he was a Banneker-Key scholar. He obtained his Biochemistry B.S. degree and participated in a Gemstone undergraduate interdisciplinary research project studying prison overcrowding in the US. After 4 years the Gemstone project culminated in a presentation at the November 2000 American Society of Criminology Conference in San Francisco entitled GPS Sex Offender Tracking, and in a report to the Maryland Lieutenant Governor. Albert is happy to have the opportunity to work with BCST, since he has always been interested in the way governmental entities obtain and utilize scientific information. In the long term Albert hopes that his varied interests will lead him on a career path to improving science education and general interest in science. In his spare time Albert enjoys cooking, tennis, B&W film photography, and learning Spanish. Contact by email (albert.epshteyn@gmail.com).

Patrick Foley (COSEPUP/PGA) is currently completing his PhD at the University of Arkansas at Little Rock in Applied Physics. His research is focused upon optimization of active sound cancellation components through interactive visualization. He received a B.A. in Physics at Hendrix College in Conway, AR with a minor in Classics. For the past two years, he has worked for the Virtual Reality Center at UALR, programming and demonstrating a CAVE Automatic Virtual Environment for university guests. During the summers, he has also worked under a NASA EPSCOR grant funding research on a hybrid rocket. Patrick is unsure of his long-term career goals, and hopes that the Convocation on Rising above the Gathering Storm will help him understand the demands of the scientific community and his place within it. He is excited to gather information to help Arkansas adapt to the rapidly changing needs of scientific inquiry. Patrick enjoys fishing, Frisbee, and games of all sorts. Contact by email (airdish2@gmail.com).

Friederike Haass (NAS/PNAS) is a fifth year Neuroscience graduate student at the University of California San Francisco in Lily Jan's laboratory. For her thesis project she studies how potassium channels (proteins in the cell membrane that act as gates to regulate the flow of potassium ions) are assembled and trafficked to the right location within the cell. She grew up in Germany and studied Biology at the University of Wuerzburg. For her "Diplom" research thesis, Friederike worked in Ed Kravitz's lab at Harvard Medical School on fighting behavior in lobsters. She would like to apply her science background to work in a team environment and address questions relating as to how science affects society and what society should ask of science to solve problems. She looks forward to learning about this process during her fellowship with PNAS. Friederike participated in BioTeach for three years, planning and implementing hands-on science experiments for 7th graders. This past summer, she did a part-time internship with the California Council on Science and Technology. In her spare time, she likes to read, particularly newspapers and books on history and politics, play the violin, visit museums, and attend classical music/opera performances. Contact by email (Friederike. Haass@ucsf.edu).

Jonathan Hickman (DELS/PRB & BASC) is currently working towards his Ph.D. in Ecology and Evolution at SUNY at Stony Brook. He became interested in biogeochemistry and ecophysiology in his first two years of grad school, and for his dissertation he's examining how relatively unique aspects of the physiology of kudzu, and invasive vine, is leading to substantial impacts on ecosystems and atmospheric chemistry. During college and for several years afterwards, Jonathan's focus was distinctly non-scientific—he completed a B.A. in English and Studio Art from Vassar College in 1995, and then worked as a researcher first at the Council on Economic Priorities and then for FORTUNE magazine. He's very excited to be taking a break from academe (and the lab) for a few weeks. Jonathan feels the draw of a career in policy very strongly, but at the same time, he really enjoys doing scientific research, and it's difficult to consider severing himself from it completely. He hopes that the fellowship experience will help him reconcile those two apparently conflicting desires. In his spare time, he enjoys the odd NPR podcast, Billy Wilder movies, making music, and occasionally playing tennis or squash very poorly. Contact by email (jhickman@gmail. com).

Marc Humphrey (PGA/CISAC) earned his Ph.D. in physics from Harvard University in 2003 and his B.S. at Western Michigan University in 1997. His dissertation, conducted at the Harvard-Smithsonian Center for Astrophysics, focused on both theoretical and experimental aspects of precision measurements in atomic physics. After devoting one year to language training in Germany and France, he extended his skills to the international arena as a Peace Corps Volunteer in West Africa. His service included a ten-month water and sanitation assignment in rural Mali, followed by a data management post with the U.S. Centers for Disease Control and Prevention in Bamako. Following his Peace Corps service, Marc intends to apply his physics training and foreign policy interests to the fields of arms control and nuclear non-proliferation. He hopes to build on his experience at CISAC to become an international security policy analyst or diplomat. For many years, Marc has held a passion for traveling to distant places, experiencing diverse cultures, and learning about foreign affairs. In addition, after two years in the desert, Marc is anxious to rediscover ice and to rekindle his love of hockey. Contact by email (mhumphrey@post.harvard.edu).

Sabrina Jedlicka (PGA/COSEPUP) is currently completing her Ph.D. in Agricultural and Biological Engineering at Purdue University. Her highly interdisciplinary doctoral research is focused on the functional modulation of neuronal phenotype and neurotransmitter release via induction by rationally designed novel biomaterial peptide surfaces. Currently her materials are being applied to novel cell-silicon therapies for epilepsy. She holds a dual B.S. from Kansas State University in Chemical Science and Biological & Agricultural Engineering; while performing research in a variety of areas, including veterinary diagnostics, biomaterials, bioremediation, and developmental physiology. Sabrina is looking forward to working with COSEPUP, where she likely will focus on ethics in research and the integrity of research data. She has always been multidisciplinary in her research, academic, and career interests and hopes that a policy fellowship will allow her to utilize her talents in science, while challenging her to cultivate an understanding of ethics and policy development. In her free time, she enjoys running, hiking, exploring art museums, and reading. Contact by email (ssjedlicka@hotmail.com).

Sandra N. Ottensmann (PGA/CSTL) just received her M.S. in chemistry from Stanford University, where her graduate work focused on the synthesis of glycosyltransferase transmembrane domains for use in studying carbohydrate synthesis pathways. She received a B.S. in chemistry from the California Institute of Technology in 2005. As an undergraduate, she performed research on liquid crystalline polymers at Caltech and on thermoelectric materials at NASA's Jet Propulsion Laboratory. Sandy is excited to be working at the CSTL, where she hopes to learn how scientists and lawyers work together to create new policy decisions. Her future plans possibly include attending law school in order to gain a background in law in addition to her scientific education, so she can eventually work at the intersection of law and science. In her free time, she enjoys great food and wine, reading, rollerblading, video games and cooking. Contact by email (sandrao@alumni.caltech.edu).

Florence Roan (IOM/BGH) received a combined M.D./Ph.D. degree from Emory University in May 2003, where her graduate research focused on the regulation of cellular cytokines by human herpesvirus 8 (HHV-8; KSHV), the viral etiologic agent of Kaposi's Sarcoma. She holds a B.A. in biology and biochemistry from Rice University in Houston, Texas. She has recently completed a residency in internal medicine at Washington University in Saint Louis and will be starting a fellowship in infectious diseases at the University of Washington in July 2007. While she ultimately intends to be involved in research in infectious disease immunology and clinical practice in an academic setting, she is also very interested in the social challenges that the infectious disease field presents and hopes to be an active participant in the dialogue on public health and health policy. She is enthusiastic about her fellowship with the Forum on Microbial Threats and increasing her understanding of the underlying issues that inform our national priorities and agendas and the role of scientists in forming policy. In her free time, she enjoys technical scuba diving, good food, wine and music. Contact by email (froan@comcast.net).

Simil Roupe (NAE/DEW) is currently finishing her Ph.D. in biomedical engineering at Johns Hopkins University. Her thesis is focused on neural and vocal plasticity as a result of deafness in primates. She is interested in how the brain learns and processes language and along with a B.S.E in mechanical engineering she also received a B.A. in Spanish language from Oral Roberts University in Tulsa. Before attending college Simil worked for three years in an elementary school, and she has a strong desire to work on improving science and mathematics education especially for underrepresented groups. She is excited to begin her fellowship with the DEW program this year, and hopes the experience will give her a broader perspective on how scientists can be an influence toward socially responsible public policy. In her free time, Simil likes to hike and explore or play games with friends, and she is looking forward to meeting new people and making new friends during her time in D.C. Contact by email (similr@gmail.com).

Carolyn Williams (NAE/NAE EO) is currently completing her PhD in chemical engineering at the University of California, Los Angeles. Her dissertation research focuses on the use of synthetic gene-circuits in Escherichia coli for improved precursor and cofactor availability during secondary metabolite production. This research would create a dynamic microbial strain for industrial-level synthesis of biopharmaceuticals and other desirable products. She completed her BS in biomedical engineering at Johns Hopkins University in 2003. Carolyn is excited to be working at the NAE, where she anticipates being involved in a project to evaluate the success of different organizations at incorporating engineering concepts into standard K-12 curricula. During her fellowship, she hopes to gain insight into the process of science and engineering curriculum development and the formulation of education policy. Carolyn enjoys reading, singing, snowboarding, and theater. Contact by email (cari@ucla.edu).

Davidson Fellows Scholarship

9665 Gateway Drive, Suite B
Reno, NV 89521
(775) 852-3483 ext. 435
http://www.ditdgifted.org/Articles.aspx?ArticleID=146&NavID=4_3
http://tiny.cc/cjDD4

Description

This program recognizes and awards the extraordinary. All submissions should reflect prodigious development of talents focused on creating something of significance in Math, Science, or Technology. The Davidson Institute does not discriminate based on race, gender, religion, ethnicity or physical disability. All selection decisions are final.

Each application is examined for completeness and accuracy. Qualified entries are evaluated by an independent team of judges comprised of professionals with expertise in related domain areas. Application categories include Science, Technology, Math, Music, Literature, and Philosophy.

Recent Awards, Winning Projects & Award Winners

Alexandra Courtis (http://tiny.cc/BfZgs), 17
Davis, California
Category: Science
Project Title: "Bright Luminescent Silicon Nanoparticles for Biological Applications"
Scholarship: $50,000

A 17-year-old young woman from Davis, California, Alexandra Courtis developed a new method of creating luminescent silicon nanorods and quantum dots, used in biomedical imaging and cancer treatments to track biological processes. While traditional production methods of quantum dots are very costly, Alexandra used sodium silicide and ammonium bromide to produce highly luminescent particles making the synthesis of silicon nanoparticles commercially viable on a large-scale. Her research is considered a major advancement in the imaging of cancerous tumors at the cellular level and directed tumor targeting.

Yale Fan (http://tiny.cc/wU67F), 15
Beaverton, Oregon
Category: Technology
Project Title: "Applications of Multi-Valued Quantum Algorithms"
Scholarship: $50,000

A 15-year-old young man from Beaverton, Oregon, Yale Fan extended the binary quantum computational Deutsch-Jozsa and Grover algorithms to multi-valued logic problems. The Deutsch-Jozsa and Grover algorithms are among the first quantum algorithms designed for execution on a quantum computer. Yale discovered novel applications of these multi-valued algorithms and their computational advantages over the binary cases. The expanded versions of these algorithms are relevant to computer vision systems, search problems in economics, and space complexity issues in transportation, scheduling and manufacturing.

<u>**Madhavi Gavini**</u> (<u>http://tiny.cc/Af73H</u>), **17**
Starkville, Mississippi
Category: Science
Project Title: "Engineering a Novel Inhibitor of Biofilm-Encapsulated Pathogens"
Scholarship: $50,000

A 17-year-old young woman from Starkville, Mississippi, Madhavi Gavini engineered a method to inhibit the growth of biofilm-forming pathogens. Pseudomonas, an opportunistic, multi-drug resistant pathogen, produces biofilms that protect it from antibiotics and is a leading cause of death among patients with compromised immune systems. Through the combination of traditional Indian medicine and molecular biology, Madhavi identified a compound capable of penetrating and inhibiting the growth of the biofilm. This compound will be used in inhalers and antiseptic sprays and treat millions of people suffering from chronic Pseudomonas bacterial infections.

<u>**Danielle Lent**</u> (<u>http://tiny.cc/kCcUj</u>), **17**
Cedarhurst, New York
Category: Science
Project Title: "Optimizing Recycled Polymer Blends Using Supercritical Carbon Dioxide"
Scholarship: $25,000

A 17-year-old young woman from Cedarhurst, New York, Danielle Lent developed a method of recycling plastics that is cost-efficient and environmentally friendly. By exposing polymers to supercritical carbon dioxide, a phase of carbon dioxide that exhibits unique properties as a solvent, Danielle created a process of recycling that produces plastics that have equal or superior properties of the original material allowing for their continued use. Danielle's process does not release toxins and may create a net loss of carbon dioxide.

<u>**Janet Song**</u> (<u>http://tiny.cc/Dku1m</u>), **15**
Norristown, Pennsylvania
Category: Science
Project Title: "Development of a Urine Test for the Early Detection of Cancer"
Scholarship: $25,000

A 15-year-old young woman from Norristown, Pennsylvania, Janet Song used carboxylated magnetic beads to develop a urine test for the early detection of cancer. Urine has been shown to contain short-length, circulatory DNA from possible tumor sites. Janet developed a method to isolate the short-length DNA from urine and demonstrated that the use of the isolated DNA greatly increased the sensitivity in detecting a cancer-associated mutation. The use of a urine test for cancer screening would be less invasive, less unpleasant, and less expensive than current cancer screening methods, increasing compliance rates and allowing for the early detection of cancer.

Richard Alt, II (http://tiny.cc/mmiVE), 17
Fredericksburg, Pennsylvania
Category: Science
Project Title: "A Comparison of Three Seasonal Snowfall Forecasting Methods for Winter 2004-05"
Scholarship: $10,000

A 17-year-old young man from Fredericksburg, Virginia, Richard Alt compared three weather forecasting methods for accuracy in predicting snowfall with historical climate data for his hometown and synthesized this information to create a new forecasting mechanism. Through analysis and interpretation of large-scale, upper-air and surface climatological circulation patterns, dynamics, and physics, Richard created a universal forecasting method that can be used anywhere on earth with sufficient, historical weather records. Richard's research can help meteorologists compile more accurate forecasts and help public officials prepare seasonal response plans.

Billy Dorminy (http://tiny.cc/Ffugr), 15
McDonough, Georgia
Category: Technology
Project Title: "Improper Fractional Base Encryption"
Scholarship: $10,000

A 15-year-old young man from McDonough, Georgia, Billy Dorminy invented a secure method of encrypting messages using reduced redundancy representations of improper fractional bases (IFBs), a number base using improper fractions. Billy created a new method of encryption using these representations, which takes up less computer memory and uses both confusion and diffusion to hide a message. As the first secure method of encryption using IFBs, this system allows a second encrypted message to be undetectable within the body of the main message and opens a new area for encryption exploration.

Graham Van Schaik (http://tiny.cc/KePHO), 16
Columbia, South Carolina
Category: Science
Project Title: "Pyrethroid Pesticides and Their Potential to Promote Breast Cancer and Neurodegeneration"
Scholarship: $10,000

A 16-year-old young man from Columbia, South Carolina, Graham Van Schaik researched pyrethroids, chemicals found in common household and agricultural pesticides. More than 30 commercial crops are treated with pyrethroids and they have been found in meats, seeds and baby food. Graham determined the residual amounts of pyrethroids found in tomatoes and possible inhalation when used in a home environment. By extrapolating human consumption and inhalation, he found pyrethroids were retained in both cases and promoted statistically significant cellular proliferation in human breast cells, a sign of cancer, and significant neurite retraction in neurons, a sign of neurodegenerative diseases.

Nora Xu (http://tiny.cc/3AwxH), 17
Naperville, Illinois
Category: Science
Project Title: "Modeling of X-Ray Scattering for Nanocrystal Superlattice Multilayer Thin Films"
Scholarship: $10,000

A 17-year-old young woman from Naperville, Illinois, Nora Xu developed a unique method of determining the crystal structure of nanocrystalline superlattice (NCS) thin films. Nora proposed treating the NCS multilayer thin films as a set of two-dimensional lattice points with each basis in three-dimensional space. Using this model, Nora confirmed x-ray scattering pattern intensities which can be applied to molecules and atoms. Nora's research has potential in optical and electron microscopes, as a delivery system for biomolecules, and as a vector for drug delivery to cancerous tumors.

The Graphic Arts Education and Research Foundation (GAERF®)

1899 Preston White Drive
Reston, Virginia 20191
Voice: 703/264-7200
Toll Free: 1/866/381-9839
http://www.gaerf.org/about/gaerf.html
http://tiny.cc/qPGFB

http://www.gaerf.org/blasts/grants_release.html
http://tiny.cc/B5Zlg

Description

The Graphic Arts Education and Research Foundation (GAERF®) is an organization whose mission is to advance knowledge and education in the field of graphic communications by supporting programs that prepare the workforce of the future.

GAERF was founded in 1983 by the National Association for Printing Leadership (NAPL), NPES The Association for Suppliers of Printing, Publishing and Converting Technologies and the Printing Industries of America/Graphic Arts Technical Foundation (PIA/GATF). These three national associations jointly own the Graphic Arts Show Company (GASC®). GAERF was created to channel a portion of the revenues earned by GASC-managed shows, such as GRAPH EXPO® and PRINT®, into projects supporting a strong future for the industry.

Recent Awards, Winning Projects & Award Winners

RESTON, VA, January 5, 2007... Three major initiatives have received continuing funding in 2007 from the Graphic Arts Education and Research Foundation (GAERF®). These programs aim to excite high school students about careers in graphic communications, extend career information and opportunities to the deaf and hard-of-hearing, and expand a thriving nationwide web portal for graphic communications teachers and students. All three projects have previously received awards from the Foundation to support their planning and development, and the additional assistance will be used for implementation, field testing, or continuing expansion.

The International Printing Museum, Carson, CA

The GAERF grant to the International Printing Museum will subsidize the second year of a three-year project. Phase one included the research and development of interactive learning modules that teach historical graphic communications processes to high school and post-secondary students, ranging from paper-making to typesetting to historical approaches to color reproduction.

In phase two, the monies will be used to develop the hands-on lab at the International Printing Museum that will teach the learning modules, and to create the mobile graphic arts lab that will enable these same modules to be taught "on the road" to students who cannot visit the museum.

"Our goal is to supplement what teachers are already doing," says director Mark Barbour. The museum's previous experience indicates that students are extremely excited by the chance to work with historical machinery and materials. "This is like Velcro, attaching the kids to our industry," Barbour adds.

The National Technical Institute for the Deaf (NTID), Rochester Institute of Technology (RIT), Rochester, NY

In 2006, GAERF provided the National Technical Institute for the Deaf (NTID) at the Rochester Institute of Technology (RIT) with financial backing to create, test, and evaluate an interactive web site targeted toward deaf high school students that provides career exploration in graphic communications. Thomas Raco, faculty member and director of the graphic communications program at NTID notes that the continuing funding will allow for the public deployment of the web site, creation of several videos profiling deaf/hearing-impaired industry professionals, and organization of a large library of links.

"We hope to be able to test the program by next fall, with selected high schools that have significant populations of deaf students," says Raco. The site will provide extensive information about the industry and its career offerings, together with an interactive link that will enable visitors to connect online with a career counselor. "We're now looking for appropriate deaf and hard-of-hearing professionals to be in our videos, which we hope to begin shooting in January," Raco says.

GRAPHIC COMM CENTRAL, Virginia Polytechnic and State University, Blacksburg, VA

"For the GRAPHIC COMM CENTRAL (GCC) project, this year marks the end of a decade of service to the graphic communications profession as the education portal for educators, students, and those in the industry wishing to 'connect' with the education sector," says project director Mark

Sanders. Sanders noted that the web portal has expanded almost continuously in recent years, and now offers curriculum materials, discussion groups, and thousands of links to industry resources.

"This past summer, the GCC Project upgraded from the WebSTAR server application that we used successfully for about eight years to Apple's OSX server application," Sanders says, explaining this major technology migration will enable GRAPHIC COMM CENTRAL to manage its extensive contents more effectively.

Mellon Awards for Tech Collaboration

282 Alexander Rd.
Princeton, NJ 08540
609-924-9424
Christopher J. Mackie
http://matc.mellon.org/nominations
http://tiny.cc/SFnHd

Description

The Program in Research in Information Technology of the Andrew W. Mellon Foundation invites nominations for the 2008 Mellon Awards for Technology Collaboration (MATC). In support of the Program's mission to encourage collaborative, open source software development within traditional Mellon constituencies, these awards recognize not-for-profit organizations that are making substantial contributions of their own resources toward the development of open source software and the fostering of collaborative communities to sustain open source development.

The MATC awards provide the recipients with opportunities to strengthen their commitment to inter-organizational collaboration and open source software development. Awards are given at two levels: $50,000 awards to recognize important organizational contributions to open source projects which currently or potentially provide significant benefits to at least one traditional Mellon constituency; and $100,000 awards to recognize highly significant contributions to open source projects offering larger benefits to more or larger constituencies. Multiple awards may be bestowed at each level, at the discretion of the Award Committee and the Trustees of the Foundation.

Recent Awards, Winning Projects & Award Winners

http://matc.mellon.org/winners/2007-matc-awardees-announced/
http://tiny.cc/lrYgN

- American Museum of the Moving Image (Astoria, NY: www.movingimage.us) for the development and release of the OpenCollection museum collection management system (www.opencollection.org).

- Duke University (Durham, NC: www.duke.edu) for leadership and development work on the OpenCroquet open source 3-D virtual worlds environment (www.opencroquet.org).
- Open Polytechnic of New Zealand (Wellington, NZ: www.openpolytechnic.ac.nz) for leadership and development work on several open source projects including the New Zealand Open Source Virtual Learning Environment (http://eduforge.org/projects/nzvle/).

- Georgia Public Library Service of the University System of Georgia (Atlanta, GA: www.georgialibraries.org) for the development and release of the Evergreen open-source library automation system (www.open-ils.org).
- Middlebury College (Middlebury, VT: www.middlebury.edu) for the development and release of the Segue interactive learning management system.
- Participatory Culture Foundation (Worcester, MA: www.participatoryculture.org) for the development and release of the open source Miro media player (www.getmiro.com).
- Talboks- och punktskriftsbiblioteket (The Swedish Library of Talking Books and Braille: Enskede, Sweden: www.tpb.se) for the development and release of open source tools supporting the Daisy Project for talking books for the visually impaired.
- Two awards to University of Illinois (Champaign-Urbana, IL: www.illinois.edu): one award for the development and release of the Firefox Accessibility Extension (https://addons.mozilla.org/en-US/firefox/addon/1891); and one award for the development and release of the OpenEAI enterprise application integration project (www.openEAI.org).
- University of Toronto (Toronto, Ontario: www.utoronto.ca) for the development and release of the ATutor learning management system (www.atutor.ca).

Microsoft Innovative Teachers Award

1-800-342-9224 ext 300

http://www.microsoft.com/education/innovativeteachers.mspx
http://tiny.cc/5dYEs

http://www.microsoft.com/education/innovativeteachersabout.mspx
http://tiny.cc/yt0K5

http://www.microsoft.com/australia/education/pil/innovativeteachers/awards.mspx
http://tiny.cc/1XZRj

Description

Join the worldwide Microsoft Innovative Teachers program and become an active stakeholder in your profession. Network within a global community interested in education focused on 21st century learning, and be recognized for your exemplary efforts to prepare students to become productive 21st century citizens.

Our program has two primary offerings:

Innovative Teachers Forums

Regional, country-wide and worldwide annual events that reward teachers who practice elements of 21st century learning and then incorporate these skills into the student learning environment. Learn more (http://tiny.cc/b7hi0)

Innovative Teachers Network

A worldwide network of portals—local in implementation but global in reach and scope—that allows educators to share successful methodology and protocols on an international basis. Get started (http://tiny.cc/qve8n)

Recent Awards, Winning Projects & Award Winners

Andrew Douch
Wanganui Park Secondary College, Shepparton, Victoria

Andrew Douch created a virtual classroom where students and teachers share information, lessons and projects. Students are using the forum to publish oral and visual presentations they've created with various technologies, while teachers are setting up discussion groups, forums and quizzes on MSN®. A Microsoft® Office SharePoint® site enables content to be automatically distributed to students' mobile devices, inboxes and a public forum.

Andrew runs professional development on weekly basis to help colleagues use technology and as a result 80 percent of teachers at the school are using Office SharePoint sites with their classes and 20 percent are using podcasts.

"We're seeing a 10 percent improvement in student achievement in VCEA exams as a result of using these new approaches. Students are much more engaged. Podcasting removes barriers between groups, for example, gender, social, year and school groups. This is truly innovative, because it redefines the idea of 'classroom? There are more than 2000 students across the world that are joining in in the podcasts, and they often respond by sending in emails and their own content for the podcasts."

View resources (http://tiny.cc/WkXas)

Andrew Lord
Spence Primary School, Aberfoyle Primary School Campus, South Australia

How do you help students transform personal experiences into shared stories? Andrew Lord introduced digital media to help young students express themselves, build self-esteem and learn new skills. The students are using blogging and online resources to produce multimedia texts incorporating Web pages, video and audio.

"By tightly incorporating new technologies into the classroom, I've engaged students in richer tasks that promote independent thought, problem solving and critical thinking," says Andrew. "For example, they produced a CD of their own dance music, recorded an opera and created an intranet postcard service. They even made a film about school bullying – all using Microsoft-based technologies."

Because the students' work is easily viewed online, parents are more engaged in their children's learning and have a greater understanding of school directions and priorities so they can offer support.

View resources (http://tiny.cc/nnezM)

Jennifer Lobb
Anula Primary School, Northern Territory

Jennifer Lobb developed an online community where Year 4 and 5 students and their parents can participate in lessons from anywhere. Using Janison Toolbox, a component-based learning management system, students built a collaborative Web site where they can store book reviews, stories and wikis.

Accessible from school or home, this learning space enables students to interact safely with others around the world using a range of technologies. And it means students with disabilities or long-term absences can stay in touch with classmates and keep up with their studies.

Jennifer encourages students to involve their families so they can support their children through learning. Jennifer comments: "Students started out working alone, but they quickly began collaborating. Before long they would complete assignments or projects at home with their parents, then show me their joint achievements the following day."

View resources (http://tiny.cc/hI9cC)

Marie Leech & Heather Wessling
Kurwongbah State School, Petrie, Queensland

It's not easy to achieve a sustainable community when untamed critters with bad attitudes are out to spoil it. Learning how to solve these problems and more while playing the Xbox 360? game Viva Piñata? helped Marie Leech and Heather Wessling's year 6 and 7 students understand critical relationships within ecosystems. As they played, they achieved Science outcomes and developed skills in other subjects, including English, Mathematics and Art.

Viva Piñata provides a fantastical digital environment to which students must lure wild cybercreatures called piñatas. It's up to each student to choose the piñatas they want to attract, care for them and maintain a sustainable community. They can spend resources, for example, chocolate coins, to adjust their ecosystems to suit their favourite piñatas.

The game offered a valuable learning experience for teachers and students alike. Heather says, We found our role shifted from teacher to facilitator of learning experiences. Students were so enthusiastic that Marie and Heather decided to produce a chatroom devoted to the game. Marie says, Students can discuss Viva Piñata online and participate in blogs and forums to share tips and tricks."
View resources (http://tiny.cc/JgZKs)

Pat McMahon
Diamond Valley College, Diamond Creek, Victoria

For many students, there's nothing more exciting than building something. For Pat McMahon's students, it's robots - and technology skills.

Students start by recording their ideas and developing designs using Microsoft® Visual Basic® and CAD. They then construct their own programmable microcontrollers using various self-diagnostic tools and tutorials. Projects range from light-and-tune models to infrared-controlled LEDs, tanks, hexapods and robots. Some can read and display temperature, sense colour, test fabric for sun-smart qualities, run servo motors and even control pneumatic devices. The students use a variety of tools to complement their design work, including Windows Media® Player and Microsoft® Office PowerPoint®.

Pat McMahon comments: Technology enables students to understand and digitally record their experiences. They also learn from constructing, testing, programming and diagnosing faults. I've found that students are highly motivated to complete their designs and then proudly share them with others.
View resources (http://tiny.cc/UCR05)

Robin McKean and Raelene Beecher
St Hilda's Anglican School for Girls, Mosman Park, Western Australia

At St Hilda's, Year 5 students are journeying around the world without leaving the school grounds. Using GPS coordinates and Microsoft-based PDAs, Robin McKean and Raelene Beecher designed a virtual journey so that students could visit and compare different communities. At every step of the way, they're developing mapping and other skills as they collate and analyse all the data, both virtual and real.

It all started with Antarctica. Robin McKean explains: "Using Microsoft® Office, Microsoft® Photo Story and third party applications we simulated a trip to Antarctica. Students used PDAs and headphones to locate and investigate land forms, species and food webs and of course uncover environmental issues. They roamed around using the PDAs to find the next clue a little like The Amazing Race?."
View resources (http://tiny.cc/BYv7y)

Roxanne Steenbergen and Wendy Fletcher
Claremont and Lenah Valley Primary Schools, Hobart, Tasmania

Although Roxanne Steenbergen and Wendy Fletcher teach in schools that are 12 kilometres apart, their students are learning about chemistry in the same classroom.

Cool Chemistry is a virtual classroom with content developed using Microsoft technologies. It provides hands-on activities so Grade 4 and 5 students can investigate chemistry concepts. As they discover chemistry, they can share ideas, results and reports online. And with a practising chemist on hand, they can get answers to their curliest questions. They used Microsoft® Photo Story and Microsoft® Office PowerPoint® to communicate their findings to their school communities.

Roxanne says: "Primary school students don?t often have an opportunity to study chemistry, and we wanted them to experience it as a fun, exciting subject from the start. Motivation and excitement was high as children saw and heard what those in the other school were doing. They could see if experiments turned out the same way in different hands and ask the chemist why it happened."

At the end of the class students work in teams to construct an alien, a genetically engineered creature or a city of the future, then present their creation to the class. That proved fatal for the edible alien, a sentient being in the form of a cake. By the end of the class it was no more.
View resources (http://tiny.cc/gz0NB)

Tim Gorrod
Buladelah Central School, NSW

Tim Gorrod inspires Year 7 and 8 students to build technology skills and collaborate online by asking them to produce a claymation short film.

The project spans all key learning areas. Tim explains: "Students do scripting and storyboards. They compose original music, design and construct sets and produce clay figures for the stop-frame animation. Also quite a lot of calculation is involved in timing the animation. So students develop many skills across all their subjects and have fun at the same time."

The students use Microsoft technologies to make their films and communicate and collaborate using a Microsoft® Office SharePoint® Web portal. And when they?re finished, they upload their films to the portal and viewers rate them. Top-rated movies are screened at a gala night where family and friends are invited to tread the red carpet with the school?s budding filmmakers.
View resources (http://tiny.cc/tW1uC)

Todd George
Port Lincoln High School, South Australia

Todd George Port Lincoln High School, South Australia In the remote Eyre Peninsula, 44 students spread across 42,995 square kilometres are using webcams to get a fresh perspective on learning. Todd George and Peter Tokarski introduced videoconferencing to help them stay in touch and develop personal skills, community and school relationships, and educational and career opportunities through sport.

Todd has found videoconferencing a very effective way to engage isolated or disinclined students and connect them to learning. At Port Lincoln it has boosted indigenous attendance, as students who do well often go on to attend other classes. Teachers benefit too, with weekly videoconferencing greatly enhancing collaboration.

Todd says: "One disengaged Year 11 student was the only senior secondary student enrolled in his school and he stayed on because this program was offered. Now he is an engaged student, passing all subjects, with an apprenticeship on the horizon and an Australian Football Scholarship."
View resources (http://tiny.cc/zezOu)

Competition on Microsoft Office Specialist Exam

http://www.officecompetition.com/index.html
http://tiny.cc/CZyUV

http://www.officecompetition.com/participants.html
http://tiny.cc/CgHhT

Description

Any student aged 14+ years may participate in the competition by taking an eligible Microsoft Office certification exam at a Certiport Testing Center

NEH Digital Humanities Fellowships

Room 318
National Endowment for the Humanities
1100 Pennsylvania Avenue, N.W.
Washington, D.C. 20506
202-606-8200
http://www.neh.gov/GRANTS/guidelines/DH_Fellowships.html#howto
http://tiny.cc/Sh2OS

Description

NEH Digital Humanities Fellowships are intended to support individuals pursuing advanced research or other projects in the humanities that explore the relationship between technologies and the humanities; or produce digital products such as electronic publications, digital archives, or databases, advanced digital representations of extant data using graphical displays such as geographic information systems (GIS) or other digital media, or digital analytical tools that further humanistic research.

Fellowships support full-time work on a humanities projects for a period of six to twelve months. Applicants may be faculty or staff members of colleges, universities, or they may be independent scholars or writers.

IRA Presidential Award for Reading and Technology

International Reading Association
Headquarters Office
800 Barksdale Rd.
PO Box 8139
Newark, DE 19714-8139
USA
1-800-336-READ (1-800-336-7323), U.S. and Canada
+302-731-1600, elsewhere
http://www.reading.org/association/awards/teachers_presidential.html
http://tiny.cc/PzQmS

Description

The Presidential Award for Reading and Technology honors educators in grades K–12 who are making an outstanding and innovative contribution to the use of technology in reading education. There will be one grand-prize winner, seven U.S. regional winners, one Canadian, and one international winner. All entrants must be educators who work directly with students ages 5–18 for all or part of the working day.

Recent Awards, Winning Projects & Award Winners

Grand prize winner
Larry Ferlazzo

Regional winners
Kathy Cassidy
Rachael Ogbin
Janette C. Stubbs
Eric Benson
Sara R. Van Abel
Jo Ann Merritt
Amy Cantrell
Eric Langhorst
Helena Marie Stevens

Reuters Digital Vision Fellowship

210 Panama Street
Stanford, CA 94305-4115
1 650 724 4069
Stuart Gannes
http://rdvp.org/become/faq
http://tiny.cc/kcW3G

Description

Each year, the RDVP hosts an elite group of seasoned professionals from around the world
at Stanford. These Fellows work on interdisciplinary projects that utilize information and
communication technologies (ICTs) to address real needs in underserved communities. RDVP
Fellows bring a unique understanding of the realities of a particular emerging market or community
to the Program. During their nine-months on campus, they collaborate with Stanford faculty and
students, private sector firms, and non-governmental organizations (NGOs) to translate this market
knowledge into culturally relevant and sustainable product and service concepts. The end goal of the
RDVP is two-fold: accelerate community development and acquire valuable market knowledge.

Recent Awards, Winning Projects & Award Winners

Michael Chertok (http://tiny.cc/HeEM2)
RETOOL: Re-engineering Employment Training through Outsourcing Opportunities in LDCs

Isha Garg (http://tiny.cc/UBCU9)
Disease Surveillance
India

Shashank Garg (http://tiny.cc/02Yop)
Mobile, Integrated Disease Surveillance System
India

Marvin Hall (http://tiny.cc/MPIfr)
Robotics Stimul-I
Jamaica

Nam Mokwunye (http://tiny.cc/kWRda)
100 Nigerian Universities To Become Digital Campuses
Nigeria

Ahmad Atif Mumtaz (http://tiny.cc/7gDI2)
Tele-Health-Care for Disaster Relief
Pakistan

Seymour Cray Computer Science and Engineering Award

1828 L St., NW Suite 1202
Washington, DC 20036-5104
Pamela Kemper (Awards Administrator)
http://awards.computer.org/ana/award/viewHomepage.action
http://tiny.cc/RkHpq

Description

The Seymour Cray Computer Science and Engineering Award, also known as the Seymour Cray Award, is an award (http://tiny.cc/LuLvW) given to recognize significant and innovative contributions in the field of high-performance computing (http://tiny.cc/fygLh). The award honors scientists who exhibit the creativity (http://tiny.cc/pVy4M) demonstrated by Seymour Cray (http://tiny.cc/JWBtl), founder of Cray, Inc. (http://tiny.cc/VmolZ) and an early pioneer of supercomputing (http://tiny.cc/u6Sz2). The winner receives a crystal memento, certificate (http://tiny.cc/MCTuZ), and US$ (http://tiny.cc/rkS11) 10,000.

Recent Awards, Winning Projects & Award Winners

Ken Batcher (http://tiny.cc/vhpJw), 2007. "For fundamental theoretical and practical contributions to massively parallel computation, including parallel sorting algorithms, interconnection networks, and pioneering designs of the STARAN (http://tiny.cc/ATwU5) and MPP (http://tiny.cc/rE4i8) computers."

SRC Master's Scholarship Program

Semiconductor Research Corporation
1101 Slater Road, Suite 120
Durham, NC 27703
(919) 941-9400
http://grc.src.org/member/about/aboutmas.asp
http://tiny.cc/BxdsP

http://grc.src.org/member/about/aboutmas.asp#apply
http://tiny.cc/Y2v24

Description

The Master's Scholarship Program addresses issues of improving educational opportunities at the master's level for students in under represented minority categories. The objectives of the program are: 1) to encourage academically gifted U.S./permanent resident students in these populations to pursue graduate research in areas consistent with SRC Global Research Collaboration (GRC) goals, and 2) to develop a cadre of highest quality minority candidates for doctoral study and hire by GRC companies.

The Master's Scholarship Program was created in 1997 for the purpose of attracting qualified students who are also in under represented minority categories to graduate study in areas of interest to the semiconductor industry. In 1999, the program was opened to women as a category and has since been opened to under under represented students holding refugee or political asylum status in the U.S. Currently, the Master's Scholarships are administered by either GRC or the SRC Education Alliance.

The Tech Museum Awards

201 South Market Street   San Jose, CA 95113
(408) 795-6338
Amanda Reilly
http://www.techawards.org/nominate/
http://tiny.cc/vFUhG

Description

The Tech Awards program inspires global engagement in applying technology to humanity's most pressing problems by recognizing the best of those who are utilizing innovative technology solutions to address the most urgent critical issues facing our planet. People all over the world are profoundly improving the human condition in the areas of education, equality, environment, health, and economic development through the use of technology. It is the goal of The Tech Awards to showcase their compelling stories and reward their brilliant accomplishments.

Recent Awards, Winning Projects & Award Winners

Diagnostics Development Unit, University of Cambridge & Diagnostics for the Real World Ltd.(http://tiny.cc/yGAAv)
(Cambridge, U.K.)

Emulsified Zero-Valent Iron (EZVI) Team (http://tiny.cc/1AAau)
(Kennedy Space Center, Florida)

Fundacion Terram (http://tiny.cc/3RCqc)
(Santiago, Chile)

Joe David Jones, Skyonic Corporation (http://tiny.cc/G4qAx)
(Austin, Texas USA)

Marc Andre Ledoux, Consortium SudEco Industrie (http://tiny.cc/pnoYG)
(Montreal, Canada)

P&G's Children's Safe Drinking Water Program (http://tiny.cc/rCE1m)
(USA)

PATH, Vaccine Vial Monitor (http://tiny.cc/l1CIp)
(Seattle, WA U.S.)

Solar Sailor (http://tiny.cc/sDaFi)
(Chatswood, Australia)

Vaxin Inc., Rapid-Response Bird Flu Vaccine
(http://tiny.cc/OeZrZ)
(U.S.)

Thomson ISI Outstanding Information Science Teacher Award

1320 Fenwick Lane, Suite 510
Silver Spring, MD 20910, USA
(301) 495-0900
http://www.asis.org/awards/outstandingteacher.html
http://tiny.cc/14as6

Description

The Thomson ISI Citation Analysis grant supports either research underway that is based on citation analysis by encouraging and assisting individuals in this area of study with a grant of $3,000 from the Thomson Institute for Scientific Information. Citation analysis is broadly defined, including but not limited to analyses using resources developed by Thomsosn ISI.

Recent Awards, Winning Projects & Award Winners

The ISI/ASIST Outstanding Information Science Teacher Award is presented each year to an individual who has demonstrated sustained excellence in teaching information science. In 2007, the honoree is Peter Ingwersen, research professor at the Department of Information Studies, Royal School of Library and Information Science in Copenhagen. He is a distinguished researcher and scholar whose contributions include, among others, suggesting cognitive approaches to interactive information retrieval theory and coining the term Webometrics to describe quantitative studies of the Web. His list of publications is impressive, his professional service is outstanding and his influence on the field is further enhanced through his teaching.

Verizon Tech Savvy Awards

http://www.famlit.org/site/c.gtJWJdMQIsE/b.2180327/
http://tiny.cc/CEmNX

http://literacynetwork.verizon.org/TLN/techsavvyawards
http://tiny.cc/dl8Wm

Description

The Verizon Tech Savvy Awards are the first national award designed to provide an incentive for grassroots, community-based nonprofit organizations and schools to create programs that demystify technology for parents, enabling them to better guide their children in the use of new media. The awards honor sustainable family literacy programs that help parents bridge the widening gap between adults' and children's understanding of technology. Those two generations must learn about technology together, so parents can be effective teachers and advocates to ensure that their children are literate in technology and prepared for the 21st century workforce. The awards are run by the esteemed National Center for Family Literacy (NCFL) with generous funding by the Verizon Foundation.

Recent Awards, Winning Projects & Award Winners

National Winner:
Enemy Swim Day School
Waubay, SD
Enemy Swim Day School connects generations through ICT literacy and the power of storytelling. The organization's RealeBook project increases parents' technology skills by teaching them to write and publish a children's book. Because the books incorporate the Dakota language, native to the

people of the Lake Traverse Reservation, the children gain a greater understanding of their heritage, increased respect for their parents and improved literacy skills.

East Region Winner:
Rhode Island Family Literacy Initiative

Providence, RI

The Rhode Island Family Literacy Initiative (RIFLI) uses the community library to provide ICT literacy programming to families for which English is a second language. In direct response to the growing immigrant community in Rhode Island, the program combines an ESL teacher with a technology instructor and a children's teacher to increase tech skills while improving English comprehension skills.

Midwest Region Winner:
Iowa Central Community College

Fort Dodge, IA

The Iowa Central Community College Adult Literacy Program empowers parents to be their child's first and best teacher. Using ICT literacy instruction, adult students learn how to use the Internet to communicate with their child's teacher through e-mail, to gain knowledge about Web sites that their children visit, to enhance writing skills, and to improve basic computer skills for job retention.

Mountain/Southwest Region Winner:
Forrest Outreach Foundation

Addison, TX

Forrest Outreach Foundation's Click-for-Success program seeks out the most economically disadvantaged families and brings ICT literacy instruction to them. Through weekly Computer Club classes, children improve their ICT skills. These improvements are reinforced during home visits where parents join students in using the hardware, software and Internet access provided by the program. Mentors work to establish the interconnectivity between parents and children furthering their education and skills together.

West/Northwest Region Winner:
Little Tokyo Service Center Community Development Corporation

Los Angeles, CA

Little Tokyo Service Center's DISKovery Angelina program provides ICT training to low-income immigrant families living in and around the Angelina Apartments community. Program participants learn to use computers to navigate the challenges of everyday life, including public transportation, housing information, child care programs and legal services. Through regular "Mommy and Me" and "Papi and Me" classes, students are transformed into teachers as they instruct their children how to use computers and the Internet to access educational tools and other resources.

Category: Libraries & Museums

AASL Information Technology Pathfinder Award

50 E. Huron Chicago, IL 60611
1-800-545-2433
http://www.ala.org/ala/aasl/aaslawards/itpathfinderawd/aaslinformation.cfm
http://tiny.cc/XEN1R

Description

Established in 1985 (as the Microcomputer in the Media Center Award), the award recognizes and honors a school library media specialist demonstrating vision and leadership through the use of information technology to build lifelong learners. This award, $1,000 to the school library media specialist and $500 to the library, is given in two categories--elementary (K-6) and secondary (7-12). Applicants must be AASL personal members.

ALISE Award for Library & Information Science Education

65 East Wacker Place, Suite 1900
Chicago, IL 60601-7246 USA
1 312 795 0996
Kathleen Combs (Executive Director)
http://www.alise.org/mc/page.do?sitePageId=55539
http://tiny.cc/mGZQJ

Description

The Association now known as the Association for Library and Information Science Education (ALISE) was founded as the Association of American Library Schools. The original association grew out of a series of informal meetings of library school faculty at American Library Association conferences which was known as the Round Table of Library School Instructors. The Round Table voted in 1915 to form a permanent organization and to be identified as the Association of American Library Schools. The Association has provided a forum for library educators to share ideas, to discuss issues, and to seek solutions to common problems. In 1983, the Association changed its name to its present form to reflect more accurately the mission, goals, and membership of the Association.

IMLS 21st Century Museum Professionals Grant

1800 M Street NW, 9th Floor
Washington, DC 20036-5802
202-653-4685
Christopher J. Reich (Senior Program Officer)
http://www.imls.gov/applicants/submitting.shtm
http://tiny.cc/EMpmK

Description

Museum professionals need high levels of knowledge and expertise as they help create public value for the communities they serve. The purpose of the 21st Century Museum Professionals program is to increase the capacity of museums by improving the knowledge and skills of museum professionals. 21st Century Museum Professionals grants are intended to have an impact upon multiple institutions by reaching broad groups of museum professionals throughout a city, county, state, region, or the nation.

Grants fund a broad range of activities, including the development and implementation of classes, seminars, and workshops; resources to support leadership development; collection, assessment, development and/or dissemination of information that leads to better museum operations; activities that strengthen the use of contemporary technology tools to deliver programs and services; support for the enhancement of pre-professional training programs; and organizational support for the development of internship and fellowship programs.

Recent Awards, Winning Projects & Award Winners

Art Education for the Blind – New York, NY
Year: 2007
Amount: $77,050
Grant: 21st Century Museum Professionals
 Art Education for the Blind (AEB) will complete the production and online launch of its "Handbook for Museums and Educators," a practical guide designed to facilitate the process of creating accessible programming for people with visual impairments or other disabilities. AEB will work with over ten museums to pilot and evaluate tools involving the development of accessible art education programs, disability awareness training for museum staff, and the creation of employment opportunities for persons with disabilities. Available both online and in CD format, the handbook's multimedia features will offer effective, user-friendly teaching tools, enabling users to select, download, and customize information and components most pertinent to their institutions' needs.

Seton Hall University – South Orange, NJ
Year: 2007
Amount: $209,487
Grant: 21st Century Museum Professionals

The newly founded Institute of Museum Ethics at Seton Hall University will launch a range of educational initiatives designed to help museum professionals create more transparent, accountable, and socially responsible institutions. Funding will support the introduction of two new courses on museum ethics in association with the University's M.A. program in Museum Professions that will be open to both graduate students and working professionals; a national conference on museum ethics; public lectures; workshops for University faculty on infusing ethics across the museum studies curriculum; and the design and launch of a unique web portal that will become a national resource featuring an ethics listserv, media feeds, and bibliographies and other tools to help museum professionals incorporate ethics into ongoing operations.

Essex County Historical Society – Elizabethtown, NY
Year: 2007
Amount: $338,585
Grant: 21st Century Museum Professionals

Staff and volunteers of eight heritage centers within the Lakes to Locks Passage corridor of northern New York will receive training in best practices for museum operations in this comprehensive program coordinated by the Essex County Historical Society. The three-year project will include eleven workshops on leadership and organizational structure, staff and volunteer training, mission and planning, collections care, and financial stability. Funding will also support hiring two "circuit riders" to help the heritage centers implement and reinforce the training and develop cultural heritage programming for visitors throughout the Lake Champlain region. Sixty cultural organizations in the surrounding region will be invited to participate in the training workshops, potentially improving skills and capacity building for over 200 museum professionals.

Vermont Museum and Gallery Alliance – Vergennes, VT
Year: 2007
Amount: $29,848
Grant: 21st Century Museum Professionals

The Vermont Museum & Gallery Alliance will select eight museums, historical societies, and galleries throughout Vermont to participate in an intensive collections care management program. The participating institutions will benefit from a series of workshops, followed by a self-assessment of specific needs in their own facilities. A graduate-level intern and the Project Director will then work with each organization on site-specific projects. Information and resources will be shared through an e-mail group and results of the projects will be shared more broadly through conference presentations. The three-year project will provide hands-on training and job skills for museum professionals and result in eight small institutional models in collections care, exhibition, and documentation techniques.

IMLS Museums for America

1800 M Street NW, 9th Floor
Washington, DC 20036-5802
202/653-4634
Sandra Narva (Senior Program Officer)
http://www.imls.gov/applicants/grants/forAmerica.shtm
http://tiny.cc/2ESC3

Description

Museums for America is the Institute's largest grant program for museums, supporting projects and ongoing activities that build museums' capacity to serve their communities.

Museums for America grants strengthen a museum's ability to serve the public more effectively by supporting high-priority activities that advance the institution's mission and strategic goals. Museums for America grants are designed to be flexible: funds can be used for a wide variety of projects, including: ongoing museum work, research and other behind-the-scenes activities, planning, new programs, purchase of equipment or services, and activities that will support the efforts of museums to upgrade and integrate new technologies.

Recent Awards, Winning Projects & Award Winners

Adams Museum and House – Deadwood, SD
Year: 2007
Amount: $50,153
Grant: Museums for America - Sustaining Cultural Heritage

The Adams Museum and House will create a fully integrated database system to manage its collections, thus making them more accessible to staff, the public, and researchers. The project will include upgrading to PastPerfect software and improving the information recorded in the database.

Arboretum at UNLV – Las Vegas, NV
Year: 2007
Amount: $63,107
Grant: Museums for America - Supporting Lifelong Learning

The Arboretum at the University of Nevada Las Vegas will use its grant to develop the Virtual Arboretum, a Web site that will provide public Internet access to photographic and text-based information about plants native or adaptive to the harsh growing conditions of the eastern Mojave Desert, where the cooperating institutions are located.

Arizona-Sonora Desert Museum – Tucson, AZ
Year: 2007
Amount: $149,999
Grant: Museums for America - Sustaining Cultural Heritage

The Arizona-Sonora Desert Museum (ASDM) will add the newly acquired Kerstitch Collection of Sea of Cortez marine life images to its digital collection and expand the terrestrial collection produced in an earlier phase of this project. Working in partnership with the University of Arizona

Library, the museum will add species narratives and descriptions of species attributes, and will enhance the user interface and search functionalities for audiences at various levels. This grant will help the museum implement a metadata harvesting protocol and high-resolution image downloading mechanisms.

Buffalo Bill Historical Center – Cody, WY
Year: 2007
Amount: $148,076
Grant: Museums for America - Sustaining Cultural Heritage

The Buffalo Bill Historical Center will digitize photographic images from five archival collections housed in the McCracken Research Library in the Historical Center. The images comprise significant Native American, natural history, and Western American history collections that are representative of the five museums of the Historical Center. The goal in digitizing these collections is to preserve the original material and broaden public access to the photographs. The digitized images will be cataloged and made available for worldwide dissemination through the Historical Center's Web site. This project will fulfill institution strategic imperatives to improve the stewardship of the collections, build an offsite audience, and increase awareness of the world-class research material in the McCracken Research Library and archives.

Burchfield-Penney Art Center – Buffalo, NY
Year: 2007
Amount: $149,465
Grant: Museums for America - Sustaining Cultural Heritage

The Burchfield-Penny Art Center will use grant funds to hire an assistant registrar to convert multiple inventory systems, including paper records and older digital files into one central electronic inventory system (The Museum System). The inventory will be supplemented with digitial images of the collection, allowing more access for interpretation, exhibition and research.

Preservation and Access: Humanities

Collections and Resources

Division of Preservation and Access
Room 411
National Endowment for the Humanities
1100 Pennsylvania Avenue, NW
Washington, DC 20506
202-606-8570
http://www.neh.gov/grants/guidelines/Collections_and_Resources.html
http://tiny.cc/7LHd2

Description

These grants support research and development projects that address major challenges in preserving or providing intellectual access to humanities resources. Applicants should define a specific problem, devise procedures and potential solutions, and evaluate findings. Successful proposals ought to have broad applicability to the humanities. NEH encourages applications that will explore new uses of digital technology in the humanities.

See Full Listing with Recent Winners Under College – University.

Gale/Library Media Connection TEAMS Award

27500 Drake Rd.
Farmington Hills, MI 48331
1-800-877-GALE
http://www.galeschools.com/pdf/TEAMS-form.pdf
http://tiny.cc/WUWVp

Description

The Gale/Library Media Connection TEAMS Award recognizes and encourages the critical collaboration between the teacher and media specialist to promote learning and increase student achievement.

Category: **Non-Profits**

CyberLearning Matching Grants

4926-C Eisenhower Ave,
Alexandria, VA. 22304
(703) 823-9999
http://www.cyberlearning.org/links/grants.asp
http://tiny.cc/aCZqK

http://www.cyberlearning.org/links/partner_info_request.asp
http://tiny.cc/mBTXV

Description

Our primary mission is to provide the highest quality education to all, especially the disadvantaged, at the lowest fee. We provide up to 95% matching grants to all eligible organizations including schools, colleges, non-profits, workforce development programs, banks, government agencies and corporations. Matching grants may be used to access our 3,000 plus high-quality online courses in IT (Information Technology- all levels and almost all topics), Management (Business Math) and TestPrep (Barrons SAT, TOEFL, GRE, GMAT…).

Recent Awards, Winning Projects & Award Winners

- New Jersey Dept. of Education $4,000,000
- Westbury, NY Public Schools $2,800,000
- Puerto Rico Department of Education $5,000,000
- Louisiana Public Schools $2,000,000
- Mississippi Public Schools $2,000,000
- Collier County, FL School District $700,000
- Pearsall ISD, Tx $560,000
- Oklahoma Public Schools $600,000
- Massac County, IL School District $307,000
- Siuslaw, OR School District $250,000
- West Washington Schools, IN $100,000
- Rutgers University, NJ $60,000
- Shoreline Community College, WA $50,000
- University of Jordan, Amman, Jordan $100,000
- Stamford Education Foundation $50,000
- Greater Kansas City Community Foundation $30,000
- Owen County Learning Network Foundation $30,000
- U.S Department of Commerce $50,000
- Nevada State IT Dept $40,000
- Fairfax County, VA $30,000

- Verizon $60,000
- Learn In USA $50,000
- Analytical Sciences Inc $30,000

The Dell Foundation Literate Communities Grants

1-800-915-3355

http://www.dell.com/content/topics/global.aspx/about_dell/values/community_outreach/literate_comm?c=us&l=en&s=corp

http://tiny.cc/BQrLd

Description

Through effective and strategic community partnerships, Dell supports educational and literacy services programs that address the critical and most basic educational needs of its neighbors in Dell Communities - prerequisites to success in the digital world.

The Dell Foundation solicits competitive applications from 501 (c)(3) non-profit organizations for a number of partnerships every two years.

Recent Awards, Winning Projects & Award Winners

SciWorks, The Science Center and Environmental Park of Forsyth County: The mission of SciWorks is to promote scientific literacy, life-long learning and an appreciation of the sciences by providing innovative educational and recreational experiences for all people through interactive programs and exhibits, collections, an environmental park and unique facilities. Dell Foundation Funding will underwrite costs associate with the 'Science Education Programs '. The program provides science and math learning experiences not feasible in the classroom and enables families to enjoy informal science and math learning.

KLRU TV: The PBS station, KLRU, educates, informs and enlightens viewers through broadcasts reaching over 500,000 households in Central Texas. Funding from The Dell Foundation will support two programs: Sesame Street and the Ready to Learn Service . Sesame Street children's programming series prepares children to start school and continue lifelong learning through a variety of scientifically and time-tested techniques. The Ready to Learn program serves schools districts through parent, teacher and student workshops and provides curriculum materials.

Dell TechKnow program

1-800-915-3355

http://www.dell.com/content/topics/global.aspx/sitelets/solutions/industry_application/pub_solutions/programs/dell_techknow?c=us&cs=RC1084719&l=en&s=k12

http://tiny.cc/kW2Vq

Description

Dell TechKnow is a program designed and offered by Dell to provide in-depth technology literacy and 21st Century skills to students. TechKnow students complete approximately 40 hours of hands-on training in which they learn technology concepts including how to identify, troubleshoot and resolve common IT problems. They then have the opportunity to apply these concepts in an instructional help desk environment where they operate, maintain and support computer hardware and software.

Dell TechKnow is one example of Dell's ongoing commitment to help students develop the skills and experiences they need to be successful in today's workforce.

HP Microenterprise Development Program

http://www.hp.com/hpinfo/grants/us/programs/index.html
http://tiny.cc/pOqKA

http://www.hp.com/hpinfo/grants/us/programs/microenterprise/recipients.html
http://tiny.cc/9pebD

Description

The HP Microenterprise Development Program is designed to support nonprofit microenterprise development agencies in the U.S. that serve clients in low-income communities.

We seek to advance the use of technology in microenterprise development programs in order to improve the efficiency, effectiveness and sustainability of microenterprises in underserved communities. HP's investments focus not only on providing technology access to microenterprises, but also on training microenterprises on how to use technology to build and grow their business.

Recent Awards, Winning Projects & Award Winners

- Microbusiness Advancement Center, Tucson
- Southern Good Faith Fund, Pine Bluff
- Agriculture & Land Based Training Association, Salinas
- CHARO Community Development Corporation, Los Angeles
- Mutual Assistance Network of Del Paso Heights, Sacramento

ING DIRECT Planet Orange Financial Literacy Grants

1 S. Orange St.
Wilmington, DE 19801
(02) 9028 4657
http://home.ingdirect.com/about/about.asp?s=News06
http://tiny.cc/voR2Z

www.orangekids.com/awards
http://tiny.cc/H1Nz3

https://secure4.easymatch.com/ingdirectgrant/CustomerContent/Grants/Guidelines.asp
http://tiny.cc/a2evv

Description

The Planet Orange Financial Literacy Awards (www.orangekids.com/awards (http://tiny.cc/nnLdJ), launched by ING DIRECT, the nation's largest direct bank, will offer $100,000 in grants to kindergarten through eighth grade teachers to implement financial literacy projects and programs into their curriculums.

The awards are named after Planet Orange (orangekids.com), the educational Web site launched by ING DIRECT in 2002 to teach kids about money management basics.

Recent Awards, Winning Projects & Award Winners

Just click on the state below to see the recipients:

- Arkansas (http://tiny.cc/wDCKv)
- Arizona (http://tiny.cc/uBghB)
- California (http://tiny.cc/QSLA8)
- Connecticut (http://tiny.cc/ah6Ka)
- Delaware (http://tiny.cc/v0Y24)
- Florida (http://tiny.cc/qdvdg)
- Georgia (http://tiny.cc/SeRaj)
- Hawaii (http://tiny.cc/AXo1L)
- Illinois (http://tiny.cc/AdzEq)
- Indiana (http://tiny.cc/eg6Hb)
- Kansas (http://tiny.cc/AEWT5)
- Louisiana (http://tiny.cc/jgxI4)
- Massachusetts (http://tiny.cc/IYV2b)
- Michigan (http://tiny.cc/cdSDj)

- North Carolina (http://tiny.cc/hmGq9)
- New Hampshire (http://tiny.cc/pgaPd)
- New Jersey (http://tiny.cc/C0Bts)
- Nevada (http://tiny.cc/P0W3R)
- New York (http://tiny.cc/suk2A)
- Ohio (http://tiny.cc/k3VcM)
- Oklahoma (http://tiny.cc/AdRKp)
- Pennsylvania (http://tiny.cc/jrVW0)
- South Carolina (http://tiny.cc/FnCMN)
- Texas (http://tiny.cc/KY5Iq)
- Utah (http://tiny.cc/az9lc)
- Virginia (http://tiny.cc/L1ghJ)
- West Virginia (http://tiny.cc/kfa1f)
- Wisconsin (http://tiny.cc/c8tkt)

METLIFE Foundation Grants

27-01 Queens Plz. N. Long Island City, NY 11101-4007
(212) 578-6272
Sibyl C. Jacobson, C.E.O
http://www.metlife.com/Applications/Corporate/WPS/CDA/PageGenerator/0,4132,P296,00.html
http://tiny.cc/fkZYc

Description

MetLife Foundation was established in 1976 by MetLife for the purpose of supporting educational, health and civic and cultural organizations. Our goals are to strengthen communities, promote good health and improve education. The Foundation continues a tradition of corporate contributions (http://tiny.cc/GabEz) and community involvement begun by MetLife in the 19th century.

Motorola Innovation Generation Grants

1303 East Algonquin Road
Schaumburg, Illinois 60196
USA
847 576 6200
http://www.motorola.com/content.jsp?globalObjectId=8152
http://tiny.cc/DnZ1c

Description

With an interest in sparking a love for science and inspiring the next generation of inventors, Motorola and the Motorola Foundation help cultivate the next generation of skilled scientists and engineers needed to create tomorrow's breakthrough ideas.

See Full Listing with Recent Winners Under College – University Category.

FINRA Investor Education Foundation

1735 K Street, NW
Washington, D.C. 20006-1506
(202) 974-2842
John Gannon (Executive Director)
http://www.finrafoundation.org/grants.asp
http://tiny.cc/0lXCq

Description

The NASD Investor Education Foundation, established in 2003, supports innovative research and educational projects that give investors the tools they need to better understand the markets and the basic principles of financial planning. The Foundation has awarded more than $2.4 million in total to organizations for educational programs and research projects targeting the underserved segments of the population. For details about grant programs and other new initiatives of the Foundation, visit www.nasdfoundation.org.

NEC Grants for the Disabled

2950 Express Drive South, Suite 102, Islandia, NY 11749-1412
(631) 232 2212
http://www.necfoundation.org/guidelines/guidelines.htm
http://tiny.cc/snpdi

Description

Established by NEC Corporation, the NEC Foundation of America supports programs with national reach and impact in assistive technology for people with disabilities. The foundation makes cash grants to nonprofit organizations in support of the development, application, and use of technology by and for people with disabilities. All proposals should demonstrate national reach and impact.

Recent Awards, Winning Projects & Award Winners

American Foundation for the Blind
New York, NY

Toward the development and implementation of the *AFB Senior Site*, a one-stop, authoritative web site for people who are experiencing vision loss, as well as for their family members and friends. *The Site* will offer tools, techniques and information on living independently and productively with vision loss, and offer practical techniques to deal with changing eyesight.
www.afb.org

American Institutes for Research (AIR) for its National Center for Technology Innovation (NCTI)Washington, DC

To expand *Tech Matrix*, a nationally recognized online review of assistive and learning technology features available in commercial technologies for Reading and Math instruction, to include two additional matrices in Early Reading and Writing and to upgrade the Web-platform of **Tech Matrix** to a content management system in order to add interactive features and ensure better site management.
www.air.org
www.nationaltechcenter.org

Friends of Disabled Adults and Children, Too!, Inc. (FODAC)
Stone Mountain, GA

To facilitate the transfer of FODAC's best practices and standards for recycling assistive technology for people with mobility impairments, as part of a new federal *ReUse of Assistive Technology* initiative. FODAC will serve as the national model and cornerstone for this national project which will ultimately include eleven additional 'depots' across the U.S. which will, in turn, organize their respective regional networks as FODAC will do in the six states in the Southwest.
www.fodac.org

National Federation of the Blind
Baltimore, MD

To sponsor the *NFB Youth Slam*, the largest gathering of blind youth ever, to take place in Baltimore in the summer of 2007 in partnership with Johns Hopkins University's Whiting School of Engineering and the National Aeronautics and Space Administration (NASA). The "NEC Cluster" of 40 participants will be part of a four-day event comprised of two hundred blind high school students and one hundred blind mentors and instructors convened to experience Science, Technology, Engineering and Math (STEM) subjects typically kept out of reach of blind students. The objective is to develop, apply and use assistive technology approaches and techniques that enhance the participation of blind youth in STEM and encourage them to pursue careers in STEM fields. This information will be featured on www.blindscience.org for on-going use by students, parents and teachers from around the country.

NEH Preserving & Accessing Reference Materials

Division of Preservation and Access
Room 411
National Endowment for the Humanities
1100 Pennsylvania Avenue, NW
Washington, DC 20506
202-606-8570
http://www.neh.gov/GRANTS/guidelines/referencematerials.html
http://tiny.cc/8Ihfc

Description

These grants support projects that create reference works and research tools.

See Full Listing with Recent Winners Under College – University Category.

NPower Technology Innovation Award

NPower Greater DC Region
2001 S Street, NW
Suite 630
Washington, DC 20009
(202) 234-9670
http://www.npowergdcr.org/events/technology+innovation+award/index.htm
http://tiny.cc/FnGyq

Description

The NPower/Accenture Technology Innovation Award honors nonprofits in the metro Washington, DC area whose innovative use of technology has helped them improve key aspects of their operations and more effectively fulfill their missions.

Recent Awards, Winning Projects & Award Winners

RAINN (Rape, Abuse & Incest National Network) (http://tiny.cc/i2DHn) was recognized for their National Sexual Assault Online Hotline, the first secure web-based crisis hotline providing live and anonymous support.

Fairfax Symphony Orchestra (http://tiny.cc/nbMcF) was recognized for use of podcasting to bring the Orchestra online.

GlobalGiving (http://tiny.cc/lkqKe) was recognized for GiveCertificates, online gift certificates that can be redeemed to support a specific charity.

RGK Foundation Grants

1301 West 25th Street - Suite 300 - Austin, Tx 78705-4236
(512) 474-9298
http://www.rgkfoundation.org/guidelines.php
http://tiny.cc/9oeG6

Description

RGK Foundation awards grants in the broad areas of Education, Community, and Medicine/Health. The Foundation's primary interests within Education include programs that focus on formal K-12 education (particularly mathematics, science and reading), teacher development, literacy, and higher education.

Sun Academic Excellence Grant

4150 Network Circle
Santa Clara, CA 95054
1-800-786-0404
http://www.sun.com/solutions/landing/industry/education/aeg.xml
http://tiny.cc/UVAU3

Description

The Sun Academic Excellence Grant program has helped numerous schools kick-start their projects by providing equipment grants and access to free training and certifications.

Sun Microsystems Foundation Open Gateway Grants Program

901 San Antonio Road, M/S UPAL01-462, Palo Alto, CA 94303
650.336.0487
http://www.sun.com/aboutsun/comm_invest/ogp/about.html
http://tiny.cc/Gqjkn

Description

Provides hardware and software grants, training, and technical support to: assist schools, particularly in economically disadvantaged communities, in making the transition to network computing; assist schools in utilizing network-based tools to implement new teaching strategies that improve instruction and student outcomes; and promote the full integration of technology into curriculum to help ensure that students are prepared to become information workers of tomorrow.

UPS Foundation Grants

55 Glenlake Parkway, NE
Atlanta, GA 30328
http://www.community.ups.com/philanthropy/grant.html
http://tiny.cc/U31nh
http://www.community.ups.com/downloads/pdfs/Foundation_brochure.pdf
http://tiny.cc/IP8RA

Description

Since 1981, The UPS Foundation has committed more than $1.2 million to the Hispanic Scholarship Fund. The UPS Foundation identifies specific areas where its support will clearly impact social issues. The UPS Foundation's major initiatives currently include programs that support increased nationwide volunteerism, family and workplace literacy and hunger relief. The UPS Foundation focuses on hunger http://tiny.cc/edSFo , literacy and volunteerism http://tiny.cc/FFF2S .

Category: Health

Health Information Technology (HIT)

Planning Grants

5600 Fishers Lane
Rockville, MD 20857
301-594-4465
Judy Oliver (Public Health Analyst)
http://www.grants.gov/search/search.do?&mode=VIEW&flag2006=true&oppId=16803
http://tiny.cc/s4BCI

http://www.hhs.gov/healthit/ahic/materials/03_08/phccc/casnoff_files/textonly/slide8.html
http://tiny.cc/8elKD

http://www.raconline.org/funding/funding_details.php?funding_id=1501
http://tiny.cc/ShJ8v

Description

To support health centers in structured planning activities that will prepare them to adopt Electronic Health Records (EHR) or other HIT innovations. Planning activities for EHR adoption may include readiness assessment, workflow analysis, due diligence in selecting vendor, business planning, determing specific network HIT functions. Planning activities for other HIT initiatives may include marketplace assessment, initial stages of colloboration with partners, and business planning. Applicants will need to descibe the outcome of the grant and must demonstrate progress after the first year that will lead to completing the goal after the second year. For example, if the applicant proposes to use the funds to plan for implementation of an EHR, then at the end of 2 years, grantees will have a solid plan to adopt EHRalong with indicators of success.

Medical Informatics Section/ MLA Career Development Grant
65 E. Wacker Place, Ste. 1900, Chicago, IL 60601-7246
312.419.9094 x28.
Lisa C. Fried (mlapd2@mlahq.org)

URL Website addresses where to apply or learn about
http://www.mlanet.org/pdf/grants/medinfo_app_20050712.pdf
http://tiny.cc/P5b0o

Description

This award provides up to two individuals $1500 to support a career development activity that will contribute to advancement in the field of medical informatics. The award was established in 1996 by the Medical Informatics Section http://tiny.cc/Vgrih .

NLM Exploratory Innovations in Biomedical Computational Science and Technology (BISTI) Grants (R21)

Center for Bioinformatics and Computational Biology
NIGMS 45 Center Drive, Room 2AS.55k, MSC 6200
Bethesda, MD 20892-6200
(301) 451-6446
Peter Lyster, Ph.D. (Program Officer)
http://grants.nih.gov/grants/guide/pa-files/PAR-06-411.html
http://tiny.cc/Z70cN

http://www.grants.gov/search/search.do?mode=VIEW&oppId=9509
http://tiny.cc/YUTgS

Description

Support for computational science & tool development for biomedical research. These funding opportunity announcements (FOAs) support fundamental research through the NIH Research Project Grant (R01) award mechanism and exploratory/developmental research through the NIH Exploratory/Developmental Research Grant (R21) award mechanism. This program expires May 8, 2009 unless reissued. Only electronic applications are accepted.

Recent Awards, Winning Projects & Award Winners

ARONSKY, DOMINIK
5-R21-LM009002-02
VANDERBILT UNIVERSITY
Managing ED Diversion with Information Technology http://tiny.cc/H4VPg

HAUSKRECHT, MILOS (New Investigator)
1-R21-LM009102-01A1
UNIVERSITY OF PITTSBURGH AT PITTSBURGH
Evidence based anomaly detection in clinical databases http://tiny.cc/hzVFN

PATRICK, SALLY M.
5-G08-LM008549-03
UNIVERSITY OF UTAH
Utah Consumer Health Information Infrastructure http://tiny.cc/NsOsa

SLONIM, DONNA (New Investigator)
1-R21-LM009411-01A1
TUFTS UNIVERSITY MEDFORD

Evaluating Biological Networks by Mining Public Data http://tiny.cc/BeQsQ

SZALLASI, ZOLTAN
5-R21-LM008823-02
CHILDREN'S HOSPITAL BOSTON
Extracting reliable information from microarray data http://tiny.cc/nYlkH

TIWARI, HEMANT K. (New Investigator)
1-R21-LM008791-01A2
UNIVERSITY OF ALABAMA AT BIRMINGHAM
Multiple Imputation in Genetic Studies http://tiny.cc/mb7Uy

Planning Grant for Integrated Advanced Information Management Systems (IAIMS)(G08)

Extramural Programs
National Library of Medicine
Rockledge 1, Suite 301
6705 Rockledge Drive
Bethesda, MD 20892-7968
301-435-0714
301-496-4253
Dwight Mowery
http://grants.nih.gov/grants/guide/pa-files/par-07-238.html
http://tiny.cc/f1SV7

Description

Integrated advanced information systems (IAIMS) are comprehensive trans-organizational information management structures. In an IAIMS environment, organizations apply proven management practices and appropriate expertise about informatics and information services in order to link and relate the published biomedical knowledge base with clinical, research, educational and administrative, information, using computers and networks.

The National Library of Medicine (NLM) provides IAIMS grants to health-related institutions and organizations that seek assistance for projects to plan, deploy, evaluate and sustain a comprehensive information environment that supports organizational mission activities. Implementing an IAIMS information environment that crosses organizational and disciplinary boundaries is a complex task. IAIMS is not a grant program for the selection and installation of an electronic health record system or laboratory reporting system or other single-purpose information tool. IAIMS work usually involves integrating an array of commercial products (which may include electronic health record systems or electronic full-text journals) with local systems, resources and services and Internet-based information to create a single point of access.

Recent Awards, Winning Projects & Award Winners

GANTENBEIN, REX E
1-G08-LM009216-01
UNIVERSITY OF WYOMING
Western Regional Biomedical Collaboratory http://tiny.cc/RosQT

KO, CLIFFORD
1-G08-LM009537-01
AMERICAN COLLEGE OF SURGEONS
Plan for Extracting Intraoperative Anesthesia Data to the ACS NSQIP Database http://tiny.cc/Q140B

LIPTON, MARK S.
5-G08-LM009152-02
NEW YORK UNIVERSITY SCHOOL OF MEDICINE
New York Clinical Information Exchange Planning Project http://tiny.cc/9UoR9

TRIOLA, MARC
5-G08-LM008806-02
NEW YORK UNIVERSITY SCHOOL OF MEDICINE
NEW YORK UNIVERSITY MEDICAL CENTER IAIMS PLANNING http://tiny.cc/WcCGO

NLM Research Grants in Biomedical Informatics and Bioinformatics

Rockledge 1, Suite 301
6705 Rockledge Drive
Bethesda, MD 20892
(301) 594-4882
Dr. Valerie Florance
http://grants.nih.gov/grants/guide/pa-files/PA-06-094.html
http://tiny.cc/MzUw4

Description

Support for rigorous scientific research in biomedical informatics and bioinformatics. NLM Express Research Grant applications are limited to a 15-page research plan and to a modular budget. The scope of interests is outlined in the funding opportunity announcement.

Recent Awards, Winning Projects & Award Winners

ALTMAN, RUSS BIAGIO
5-R01-LM005652-12
STANFORD UNIVERSITY
Annotating functional sites in 3D biological structures
http://tiny.cc/hZT9F

ASH, JOAN S.
2-R56-LM006942-07A1
OREGON HEALTH & SCIENCE UNIVERSITY
Clinical Decision Support in Community Hospitals: Barriers & Facilitators
http://tiny.cc/UeQ1s

BAHAR, IVET
5-R01-LM007994-04
UNIVERSITY OF PITTSBURGH AT PITTSBURGH
Alignment-independent Classification of Proteins
http://tiny.cc/7a5NZ

BOWDEN, DOUGLAS M.
5-R01-LM008247-03
UNIVERSITY OF WASHINGTON
Spatial Information Management Resources for Human Brain
http://tiny.cc/giJP3
Project Website: http://braininfo.rprc.washington.edu/indexabout.html
http://tiny.cc/UKjZ0

BREM, HAROLD
5-R01-LM008443-03
COLUMBIA UNIVERSITY HEALTH SCIENCES
Diabetic Foot and Pressure Ulcer Databank
http://tiny.cc/9XP8F

BRENNAN, PATRICIA F
5-R01-LM006249-07
UNIVERSITY OF WISCONSIN MADISON
Custom Computer Support: Home Care of CABG Patients
http://tiny.cc/5U473

CANNON ALBRIGHT, LISA A.
1-R01-LM009331-01
UNIVERSITY OF UTAH
Analysis of the Familial Component to Disease in a Biomedical Resource w/Link...
http://tiny.cc/A0vbE

CHAPMAN, WENDY W. (New Investigator)

1-R01-LM009427-01
UNIVERSITY OF PITTSBURGH AT PITTSBURGH
NLP Foundational Studies & Ontologies for Syndromic Surveillance from ED Reports
http://tiny.cc/qtBgZ

CIMINO, JAMES J.
5-R01-LM007593-05
COLUMBIA UNIVERSITY HEALTH SCIENCES
Infobuttons to Improve Information Access in Order Entry
http://tiny.cc/dBBQk
Project Website: http://www.dbmi.columbia.edu/cimino/Infobuttons.html
http://tiny.cc/s67WX

COHEN, AARON M. (New Investigator)
1-R01-LM009501-01
OREGON HEALTH & SCIENCE UNIVERSITY
Assisting Systematic Review Preparation Using Automated Document Classification
http://tiny.cc/0mlQ8

COOPER, GREGORY F
5-R01-LM008374-03
UNIVERSITY OF PITTSBURGH AT PITTSBURGH
Learning Patient-Specific Models from Clinical Data
http://tiny.cc/PNeN4

CORK, ROBERT JOHN
5-R01-LM007591-06
LOUISIANA STATE UNIV HSC NEW ORLEANS
Enhancements to a human embryo, serial-section database
http://tiny.cc/MtOZW
Project Website: http://virtualhumanembryo.lsuhsc.edu/
http://tiny.cc/NoFcH

CRAVEN, MARK W.
2-R01-LM007050-04A2
UNIVERSITY OF WISCONSIN MADISON
Adaptive Information Monitoring and Extraction
http://tiny.cc/sizcP

DEE, FRED R
1-R01-LM009121-01A1
UNIVERSITY OF IOWA
Competencies Training & Assessment in Laboratory Medicine Using Patient Simulations
http://tiny.cc/20oMh

DOCTOR, JASON N.

1-R01-LM009157-01A1
UNIVERSITY OF SOUTHERN CALIFORNIA
Detecting Errors in Blood Labs Using Bayesian Networks
http://tiny.cc/dAK5S

EFFKEN, JUDITH A. (contact); CARLEY, KATHLEEN M.; VERRAN, JOYCE A. (New
Investigators)
1-R01-LM009516-01A1
UNIVERSITY OF ARIZONA
DyNADS: A Dynamic Network Analysis Decision Support Tool for Nurse Managers
http://tiny.cc/3JVxU

FLOUDAS, CHRISTODOULOS ACHILLEUS
1-R01-LM009338-01
PRINCETON UNIVERSITY
Peptide and Protein Identification via Tandem MS and Mixed-Integer Optimization
http://tiny.cc/m3hlW

FORAN, DAVID J.
1-R01-LM009239-01A1
UNIV OF MED/DENT NJ-R W JOHNSON MED SCH
Image Mining for Comparative Analysis of Expression Patterns in Tissue Microarray
http://tiny.cc/Q3HaN

FRIEDMAN, CAROL
5-R01-LM008635-03
COLUMBIA UNIVERSITY HEALTH SCIENCES
A Biomedical Natural Language Processing Resource
http://tiny.cc/5EEhn

HAYNES, R. BRIAN
5-R01-LM006866-07
MCMASTER UNIVERSITY
Clinical Search Retrieval from Four Electronic Databases
http://tiny.cc/Q7CXa

HUNTER, LAWRENCE E.
3-R01-LM008111-03S1
UNIVERSITY OF COLORADO DENVER/HSC AURORA
Technology Development for a MolBio Knowledge-Base
http://tiny.cc/QCnu8

KARP, PETER D. (New Investigator)
1-R01-LM009651-01
SRI INTERNATIONAL

Pathway Prediction and Assessment Integrating Multiple Evidence Types
http://tiny.cc/DPxyO

KARSH, BEN-TZION
1-R01-LM008923-01A1
UNIVERSITY OF WISCONSIN MADISON
The Value of CPOE in Pediatric Inpatient Units and Its Impact on Safety and Work
http://tiny.cc/UH0BH

LI, JING
5-R01-LM008991-02
CASE WESTERN RESERVE UNIVERSITY
Efficient Analysis of SNPs & Haplotypes with Applications in Gene Mapping
http://tiny.cc/pqhES

LU, XINGHUA (New Investigator)
1-R01-LM009153-01A1
MEDICAL UNIVERSITY OF SOUTH CAROLINA
Automatic Literature-based Protein Annotation
http://tiny.cc/1n9xY

MANDL, KENNETH D.
5-R01-LM007677-05
CHILDREN'S HOSPITAL BOSTON
Disease Surveillance in Real Time: Geotemporal Methods
http://tiny.cc/inXLR

MENDONCA, ENEIDA A
5-R01-LM008799-02
COLUMBIA UNIVERSITY HEALTH SCIENCES
Answering Information Needs in Workflow
http://tiny.cc/RUxSD

MILLER, RANDOLPH A.
3-R01-LM007995-03S1
VANDERBILT UNIVERSITY
TIME:(Tools for Inpatient Monitoring using Evidence)for Safe & AppropriateTesting
http://tiny.cc/Cz4qu

MILLER, RANDOLPH A.
2-R01-LM007995-04
VANDERBILT UNIVERSITY
TIME:(Tools for Inpatient Monitoring using Evidence)for Safe & AppropriateTesting
http://tiny.cc/iKZV0

MOONEY, SEAN D. (New Investigator)

1-R01-LM009722-01
INDIANA UNIV-PURDUE UNIV AT INDIANAPOLIS
Informatic profiling of clinically relevant mutation
http://tiny.cc/zpy72

MOORE, JASON H.
5-R01-LM009012-02
DARTMOUTH COLLEGE
Machine Learning Prediction of Cancer Susceptibility
http://tiny.cc/bYKrM

MORIYAMA, ETSUKO (New Investigator)
1-R01-LM009219-01A1
UNIVERSITY OF NEBRASKA LINCOLN
Efficient and Sensitive Mining System for G-Protein Coupled Receptors
http://tiny.cc/9b06K

MOULT, JOHN
2-R01-LM007174-06A1
UNIVERSITY OF MD BIOTECHNOLOGY INSTITUTE
Analysis of the Functional Impact of Coding region SNPs
http://tiny.cc/JmKeJ

OHNO-MACHADO, LUCILA
1-R01-LM009520-01
BRIGHAM AND WOMEN'S HOSPITAL
Assessing quality of individual predictions in medical decision support systems
http://tiny.cc/pJiW4

PANI, JOHN R
5-R01-LM008323-03
UNIVERSITY OF LOUISVILLE
Histological Reasoning: Visual Cognition in Microanatomy
http://tiny.cc/WpcgR

PEARSON, WILLIAM R
5-R01-LM004969-18
UNIVERSITY OF VIRGINIA CHARLOTTESVILLE
Comparison of Protein Sequences and Structures
http://tiny.cc/AI7VK

PERL, YEHOSHUA
5-R01-LM008445-02
NEW JERSEY INSTITUTE OF TECHNOLOGY
Partitioning to Support Auditing and Extending the UMLS
http://tiny.cc/GTwMK

QUACKENBUSH, JOHN
5-R01-LM008795-02
DANA-FARBER CANCER INSTITUTE
TM4: Software for High-Dimensional Data Analysis
http://tiny.cc/hhKsk

RACKOVSKY, SHALOM R
5-R01-LM006789-06
MOUNT SINAI SCHOOL OF MEDICINE OF NYU
Optimized Protein Informatics
http://tiny.cc/Rqkz0

ROST, BURKHARD
2-R01-LM007329-05
COLUMBIA UNIVERSITY HEALTH SCIENCES
Improve predictions of structure and function by PredictProtein
http://tiny.cc/lop27
Project Website: http://www.predictprotein.org
http://tiny.cc/CaNsb

SALZBERG, STEVEN L.
2-R01-LM006845-08
UNIVERSITY OF MARYLAND COLLEGE PK CAMPUS
Computational Gene Modeling and Genome Sequence Assembly
http://tiny.cc/igVXM

SHAVLIK, JUDE W
5-R01-LM008796-02
UNIVERSITY OF WISCONSIN MADISON
Machine Learning and Visualization in Structural Biology
http://tiny.cc/uFbIY

SHIFFMAN, RICHARD N.
2-R01-LM007199-04A1
YALE UNIVERSITY
Improving Guideline Development and Implementation
http://tiny.cc/PYgZQ

SIM, IDA
5-R01-LM006780-08
UNIVERSITY OF CALIFORNIA SAN FRANCISCO
The Trial Bank Project
http://tiny.cc/WYfjU

SLACK, WARNER V.

5-R01-LM008255-03
BETH ISRAEL DEACONESS MEDICAL CENTER
Cybermedicine for the Patient and Physician
http://tiny.cc/Bg9Ne

STARREN, JUSTIN B
5-R01-LM007663-04
MARSHFIELD CLINIC RESEARCH FOUNDATION
Managing Large Complex Data Streams/Outpatient Practice
http://tiny.cc/SoGEu

WONG, STEPHEN T.C.
5-R01-LM008696-03
BRIGHAM AND WOMEN'S HOSPITAL
Cell tracking and analysis for time-lapse microscopy
http://tiny.cc/ezPYo
Project Website: http://neuroinformatics.harvard.edu/projects/ii001.htm
http://tiny.cc/4GmHx

WONG, STEPHEN T.C.
1-R01-LM009161-01A1
BRIGHAM AND WOMEN'S HOSPITAL
Neuronal Spines Tracking and Analysis for Time-Lapse, 3D Optical Microscopy
http://tiny.cc/BcOTR

XU, XIE GEORGE
1-R01-LM009362-01
RENSSELAER POLYTECHNIC INSTITUTE
4D Visible Human Modeling for Radiation Dosimetry
http://tiny.cc/vEeAq

YU, HONG (New Investigator)
1-R01-LM009836-01A1
UNIVERSITY OF WISCONSIN MILWAUKEE
HERMES - Help physicians to Extract and aRticulate Multimedia information from li
http://tiny.cc/J4pQm

ZENG, QING
5-R01-LM007222-05
BRIGHAM AND WOMEN'S HOSPITAL
Vocabulary Support for Consumer Health Informatics
http://tiny.cc/wzWxm

NCRR's Science Education Partnership Awards (SEPA)

Division for Clinical Research Resources
http://tiny.cc/HkzDK
National Center for Research Resources
National Institutes of Health
One Democracy Plaza, Room 916
6701 Democracy Boulevard, MSC 4874
Bethesda, Maryland 20892-4874 (20817 for express mail)
301-435-0805
L. Tony Beck, Ph.D. (Program Officer)
http://www.ncrr.nih.gov/science_education_partnership_awards/
http://tiny.cc/fD647

http://www.ncrr.nih.gov/science_education_partnership_awards/20071113.asp
http://tiny.cc/YvsMe

http://www.ncrrsepa.org/
http://tiny.cc/M9zUq

Description

The Science Education Partnership Award (SEPA) Program funds grants for innovative educational programs. Such projects create partnerships among biomedical and clinical researchers and K-12 teachers and schools, museums and science centers, media experts, and other educational organizations. SEPA is sponsored by the National Center for Research Resources (NCRR), part of the National Institutes of Health (NIH).

Recent Awards, Winning Projects & Award Winners

Texas A&M University System
College Station, TX
Science Promotion in Rural Middle Schools
Grant No. R25 RR022711-01A2
Award: $1,351,569
Principal Investigator
Larry Johnson, Ph.D.
E-mail: LJOHNSON1@TAMU.EDU

Abstract (provided by applicant):

Long-term goals are to develop, evaluate, and disseminate nationwide an engaging Rural Science Promotion Model that integrates biomedical sciences into middle schools to enhance understanding of the value and ethics of research and the clinical trial process. Research education and careers will be fostered through development of interactive curricula, professional development, and classroom visits from local veterinarians. Rural schools have a prevalence of environmentally-related and zoonotic diseases, difficulty in recruiting science teachers, and less interaction with scientific professionals who could influence their career choices. Middle school is the prime developmental period for social skills and academic competence. Information on the history of drug and medical device development and associated diseases will be integrated into science curricula and disseminated into rural (and other), underserved settings through veterinarians' school visits and follow-up lessons teachers present. Specific aims are to: 1) develop curricular materials (Veterinarians' Black Bags [VBBs] of hands-on and demonstrational materials, follow-up lessons, and pamphlets) directed at K-12 and the general public that support local veterinarians' visits into rural public middle schools to promote science, understanding of the clinical trial process, and responsible use of animals in research; 2) provide professional development for public school teachers (on how to present follow-up lessons), for veterinary students (course work elective on communication through outreach), and for veterinarians (continuing education training with public school communication strategies and streaming videos on how to present materials in the VBBs); and 3) promote the application of science and value of biomedical and clinical research by veterinary students and local veterinarians' visits into rural public middle schools. They will illustrate the use of scientific method in disease diagnosis, promote understanding of the problem-solving value of biomedical research funded by NIH to address animal and human health issues, and promote careers in science and biomedical fields. Phase I will develop the model of veterinarians in the public school classroom in Texas, and Phase II will disseminate the model and materials nationwide. Public understanding of the process and accomplishments of animal research for both animal and human health will be enhanced. Likewise, knowledge of the process by which drugs and medical devices (appliances) become approved and available for public use will be promoted. Through this unique, Rural Science Promotion Model, a larger number of underrepresented students throughout Texas and the nation will be encouraged to enter and remain in science academic tracks to better meet the nation's needed scientific and biomedical workforce.

Brown University
Providence, RI
Project ARISE: Advancing Rhode Island Science Education
Grant No. RR022719-01A1
Award: $636,131
Principal Investigator
John Stein
Phone: 401-863-2263
E-mail: john_stein@brown.edu

Abstract (provided by applicant):

Project ARISE: Advancing Rhode Island Science Education is a professional development program for teachers, designed to engage students in inquiry-based approaches to learning about science, bring cutting-edge research into the classroom, and improve the understanding of the relevance of science to everyday life. The core of Project ARISE is a year-long program for Rhode Island high school science teachers that will be co-taught by university faculty and graduate students. The goal of the program is to develop the tools and perspective that will enable high school teachers to integrate national science education standards and high-level concepts in molecular and genomic biology, bioinformatics, neuroscience, and physiology into their high school science classroom. During the first year of the program, Brown faculty and staff will work with a science education specialist from the Rhode Island Department of Education, high school science teachers, and an evaluation expert from the Education Alliance to design and refine course modules, mobile laboratory projects, and lesson plans focused on an inquiry-based approach to science and the broad-based concepts that are integral to it. During the summers of the program, Brown faculty members and graduate students will team-teach a two-week course to 15 Rhode Island high school science teachers selected as fellows, who will learn active, inquiry-based teaching methods that will assist them in achieving the national science education standards for teacher professional development and for science teaching. Fellows will have access to mobile laboratory equipment as well as qualified scientific advisors during the school year, so that they may implement new curriculum and concepts in their classrooms and conduct professional development in-service workshops. With the guidance of scientific advisors and trained fellows, students will define a research question, write an application for exploration, carry out and interpret controlled experiments, and report their findings at the Nature of Discovery Symposium held at Brown University at the end of the school year. Lesson plans for middle and high school teachers developed by fellows will be posted on the Project ARISE Web site and will be presented to invited teachers at a meeting held at Brown University.

Imaginarium, Inc.
Anchorage, AK
North Star (Phases I and II)
Grant No. RR023272-01
Award: $1,346,509
Principal Investigator
Christopher Cable
Phone: 907-276-3179
E-mail: ccable@imaginarium.org

Abstract (provided by applicant):

Alaska is a vast state equal to the combined areas of Texas, California, New York, Pennsylvania, Florida, Massachusetts, Virginia and Vermont, yet it has half the road miles of Maryland, a state 56 times smaller and with a population of just 626,932. Alaska's physical size, lack of road access to most communities, natural barriers, and some of the earth's harshest weather have limited the state's ability to educate its citizens, provide adequate health care, and even to provide public water and sewer systems for everyone. Alaska also relies heavily on outsiders to fill its need for most professionals, such as educators, scientists, and health professionals. Unfortunately, these outsiders often don't appreciate Alaska's extreme conditions or remoteness. They usually leave the state after serving only a few months or semesters. If this trend is to change, Alaska must begin to identify, recruit, and educate its own youth to become tomorrow's teachers, scientists, and health professionals. The North Star program proposes to design and implement a five-year, outcome-based Phase I/II plan that brings together the Imaginarium Science Discovery Center, the University of Alaska Anchorage Department of Biological Sciences, Providence Alaska Hospital, and a statewide advisory committee to provide: 1) twenty-five educationally and/or economically disadvantaged Alaskan high school students (predominantly Alaska Natives from rural villages) with direct access to biomedical research mentors to guide and support student research projects; 2) a six-week summer institute focusing on a pre-med curriculum and job shadowing opportunities; 3) school-year internships for 60 educationally and/or economically disadvantaged Anchorage students in grades 8-12 at the Imaginarium for direct access to science and health content, training on delivering research-based demonstrations, and exhibit building for the public; 4) professional development for 200 teachers across Alaska focusing on inquiry-based, hands-on learning techniques, and supplemental health and science curricula; 5) a means for university and hospital researchers with direct access to the general public to disseminate their research methods and results in public venues; and 6) a Web site for showcasing student and biomedical research methods and results, a participant forum for blogging, pages for sharing their research projects, and links to other resources. The North Star program will be evaluated by an independent evaluation firm with student matriculation rates tracked and career paths followed.

Oklahoma City Community College
Oklahoma City, OK
Biotechnology/Bioinformatics Discovery!
Grant No. RR017282-04
Award: $538,213
Principal Investigator
Charlotte Mulvihill
Phone: 405-682-1611, ext. 7225
E-mail: cmulvihill@occc.edu

Abstract (provided by applicant):

Oklahoma City Community College, in partnership with the University of Oklahoma Health Sciences Center (OUHSC) and teacher-leaders throughout Oklahoma, will expand the phase I Biotechnology/Bioinformatics Discovery! project to rural Oklahoma and disseminate curricula to a national audience. The broad goals of the project are to enhance science education through professional development for teachers, improve student success in science—especially among underrepresented groups—so that more students will enter college and choose careers in the health sciences, and to increase awareness of the contributions of the biomedical research enterprise. At least three of the four geographic regions of rural Oklahoma are targeted and the project will focus on isolated rural schools with large numbers of students from underrepresented groups in science. The Native American networks developed by OUHSC will be a primary resource. High quality inquiry modules for laboratory experiments for high school students have been prepared and are ready for adaptation to middle school students. Teacher-participants will attend summer institutes and then implement laboratory experiments for their students, using the learning cycle as the pedagogical approach (explore, develop concept, apply/extend). The quality and content of the laboratory experiments are derived from peer-reviewed national projects to give students experiences with science content and technology that would not otherwise be available. Project personnel provide the laboratory modules for classrooms along with in-class support for the teacher, as requested. Project coordinators will make regular visits to each region. A teacher-leader for each rural region will become an active member of the implementation plan. Teacher-leaders will help set up a regional equipment loaner center, and will form a mock biotechnology company with their students to learn how to prepare module materials locally. Capstone activities to celebrate and promote the health sciences will occur regularly for students and their teachers with the aid of OUHSC partners. A DVD and learning module focused on clinical trials, tailored to student audiences, will be one project outcome. An external evaluator will provide formative feedback for continuous improvement as well as a summative evaluation. Data measures will include classroom observations, teacher surveys at baseline, post-workshop, and post module implementation, student surveys pre- and post-implementation, student acquisition of science process skills, and student interest in science and health careers at baseline and post-capstone experiences.

University of Miami Coral Gables
Coral Gables, FL
Heart Smart
Grant No. RR023279-01
Award: $1,360,053
Principal Investigator
Patrice Saab
Phone: 305-284-5472
E-mail: psaab@miami.edu

Abstract (provided by applicant):

The University of Miami's Department of Psychology, in collaboration with the Miami Museum of Science & Planetarium, will create a hands-on traveling exhibit, complementary classroom, and Web-based resources aimed at raising awareness about cardiovascular disease risk factors, and strategies for reducing these risks and improving personal health. The Heart Smart exhibit and educational resources will: 1) serve to highlight the distribution of cardiovascular risk factors across Miami-Dade County's diverse population; 2) communicate the range of disorders associated with the risk factors, including obesity, diabetes, and coronary disease; and 3) communicate the critical importance of controlling cardiovascular risk through nutrition, activity, and stress management. Besides raising awareness about this public health challenge, the project will break new ground by demonstrating how an urban science museum, in collaboration with a research university, can serve as an environment for not only communicating, but also conducting, scientific research. University of Miami graduate students and researchers will be involved in the development, training, implementation, data collection, and data analysis aspects of the exhibit. Through this participation, they will have access to the emerging data sets generated by the exhibit, informing theses, dissertations, and scientific publications related to ongoing areas of cardiovascular research. The university and the museum also will conduct a health education evaluation project to assess the effectiveness of a museum-based informal learning curriculum and its impact on student knowledge and behavior. The study will build on previous University of Miami research that has involved county-wide blood pressure screening of 10th grade public school students, indicating substantial numbers with elevated blood pressure and attendant risk factors. The evaluation project will explore the extent to which 10th graders engaging in an enhanced museum experience and playing a "cardiovascular debate game" display greater gains in cardiovascular health knowledge and improvements in behavior than their peers. Following the development, pilot testing, and implementation of the exhibit, the museum will disseminate the exhibit to a variety of alternative venues including libraries, local hospitals, high schools, and university settings. The project Web site will include continuously updated displays of the data collected at each venue, a downloadable version of the debate game, and links to related online public health resources.

University of Rochester
Rochester, NY
LSLC: Strengthening Connections Between Scientists and Classroom Learning (Phase I & II)
Grant No. RR023285-01
Award: $1,333,052
Principal Investigator
Dina Markowitz
Phone: 585-275-3171
E-mail: dina_markowitz@urmc.rochester.edu

Abstract (provided by applicant):

The Life Sciences Learning Center (LSLC), a science education laboratory at the University of Rochester Medical Center (URMC), provides secondary school students and teachers with the opportunity to learn about and experience hands-on scientific inquiry. The long-term goals of the LSLC are to provide resources to K-12 teachers, and to create an opportunities for interaction with University of Rochester biomedical research science faculty, graduate students, and post-doctoral fellows. The LSLC will utilize funding from a SEPA Phase I & Phase II grant to create and disseminate comprehensive curricula that directly reflect biomedical research performed at the URMC. This project will bring together scientists and science educators in developing and disseminating four curriculum modules focused on NIH-funded biomedical research that is being undertaken by URMC scientists. These modules will provide learning and teaching strategies to engage student interest, support learning of biological concepts, and foster an awareness and understanding of biomedical research. These curriculum modules will be standards-based and will integrate classroom activities, laboratory activities, and computer activities. The topics of the four modules will be: 1) use of neural stem cells as gene therapy vectors; 2) genomic technologies to identify pandemic-specific genes of vibrio cholerae; 3) therapies and molecular changes in the brain that result in the recovery of visual functions after brain damage; and 4) physiological and molecular effects of ultrafine air particulates. Classroom-ready versions of each module will be disseminated throughout New York State via a partnership with the New York State Biology-Chemistry Professional Development Mentor Network. Nationwide dissemination of the curricula will be facilitated through workshops, a Web site, and laboratory supply kits that will be loaned to teachers. Local dissemination of the curricula will be facilitated by URMC graduate students and post-doctoral fellows who will be trained to lead LSLC laboratory sessions. The LSLC will implement a comprehensive mixed-methods evaluation consisting of process and outcomes measures, employing both quantitative and qualitative methodologies. Furthermore, the project will assess the implementation of the curricula and the impact of the curricula on student content knowledge.

University of Utah
Salt Lake City, UT
Genome Science for Health: Web-Based Curricula for Biology, Phase I & II
Grant No. RR023288-01
Award: $1,349,482
Principal Investigator
Louisa Stark
Phone: 801-585-0019
E-mail: louisa.stark@genetics.utah.edu

Abstract (provided by applicant):

The Genetic Science Learning Center (GSLC) at the University of Utah will utilize its synergistic expertise in education, science, and technology to educate secondary-level life science students and teachers about the role of NIH-funded research advances and clinical trials in improving health care. The Genome Science for Health project will develop four Web-based curriculum supplement modules—on cell biology, developmental biology, molecular genetics, and clinical trials—that illustrate the continuum from basic research through translational science to clinical trials and into medical treatments. Regenerative medicine and animal research also will be addressed. The modules will employ interactive learning in a highly visual environment, an approach designed to appeal to the tech-savvy, digital-age students of today. At the same time, they will clearly address content in the national science education standards, ensuring that they are used by teachers. Two cohorts of teachers will participate in summer institutes, working with the GSLC staff to draft the modules, which will be developed using the GSLC's new, innovative ExploragraphicT Web design and ExploragraphicT Web-based curriculum development process. Formative feedback throughout the process from students, teachers, and scientists will help to direct module development from initiation through pilot testing in classrooms and revision. The modules will be widely disseminated via the highly-visible, award-winning GSLC Web site (http://tiny.cc/uGYLZ) , which received almost 3.7 million visits in 2005 from students, teachers, and the public. Professional development workshops for teachers and a summer institute will support dissemination of the curricula. The Genome Science for Health project goals are: 1) to educate secondary-level students about the role of NIH-funded basic research, translational science, and clinical trials in improving health care; 2) to engage high school life science teachers in learning about the Genome Science for Health module topics, and in developing the curriculum frameworks and learning approaches to address them; and 3) to prepare teachers to use the Genome Science for Health curricula with their students, through professional development courses and workshops at the local, regional, and national levels. The Genome Science for Health project will bring a new level of understanding to students, teachers, and the public about the process by which medical treatments are developed, as well as their potential roles in this process as clinical trial participants. Because the clinical trials module will be disseminated via the Web, it will be able to support the community engagement activities of NCRR's Clinical and Translational Science Awards across the United States.

University of Washington
Seattle, WA
Collaborations to Advance Understanding of Science and Ethics (Phase II)
Grant No. RR016284-04
Award: $542,000
Principal Investigator
Susanna Cunningham
Phone: 206-616-1963
E-mail: susannac@u.washington.edu

Abstract (provided by applicant):

Support for biomedical research is dependent on public understanding of how research is conducted and its vital importance for human health. The rapid pace of scientific innovation has resulted in new bioethical challenges that highlight both the need for access to accurate scientific information, as well as the importance of rational civic discourse. The Collaborations to Advance the Understanding of Science and Ethics (CAUSE) Phase II program addresses an unmet need for innovative educational resources that prepare science and health teachers to explore the ethical implications of research with their students. The long-term goals are to increase public awareness of the processes of health-related research, and to foster understanding of the relationship of ethics to science. CAUSE teaching materials are designed to increase student awareness of the social contexts in which research occurs, demonstrate the importance of understanding science content and the process of research, and promote the development of skills required to analyze ethical issues in the health sciences. This Phase II grant supports the transition to self-sustaining status and national dissemination of the expertise and materials developed in Phase I. The CAUSE products—an ethics primer and three curriculum units (HIV Vaccine Clinical Trials, Stem Cell Research, and Genetic Testing)—will be disseminated through two major methods. First, an online course for educators will be developed in collaboration with the University of Washington Distance Learning Department. Once created, pilot-tested, and revised, this course will become self-sustaining and available to all U.S. teachers. Second, CAUSE will offer educators professional development in various workshops/institutes, to ensure that teachers will use the program resources as well as train their colleagues in utilizing the materials. Dissemination will capitalize on the investment made in Phase I, effectively leveraging the work already completed. Educational use of the CAUSE program products will assist in the preparation of citizens who can analyze the ethical and scientific dimensions of future policy decisions about research-related issues, as well as their own health choices.

West Virginia University
Morgantown, WV
West Virginia H ealth Sciences and Technology Academy (HSTA) Students Design Public
Health Clinical Trials
Grant No. RR023274-01
Award: $1,332,904
Principal Investigator
Anne Chester
Phone: 304-293-2323
E-mail: achester@hsc.wvu.edu

Abstract (provided by applicant):

The Health Sciences and Technology Academy (HSTA) of West Virginia University will implement this Phase I and II SEPA project with mock clinical trial protocol as a format to bring together biomedical and clinical researchers, university faculty, and community to disseminate science education to 9th-12th grade underrepresented students, their high school teachers, and to the general public. Critical components of clinical trials will be embedded in population-appropriate and age-appropriate context, and inquiry-based experiences using diabetes as the disease system and life-style interventions focused on nutrition and exercise. Clinical trials protocol curriculum will be designed by both HSTA teachers and university faculty and used for both campus summer programming and academic year, community-based, student research projects. In W.Va., over 43 percent of children have been classified as at-risk or overweight. In the last decade, W.Va. has recorded the highest diabetes-related deaths in the nation, though it is believed to have a high prevalence of modifiable risk factors for diabetes and obesity. The objectives of this application are to demystify clinical trials for the general public with special attention to under-served populations and to improve the health of the state through education. The goal is to guide students and teachers in research projects involving life-style interventions for obesity and diabetes in communities where they transmit their new knowledge and understanding of research and clinical trials protocol to parents and community members. By doing so, teachers will address critical barriers to progress in healthy lifestyles and demystify clinical trials research through the use of a novel teaching method. In addition, the project will raise the level of science training for both teachers and students involved; excite teachers to incorporate the mock clinical trial protocol curriculum in their classrooms; provide academic enrichment in science and math to better prepare under-represented students for academic success in college; and stimulate student interest towards biomedical research with particular attention to under-represented students.

Wheeling Jesuit University
Wheeling, WV
CyberSurgeons Live Simulation and PBL Development and Dissemination
Grant No. RR023299-01
Award: $1,350,000
Principal Investigator
Bruce Howard
Phone: 304-243-8720
E-mail: howard@cet.edu

Abstract (provided by applicant):

The Center for Educational Technologies (CET) will implement a five-year Phase I & II development and dissemination project called CyberSurgeons. Through this project, the CET will increase the knowledge of high school students taking biology, physiology, or related classes. In particular, students will gain a greater understanding of human pathophysiology and the process of biomedical research and clinical trials. The project will influence the future of public health through encouraging students' future participation in the clinical research enterprise and promoting greater career awareness of occupations in these fields. The CET will develop two components for students based on national standards. The first component is the CyberSurgeons live simulation, conducted through distance learning technologies. The simulation features students working as part of a high-tech "remote trauma unit" in medical-surgical teams to diagnose and treat an ailing researcher deep in the rain forests of Ecuador. The second component is an online CyberSurgeons problem-based learning (PBL) module, which features a "problem" about the quality of a cancer drug, with case studies, science articles, datasets, and charts to analyze; hands-on, inquiry-based activities; and teacher support materials. Both components include optional activities promoting awareness of careers in biomedicine. During the development process, the CET will conduct design-based evaluation. The live simulation and PBL components will each have two cycles of development, classroom testing, formative evaluation, and revisions. An external evaluator will conduct a summative research study, utilizing a quasi-experimental design to demonstrate the effectiveness of the modules in classrooms. Dependent measures will be science literacy, science-related attitudes, and career development. Program dissemination will utilize a multimodal, multifaceted approach with the goal of program sustainability past the grant period. In the first three years, partnerships will involve three school districts in the development and testing process. In the final two years, the program will be promoted regionally, then nationally—doubling program outreach each year. Additionally, the program will be promoted among informal science education entities such as science centers and Challenger Learning Centers. Other dissemination means include conferences, workshops, promotional mailings, and research papers.

NLM Understanding and Promoting Health Literacy Research Grants

Rockledge 1, Suite 301
6705 Rockledge Drive
Bethesda, MD 20892
301.594.4882
Dr. Hua-Chuan Sim
http://grants1.nih.gov/grants/guide/pa-files/PAR-07-020.html
http://tiny.cc/g5j8K

Description

The goal of these Program Announcements is to increase scientific understanding of the nature of health literacy and its relationship to healthy behaviors, illness prevention and treatment, chronic disease management, health disparities, risk assessment of environmental factors, and health outcomes including mental and oral health.

Biomedical Information Science and Technology Initiative (BISTI)

6705 Rockledge Drive, Room 2207, MSC 7987
Bethesda, MD 20892-7987
(301) 594-6584

http://grants.nih.gov/grants/submitapplication.htm

http://tiny.cc/tNgND

Description

The Biomedical Information Science and Technology Initiative Consortium (BISTIC) was established in May 2000 and is composed of senior-level representatives from the NIH centers and institutes and representatives of other Federal agencies concerned with bioinformatics and computational applications. The mission is to make optimal use of computer science and technology to address problems in biology and medicine. In support of this mission, the BISTIC coordinates research grants, training opportunities, development of associated research and training resources, and scientific symposia associated with biomedical computing.

Recent Awards, Winning Projects & Award Winners

KOHANE, ISAAC S.
BRIGHAM AND WOMEN'S HOSPITAL
Informatics for Integrating Biology and the Bedside(RMI)
http://tiny.cc/uiXPZ

CALIFORNIA TEACHER TELLS HOW
HE WON TECH EQUIPMENT - GRANTS GALORE FOR HIS CLASSROOM

BY BRYAN FECI
USSENTERPRISE02@COMCAST.NET

Dear Readers,

Many teachers wonder where are all the grants? The following are grants proposals I have written over the past 4 years. Most continue to be offered in subsequent years. Most of them I have found simply by using Internet searches such Google and Yahoo. Local county offices and teacher associations such as NEA also offer current grant resources. My name is Bryan Feci. I teach fourth grade at Holly Oak Elementary School which is located in the Evergreen School District of San Jose. I have been teaching for 7 years.

Over these past years, I've participated in numerous professional development programs in writing, differentiating instruction, second language development, and technology.

Due to successful winning grants, I have obtained the following materials for my classroom: 15 classroom laptop computers from various grants, 1 laptop storage cabinet, 1 scanner, 6 digital cameras, 10 electronic thesauruses, 1 wireless networked printer/copier/scanner, 1 document camera, 1 LCD projector, 5 electricity kits with 16 investigations, 5 static electricity kits, a river model kit to study erosion, Pangaea model, earthquake fault model and demonstration kit, rock and mineral test kits and samples, licensed copies of 2 math computer software applications, a classroom field trip, and miscellaneous technologies such as replacement keyboards and mice, headphones, CD's, and DVD's.

DONOR'S CHOOSE (http://www.donorschoose. org) is an Internet-based grant program. Teachers all over the United States design a grant proposal to post on the Donor's Choose Website. Sponsors will go online and search for classroom projects based on type of materials requested, grade level, subject, or by location. Teachers spend points when a proposal is posted and earn points when fulfilling grant agreements.

A proposal may be posted at any time, once reviewed by the Donor's Choose staff. Many proposals are funded every year. I have had 7 proposals funded in just 4 years, but an additional 4 that were never funded. Unfunded proposals expire after 8 months. When a proposal is funded, the Donor's Choose staff purchases the supplies and mails them to the teacher's classroom making it unnecessary to worry out teacher reimbursements.

The proposals that have been funded for me have been for electricity kits, static electricity experiments, rock and mineral samples and investigations, 10 electronic thesauruses, licensed copies of 2 math software programs, river model and earthquake demonstration kits to study erosion and earthquakes, and recently a brand new MacBook Pro laptop valued at $2700.

BEST BUY offers annual technology grants of $2000 to teachers (http://communications.bestbuy.com/ communityrelations/teach.asp). I received this grant in February, 2008. My grant proposal was to buy a $1000 laptop for student use in the classroom and a wireless networked printer, scanner, copier to print student projects designed on the computer. After a field trip to local California mission, students created documentaries using movie making software from pictures taken on digital cameras. Best Buy sends the winning teachers the money in the form of a Best Buy gift card.

NATIONAL SEMICONDUCTOR offers annual grants to teachers for $2000. For this grant proposal, students created movie presentations about earthquake safety to share with other classrooms. I used the money from this winning grant to purchase another computer for students to create their movies on and to partially pay for a field trip to study earthquakes. For more information, please go to http://www.nsawards.com.

Locally in San Jose, California, the SILICON VALLEY EDUCATION FOUNDATION offers innovative grants to teachers in $500 amounts several times through the year. I was the recipient of this grant twice this school year. One purchase was for a new document camera and the second was to fund the admission fee for a special classroom field trip to the Lawrence Hall of Science at UC Berkeley. Interested applicants should visit their website at http://www.svefoundation.org.

ADOPT-A-CLASSROOM is a simple program for teachers across the United States. Teachers simply discuss their classroom needs and type of school they teach at. Donors can select classrooms they wish to fund by grade and location. Teachers can get their classrooms "adopted" once a year. This means a sponsor has donated $500 to a teacher's classroom. The teacher then completes a purchase form online and the materials are ordered and delivered to the teacher's school. This makes it unnecessary for a teacher to buy the requested supplies and be reimbursed. For more information, the website is http://www.adoptaclassroom.com.

Funding possibilities are everywhere. Sometimes you just have to be at the right place at the right time. In California, San Jose State University offered master teachers of student-teachers a $1000 CAL-MOD grant.
I just happened to have a student-teacher that semester. County offices of education sometimes offer grant writing workshops and keep lists current grant opportunities for schools and teachers.

The Santa Clara County Office of Education awarded me a $500 grant for two years in a row. The proposals I designed related to incorporating technology. One grant was used to purchase my own laptop storage cabinet for all of my laptops,

Many school districts may offer grants to their teachers. Funding is usually obtained from a grant school district office administrators write. In May, 2006, I won a $5000 LET grant through my district purchasing 3 laptops and various supplies for completing a California Gold Rush unit.

THE HISTORY CHANNEL offered $500 awards for teachers who preserve their "history" in the classroom. Through the Save Our History grant, I won $500 for preserving California history by having students design newspaper articles on the computer documenting famous California explorers. At http://wwwsaveourhistory.com, this year they are offering grants to outside agencies that partner with local schools.

The question on everyone's mind is how have I been able to write so many successful grants? In just 4 years, I have received a total of just over $28,000 in grants.

It takes a lot of time to write a successful grant, but sometimes it can take a great deal of time just to research different opportunities. In my situation, it is very worth it when you get materials for a special unit you are teaching. I get as excited as the students get and this only causes those moments to be memorable when I see the students really being the ones who benefit.

SOME OF MY FAVORITE WINNING GRANTS
BY BRYAN FECI

My name is Bryan Feci. I teach fourth grade at Holly Oak Elementary School which is located in the Evergreen School District of San Jose. I have been teaching for 7 years. Over these past years, I've participated in numerous professional development programs in writing, differentiating instruction, second language development, and technology. I've been a lead writing teacher for 2 years and have lead various workshops and staff development opportunities for the district in English Language Development and technology. I hold a BA in Liberal Studies and multiple subject teaching credential from San Jose State University. I also have an instructional technology certificate from the University of California Extension, Santa Cruz. My successes integrating technology in the classroom are made possible from my technology certificate training and from the numerous grants I have written over the past 5 years. As I like to say, I have acquired quite a fortune in classroom materials from grant writing, but it's the education that has provided me the training to know how to use technology at its fullest potential. Writing grants allows me to not just acquire new technologies, but have at least 1 project in mind that puts that new technology to a good use. Personally, I get curious about what Microsoft or Apple has come up with now, but refuse to ever want the latest gadget just for the benefit of having it. With many technologies coming out with big price tags, we need to justify obtaining them—whether by a grant or not—so that they can improve the quality of classroom instruction and student learning.

The grants I wrote were intended for only my classroom. I have never written a grant to benefit the entire school. It wasn't that I was selfish, but actually because I doubted my ability to write a successful grant. When it comes down it, a successful grant is determined by your competition. What helped me become successful with grant writing was starting with an end result in mind. Having this big picture in mind made grant writing easier. Now that I am confident with my grant writing abilities, I am very eager to take many of my colleagues up on their offers to lead a school grant committee that writes grants that benefit everyone at the school.

With every grant I write, I always design a project that will enhance instruction and learning. All of these projects vary in length of time for completion and type of project.

MY FAVORITE GRANTS

BEST BUY

One of my favorite grants was the Best Buy grant this past year. To describe the project briefly, the students created movie documentaries about the California missions using pictures taken on a class field trip to a local mission after reading about missions on an online tour of a typical California mission. The full project description is below:

History comes alive in my classroom every year when my fourth graders learn about the California Missions. Our study begins by touring through a typical mission on an online scavenger hunt. Students work collaboratively in small groups reading about different aspects of mission life and answer questions for comprehension along the way. Each online page comes with a diagram or picture for visual support. Important words are underlined allowing students to click on that link to see the definition. After our online research, students work with a partner reading online about one mission in particular and create a travel brochure about their mission using a template I created in Microsoft Word. Students provide historical facts, maps, pictures, and write about what to see at that mission.

On a class field trip to a mission, we bring along digital cameras and take pictures of different parts of the mission. Prior to the field trip to Mission San Juan Bautista, I show a short 10-minute video from Bay Area Backroads. This allows the class to know what to expect to see on the field trip and enables us to make a list of what we want to take pictures of at the mission. Common pictures include the mission bell, garden, well, and fountain, graveyard, church interior and exterior, the alter, kitchen, padre's quarters, dining hall, and the El Camino Real.

We compile all pictures and download them to all our classroom computers to use in our final project: a movie! Students use iMovie to create their own mission documentaries in groups of three using the field trip pictures. They add background music, title slides, sound effects, transitions, voice narrations, and ending credits. I burn the movies onto 1 DVD. We celebrate our hard work by watching and applauding each movie. The movies are also shown to next year's class. In the movies, students describe the historical importance of the pictures they took. For example, students will mention all the different uses of the mission bell. In the end, the hard work is worth it!

IMPACT II: SANTA CLARA COUNTY OFFICE OF EDUCATION
"WAGONS WEST"

Another of my favorite grants is the Impact II mini grant I won through the Santa Clara County Office of Education. In the grant, titled "Wagons West" students experienced being pioneers and forty-niners during 1849 in this simulation. Teams learned about this time period in American history as they made team decisions while traveling along the early trails to California. Just as pioneers did, the students learned about the dangers and risks along the way! Also similar to pioneers, students kept diary entries documenting their successes and failures. Following the project, the students typed their diary entries as a Power Point presentation and included pictures they drew themselves using a scanner. Each student was able to print out their 8 diary entries. A full description of the project is below:

"Wagons West" provides fourth graders the opportunity to relive the Wild West. In this unit, students will work cooperatively as they journey west- making decisions as pioneers. Five teams of six (each wagon train) will prepare a list of supplies to bring. With each student being allotted 10 items to fit in his wagon, it becomes important for each team to cooperatively select items. Each team will be provided a list of suggested items to select from and be encouraged to think of other items they might need. A map of the United States during the 1850's will be about 5 yards long and nearly cover the entire whiteboard.

The map displays early trail routes to California such as those used by James Beckworth. Each group will be assigned a different route of travel and start at different cities along the east coast. Since pioneers' survival depended upon cooperation, decision-making, skill, and luck, each team will be asked to make a variety decisions along the way.

Decisions involve deciding which routes to take, encounters with Native Americans, getting sick with typhoid fever, fixing wagon wheels, and experiencing many other potential pioneer problems. I will also display a power point presentation on my multimedia projector that tells a story of traveling west in a diary format. Each diary entry presents a new situation to the students that require them to discuss the possible outcomes and cooperatively decide on a course of action.

After all teams make a decision, I reveal the outcomes. This activity emphasizes cooperation for survival rather than competition. Some questions are individualized for certain trails (allows everyone to see the similarities and differences in the various routes to California). Different groups going on the same trail will have slightly different experiences also based on the decisions they make. A graphic organizer with 3 columns will be used to document question prompts given, decisions made, and outcomes. Students will be using their graphic organizers to write their own diaries using Power Point about traveling west to California.

This portion will require students to work with 2 partners from their wagon train groups (each group is now split into 2 small groups of 3). Using our 10 classroom computers, students will create their power point diaries. They will be able to include pictures downloaded online, from digital cameras, scanned, or even include an iMovie clipping since all the needed technology is available. Once finished, each group will read their power point diaries to the class and publish our writing by printing them out.

IMPACT II: SANTA CLARA COUNTY OFFICE OF EDUCATION "A MATH TWIST"

In "A Math Twist", my students created their own multiplication and division problems using Microsoft Word. Fourth graders need to be able to multiply multiple-digit numbers (i.e. 6,324x49) and divide multiple-digit numbers by single digits (i.e. 4,329/7). With Microsoft Word, a text box is created for each number in the math problem. Students solve various math problems on these "templates".

The "drawing" toolbar in Microsoft Word allows students to construct the lines and symbols needed for creating multiplication and division problems identical to what is normally written down on binder paper. Students are asked to type in the steps used to solve that problem. The Word template allows students to maintain organization in their calculations while they are learning how multiplication and long division problems are solved.

What I liked the most about this project was that students are learning math in new, meaningful ways that allow all them to be motivated and successful. Using Microsoft Word previously in the classroom, I can say with certainty that what makes this approach truly revolutionary is not so much the technology being used… it's the fact that all students are being set up to succeed.

I am very grateful for this $500 grant that I put to good use by purchasing a document camera allowing students to share their projects with the class.

NATIONAL SEMICONDUCTOR "EARTHQUAKE PREPAREDNESS DAY": $2000

In March 2008, I won the National Semiconductor grant for $2000. This grant allowed me to purchase an additional computer for classroom use and to help pay for a class field trip the Lawrence Hall of Science in Berkeley.

The first part of this project was a treasure hunt where students read various websites and answered questions about earthquakes. Students researched effective ways to prepare for an earthquake and what to do during one. A class field trip to the Lawrence Hall of Science in Berkeley allowed students the opportunity to learn about earthquakes first-hand. Students participated in 2 labs interpreting real seismic data and constructed their own buildings to withstand earthquakes. With all this learning, students created 5-minute narrated documentaries in partners using a movie-making software, iMovie, for first, second, and third graders to learn about earthquakes.

This project was one of my favorites. The class had a long day full of learning at the Lawrence Hall of Science. Despite the fact that they had to arrive at school 20 minutes early and not get back to school until 5:00 that afternoon, they still claimed it to be the best field trip of the year. I am also very pleased with how well the movies turned out. Students rose to the occasion by meeting the high expectations they were given.

The end results were 12 excellent movies with 3 weeks of work invested and 26 student leaders eager to share their movies with our school community and filled with high self-esteem. Our project ended with an award ceremony where each student received an award for his or her hard work and the chance to share their movies on their own DVD copy with their families. Any project that gets students excited about learning and wanting to share that learning with others is always worth the time put into it! For more information, the National Semiconductor Website is http://www.nsawards.com.

SILICON VALLEY EDUCATION FOUNDATION
"JUNIOR GEOLOGISTS PROJECT"

My favorite grant has been my Junior Geologists project. Funded through the Silicon Valley Education Foundation, the students visited the Lawrence Hall of Science at U.C. Berkeley to further extend our student of earthquakes. In hands-on lab activities, students learned how the earth is made up of plates that interact in various ways along faults.

We learned how to interpret real seismic data to determine the epicenter of an earthquake. In another lab, students learned about earthquake safety and preparedness by designing various types of buildings to determine the safest types of structures.

These experiences were extensions of the online reading and computer activities from class. With my class being experts on earthquakes thanks to funding from the Silicon Valley Education Foundation, students became school leaders by creating instructional movies in a narrative form that were used to teach younger students about earthquakes. After all, a unique learning experience like this has to be shared with others!

This project was accomplished in a 6 week time period. Rather than learn many scientific concepts on a surface level, our unit on earthquakes studies a single topic on a deep level that allows student learning to become meaningful. Students don't question why it is important to study earthquakes when it is being applied to their own lives. They don't just learn information for a passing grade on a test to forget about in a month. This project becomes much a part of them that it will be something they will remember for a long time. This project is probably the best example of how the grants I write are to revolutionize the way students should learn. It is not so much about the laptop computers I purchase or to have my own wireless, networked printer. Grant writing is about the special, unique experiences students when those projects are carried out. A description of my Junior Geologists grant is below:

"At the Lawrence Hall of Science on April 9, 2008, my students will participate in 2 hands-on workshops. As junior geologists, students become earthquake experts as they learn about plate tectonics and recording seismic activity. They also become safety engineers as they put simple structures under earthquake stress and discuss how to prepare for severe earthquakes. For the next 2 weeks, students create video documentaries to teach others about earthquakes.

Having this field trip experience is quite a special experience for students. I believe students learn best through hands-on experiences that also include direct instruction. That may sound amazing to you, but I see the field trip as an opportunity. As earthquake experts, students need to share this learning with our school community. What's the point in keeping all that wonderful knowledge in our heads? That is why after the field trip, students will create movie documentaries on our classroom computers to explain the causes of earthquakes and how to prepare for the BIG ONE!

In their documentaries, students will be able to explain the geological forces the cause earthquakes, technology used to record earthquakes, explain basic ways buildings are retrofitted to withstand earthquakes, and provide important ways to be prepared for a major earthquake."

The grant descriptions above came from the actual proposals I wrote. No matter how many tips I can come up with, the best one to remember of all is make your project sound important and unique.

ACTUAL GRANT PROPOSALS
FOR WINNING GRANTS TO BRYAN FECI, CALIFORNIA 4TH GRADE TEACHER

BEST BUY GRANT PROPOSAL

QUESTION #1:
USE OF INTERACTIVE TECHNOLOGY

Please respond to the following question in 2000 characters or less. If you exceed the character limit, highlight excess text to be deleted, then right click and cut or delete the text before editing the remaining response.

Tell us about the program or project you are submitting for a Best Buy Teach Award and describe how your students have used the technology products you identified earlier in creative, fun and hands-on ways to learn the curriculum in the classroom.

History comes alive in my classroom every year when my fourth graders learn about the California Missions. Our study begins by touring through a typical mission on an online scavenger hunt. Students work collaboratively in small groups reading about different aspects of mission life and answer questions for comprehension along the way. Each online page comes with a diagram or picture for visual support.

Important words are underlined allowing students to click on that link to see the definition. After our online research, students work with a partner reading online about one mission in particular and create a travel brochure about their mission using a template I created in Microsoft Word. Students provide historical facts, maps, pictures, and write about what to see at that mission.

On a class field trip to a mission, we bring along digital cameras and take pictures of different parts of the mission. Prior to the field trip to Mission San Juan Bautista, I show a short 10-minute video from Bay Area Backroads. This allows the class to know what to expect to see on the field trip and enables us to make a list of what we want to take pictures of at the mission. Common pictures include the mission bell, garden, well, and fountain, graveyard, church interior and exterior, the alter, kitchen, padre's quarters, dining hall, and the El Camino Real.

We compile all pictures and download them to all our classroom computers to use in our final project: a movie! Students use iMovie to create their own mission documentaries in groups of three using the field trip pictures. They add background music, title slides, sound effects, transitions, voice narrations, and ending credits. I burn the movies onto 1 DVD. We celebrate our hard work by watching and applauding each movie. The movies are also shown to next year's class. In the movies, students describe the historical importance of the pictures they took. For example, students will mention all the different uses of the mission bell. In the end, the hard work is worth it!

QUESTION #2:
IMPACT OF USING INTERACTIVE TECHNOLOGY

Please respond to the following question in 2000 characters or less. If you exceed the character limit, highlight excess text to be deleted, then right click and cut or delete the text before editing the remaining response.

If you answered earlier that student engagement, comprehension and/or attendance have improved as a result of being able to use technology hands-on in the classroom please describe what the impact has been.

Over the past two years, I have observed considerable difference by integrating technology into student learning. For starters, technology has made it easier for students to understand the content. The online scavenger hunt tour through the mission allows content to be broken down into manageable pieces essential to understanding.

When it comes to the travel brochure, field trip, and movie, those pieces are brought back together again for students to see the whole picture. These three projects give students the opportunity to share what they are learning with their peers. Attendance and engagement also has improved through learning using technology. Students want to come to school and remain focused as they work on their projects. Rather than complete an assignment for the sake of being able to go to recess, students take pride and ownership in their work. If they don't like a narrated recording describing how the El Camino Real is a path that connects all the missions, they record it again after coming up with a better sentence. Students also typically score higher on their Social Studies tests when technology has been integrated into curriculum compared to units that don't include this hands-on learning. Students want their projects to turn out great, they are willing to help each other, and those with focusing challenges typically are the most engaged. I've taught students with learning disabilities in writing and students who are learning English.

Some of these students have made dramatic improvements in state reading comprehension tests and state writing assessments. As you can see, this type of learning on a regular basis revolutionizes the classroom climate. Learning is not just memorization and recalling facts and details. It has become interactive. Students become active in their learning. Knowledge is not something given to them. It is something they create and discover for themselves.

QUESTION #3
BUDGET

$2,000
Hewlett-Packard Color LaserJet Printer/ Copier/ Scanner
Model: CM1015 499.99
Geek Squad® - 10' USB 2.0 A/B Cable GS-10UAB 38.99
HP Laserjet Print Cartridge- Black Q6000A 78.99
HP Laserjet Print Cartridge- Cyan Q6001A 86.99
HP Laserjet Print Cartridge- Magenta Q6003A 86.99
HP Laserjet Print Cartridge- Yellow Q6002A 86.99
=890

$10,000
Apple® MacBook™ with 13.3" Display - White
Model: MB061LL/A 1099.00
Apple® MacBook® Pro with 17" Display
Model: MA897LL/A 2799.00

QUESTION #4:
IMPACT OF TEACH AWARD

Please respond to the following question in 4000 characters or less (about 750 words). If you exceed the character limit, highlight excess text to be deleted, then right click and cut or delete the text before editing the remaining response. How will the products included in the previously listed budget improve the existing program described in this application?

Throughout this project, one emphasis I've been making is that technology used in student learning changes the classroom environment. Learning is alive and students interact to create meaning. Students are able to share their projects with classmates, but not the wider community.

I see a lot of potential for expanding on this project further by sharing their projects with family members and our school community. By being able to print out projects conveniently in our own classroom and having the resources to burn our projects onto CD's and DVD's, we can reach out to the wider community. Our projects can be used to start a History Night evening event at our school where students display their projects that bring history alive for our community to see. Students will have projects to take home and share their learning with their families. Other teachers can become inspired to integrate technology in their classrooms in similar ways.

With remarkable experiences such as these, it is easy to think big, and it becomes even easier to make these ideas a reality. Your support allows me to continue creating projects for other history units and even in other subjects allowing students to share their masterpieces with our school community and their families. My California Mission unit may bring history alive, but expanding on the possibilities gives learning a life of its own. Thank you for your consideration.

IMPACT II: SANTA CLARA COUNTY OFFICE OF EDUCATION
WAGONS WEST

"Wagons West" provides fourth graders the opportunity to relive the Wild West. In this unit, students will work cooperatively as they journey west- making decisions as pioneers. Five teams of six (each wagon train) will prepare a list of supplies to bring. With each student being allotted 10 items to fit in his wagon, it becomes important for each team to cooperatively select items. Each team will be provided a list of suggested items to select from and be encouraged to think of other items they might need.

A map of the United States during the 1850's will be about 5 yards long and nearly cover the entire whiteboard. The map displays early trail routes to California such as those used by James Beckworth. Each group will be assigned a different route of travel and start at different cities along the east coast.

Since pioneers' survival depended upon cooperation, decision-making, skill, and luck, each team will be asked to make a variety decisions along the way. Decisions involve deciding which routes to take, encounters with Native Americans, getting sick with typhoid fever, fixing wagon wheels, and experiencing many other potential pioneer problems. I will also display a power point presentation on my multimedia projector that tells a story of traveling west in a diary format.

Each diary entry presents a new situation to the students that require them to discuss the possible outcomes and cooperatively decide on a course of action. After all teams make a decision, I reveal the outcomes. This activity emphasizes cooperation for survival rather than competition. Some questions are individualized for certain trails (allows everyone to see the similarities and differences in the various routes to California).

Different groups going on the same trail will have slightly different experiences also based on the decisions they make. A graphic organizer with 3 columns will be used to document question prompts given, decisions made, and outcomes.

Students will be using their graphic organizers to write their own diaries using Power Point about traveling west to California. This portion will require students to work with 2 partners from their wagon train groups (each group is now split into 2 small groups of 3). Using our 10 classroom computers, students will create their power point diaries. They will be able to include pictures downloaded online, from digital cameras, scanned, or even include an iMovie clipping since all the needed technology is available. Once finished, each group will read their power point diaries to the class and publish our writing by printing them out.

Standards taught:

Social Studies 4.3.2. Compare how and why people traveled to California and the routes they traveled.

Writing: 1.1) Select a focus, an organizational structure, and a point of view based upon purpose, audience, length, and format requirements, 1.3) use traditional structures for conveying information, 1.7) use various reference materials as an aid to writing, 1.9) demonstrate basic keyboarding skills and familiarity with computer terminology, 1.10) edit and revise selected drafts to improve coherence and progression by adding, deleting, consolidating, and rearranging text. 2.1) Write narratives that relate ideas, observations, or recollections of an event or experience, provide a context to enable the reader to imagine the world of the event or experience, use concrete sensory details, and provide insight into why the selected event or experience is memorable.

Rubrics will be used as criteria for grading students on their power points for Social Studies standards and Writing standards (which also addresses student use of technology). Rubric strands will include 1) historical fiction (setting time and place reflects this era; description of trail during journey), 2) organizational structure, point of view, purpose, audience, 3) Narrative transitions used to convey information, 4) ability to use keyboard skills and menu headings, 5) ability to use an assortment of technology (what technology do the students use to complete the task?), 6) ability to revise and edit the power point narrative to be free of errors and contain a variety of sentences, 7) power point requirements will include a minimum number of slides, types of slides, transitions, pictures, clip art, video clipping, and background, 8) story written as first person narrative includes a required number of events from graphic organizer, 9) usage of concrete sensory details, 10) the narrative is a memorable experience, 11) ability to stay on task, work cooperatively, work safely with others, and 12) narrative is read to the class.

The success of this project depends upon the students' ability to write historical diaries that resemble those depicted in historical documents from this era.

Educational research by Robert Marzano shows that teachers should concentrate on essential instruction. Student understanding of early trail routes to California is important to allow students to compare these routes with other routes to come such as the transcontinental railroad and future highways. The simulation can be completed in 2 one-hour lessons in groups of six. The power point will take about 6-one hour sessions in groups of three. This unit can easily be modified for fifth graders.

Student prior experience throughout the year working cooperatively and using technology is helpful. Students will need to sit in clusters of six and need to see the prepared United States map. Trails on the map appear like a dot-to-dot. Students also need to see the power point sample diary narrative that I will prepare and display on my multimedia projector. Worksheets that need to be reproduced are the graphic organizer and supply lists. Questions prewritten on the graphic organizers will save essential instructional time. A laptop storage cart will adequately help students easily use, store, and maintain our classroom computers.

"Wagons West" is truly an innovative use of cooperative learning, technology, acting out historical events, visual and performing arts, reading, and writing. Content instruction is provided through the simulation and the Power Point diary I read to them. Students are motivated to learn through use of the simulation and technology. They are intrigued by the variety of scenarios that teach content and vocabulary as they learn to weigh the pros and cons involved with making decisions. They learn how to take chances and—more importantly for character development—take responsibility for their actions. Students use the technology available in my classroom as tools in the writing process. I expect all students to be excited to write for once and be even more excited to share and display their power point narratives. Students, without a doubt, take pride in their work and want to improve it. I am delighted to see that the entire unit is student-centered. Active student involvement is required every step of the way of all students. This lesson is a helpful way to incorporate technology into learning. It also allows teachers to effectively teach at-risk / low performing students, students with learning disabilities, and second language learners. "Wagons West" is absolutely a unit worthy to teach and share with educators.

A MATH TWIST ACTUAL PROPOSAL ABSTRACT OF GRANT REQUEST

Technology opens the doors towards a new and creative form of learning. With an open mind, teachers can facilitate a new way for students to learn in the 21st century. In A Math Twist, my students already have most of the resources needed: classroom computers, an LCD projector, and knowledge of how to use Microsoft Word. What would take this math program up a level would be showing and explaining how to solve their math problems with others using a document camera.

NARRATIVE:
Imagine what it would be like if students complete class assignments using computers rather than paper and pencil tasks. Here is how this scenario is possible:

Fourth graders need to be able to multiply multiple-digit numbers (i.e. 6,324x49) and divide multiple-digit numbers by single digits (i.e. 4,329/7). Therefore, my students will learn multiplication and division using various software programs on our current classroom computers. Having an LCD projector, I am able to demonstrate both the mathematical procedures and creatively Microsoft Word to extend learning.

Microsoft Word has the potential for students to practice mathematical procedures for solving multiplication and division problems. As I have done in previous years, students work on Word templates I create to solve math problems (including word problems). Text boxes are created for each number in a math problem. Students solve various math problems on these templates.

The "drawing" toolbar in Microsoft Word allows students to construct the lines and symbols needed for creating multiplication and division problems identical to what is normally written down on binder paper. In th past, I have used various math templates to differentiate for at-risk and advanced students since one size does not fit all in learning.

This project can be adjusted for many math standards. The fourth grade math and language arts standards taught in this project include: NS3.3 (Solve problems involving multiplication of multidigit numbers by two-digit numbers), NS3.4 (Solve problems involving division of multidigit numbers by one-digit numbers), MR1.2 (Determine when and how to break a problem into simpler parts), MR2.3 (Use a variety of methods... to explain mathematical reasoning), MR2.4 (Express the solution clearly using appropriate mathematical notation, terms, and clear language), LS1.4 (Give precise directions and instructions), and LS1.6 (Use traditional structures for conveying information).

EVALUATION:
Student assignments will be evaluated using rubric scores from 1 to 4. Students will earn points based on the following criteria: 1) accuracy of calculations and whether or not students show their work with regrouping when necessary, 2) accuracy of step by step instructions for solving the math problem, 3) complexity of problem solved, 4) how effective student uses textboxes, lines, arrows, word art, clip art, borders in their problems, 5) template used (whether created from scratch, continued one started for them, or a fill-

in template), and 6) how well student explains how to solve the math problem in complete sentences using the document camera.

TIMETABLE:
With 12 classroom computers and with previous experience using Microsoft Word, each student can be allotted 30-45 minutes on a computer. With less experience, it is beneficial for students to work with a partner. Giving each person a turn would likely take no more than three-45 minute sessions and one more hour for students to present their math problems to the class using the document camera.

DESCRIBE THE STUDENTS:
I prefer to think of this project as a quest—a quest to make sure all of my 30 students each year learn how to solve multiplication and division problems. Students will know how to use technology in ways unimaginable and be able to share mathematical reasoning with those around them. This activity can be modified for any grade and can benefit students of all abilities. Templates and complexity of math problems can be modified for second language learners, students with learning disabilities, or for students who are advanced learners. My fourth grade classroom contains a mix of all these abilities and every student comes away with new learning. Even by working with a partner, all student needs can be met.

MATERIALS AND FACILITIES:
This project can be done using classroom computers equipped with Microsoft Word. A document camera and LCD projector are necessary for sharing student work.

OVERALL VALUE:
Students will definitely be learning math in new, meaningful ways that allow all students to be motivated and successful. All my students, including second language learners, can be expected to share what they have learned. Using Microsoft Word previously in the classroom, I can say with certainty that what makes this approach truly revolutionary is not so much the technology being used... it's the fact that all students are being set up to succeed and that there is so much we can learn from each other.

NATIONAL SEMICONDUCTOR AWARDS GRANT $2000 + $1000

1.   What are your learning goals and objectives? (Be specific about state standards addressed and challenges for your students that the project will overcome; 500 words maximum)

What are earthquakes? How do earthquakes affect our lives in California? What should elementary students know about earthquakes to prepare for one? In this web quest unit, students will conduct research about earthquakes to determine the geological causes of earthquakes and develop an earthquake preparedness plan. (A web quest is an inquiry oriented lesson format that utilizes the Internet for research. It provides an introduction to show a purpose, explains a series of tasks, includes a list of online resources, and clarifies project expectations with an evaluation rubric.)

My fourth graders will be able to explain earthquake theories, plate tectonics, and how to be prepared for an earthquake. Towards these goals, students will know what causes an earthquake, different types of faults and the effects on the earth, how earthquakes are measured, and what to do before and during an earthquake. These objectives meet fourth grade California earth science standard 5a "Students know some changes in the earth are due to slow processes, such as erosion, and some changes are due to rapid processes, such as landslides, volcanic eruptions, and earthquakes."

One initial challenge while designing this unit has always been limiting what to study. I wanted students to know essential background concepts, how earthquakes are measured, and how to be prepared.

Another challenge is how to plan instructional activities that would be meaningful and increase understanding. I prefer instruction that incorporates hands-on activities and visual literacy. I think learning science concepts best occurs through experimentation to make it easier for students to understand what they read—

Motivation and classroom management always present a challenge when designing a unit that needs to be open enough to encourage creativity and thinking "outside the box". Students need a purpose for doing the reading online to keep them on task. Typically, organizing research as a "treasure hunt" gives the research parts the necessary structure and motivation to maintain student excitement and attention span.

Since this project is a web quest, it was also difficult to come up with a purpose for carrying out this research. After heavy thought, I eventually decided that this unit is an opportunity for my students to become school leaders in earthquake preparedness. Students will be asked to participate in an "Earthquake Preparedness Day" where they will design presentations for grade level assemblies. They will be responsible for teaching essential earthquake theories and explaining what to do during an earthquake to lower grade classrooms.

2.   How will your students achieve these goals and objectives? (Be specific about activities and student outcomes, 500 word maximum)

To prepare for Earthquake Preparedness Day, students will accomplish a series of tasks. The first task is a treasure hunt where students read various websites and answer very specific questions about plate tectonics and the theory of Pangaea. Students will explain how the continents have shifted over thousands of years and how earthquakes occur along faults when pressure is released from due to movement of plates below the surface.

They will complete a graphic organizer to help them explain cause and effect relationships in how plates interact in different ways. Categorizing questions and websites on the student research logs keeps information readily available for student access for later tasks.

In task two, students research effective ways to prepare for an earthquake and what to do during one. This means additional online reading, but this time it is to compare 2 online resources and recommend which program to follow by explaining the reasons for choosing that program. Students first conduct the research by reading the necessary websites given to them. Following this reading, the class will meet develop a criteria to evaluate a program. Our list will include criteria such as how easy is it carry out, kid-friendliness, and how it considers the needs of those who live in California.

When students are ready to begin task 3, they create their final projects to share at Earthquake Preparedness Day. In this task, students will create a 5-minute narrated documentary using a movie-making software, iMovie, for first, second, and third graders to see what earthquakes are, why they occur, what happens during an earthquake, what one can do to prepare for an earthquake, and what to do during an earthquake.

A class field trip to Los Trancos Earthquake Trail in Palo Alto will provide students the opportunity to learn about earthquakes first-hand and take up-close pictures that show changes to the earth caused by these rapid moving processes. Online pictures will be incorporated into the movies; however, students can understand the visible effects from earthquakes further by actually visiting the San Andreas Fault at Los Trancos for a hands-on field trip.

Tasks 1 and 2 require students to record their information into research logs. This means they do more than simply record the information. They also reflect on their own learning and ask questions about concepts they don't understand. Working in small teams of 2 or 3 throughout this unit allows students to respond to each other's questions. Unanswered questions are directed to me to provide additional instruction to that group or the entire class. The research logs are used continuously during task 3 as students reflect on what essential concepts are important to communicate to first, second, and third graders.

Research logs also allow students to reflect on their own learning, how the team is working cooperatively, and how they are using the various forms of technology (Internet, digital cameras, iMovie software, etc.). The research logs, therefore, are effective forms of individual assessments.

3. How will this project foster an appreciation of science, a delight in learning, or a spirit of curiosity in your students? (Be specific about how students will be engaged, 100 word maximum)

Students take on active roles evaluating their learning through reflections in research logs. They are excited to use digital cameras and iMovie software (not to mention being naturally curious and determined to learn how to use different features of that software). A safe learning environment is established for students to express what they have learned in a project-based form (in this case, the iMovie documentary). Students seem more intelligent compared with traditional forms of instruction. Students can share their learning with others, retain content for more than just a test, and actually appreciate science when content becomes meaningful.

IMPLEMENTATION PLAN

4. How will you implement your plan? (Be specific about timeline, instructional strategies, materials, 300 word maximum)

This unit occurs over a 4-week period. Longer times are required depending on student familiarity with the technology. Since the education code requires teachers to use state-adopted materials, the first week of this unit provides initial instruction about earthquakes. At the end of the first week, students write cause and effect statements using fill-in sentence frames to practice vocabulary and sentence structure after reading about earthquakes in their science textbooks.

In week 2, students conduct research using the Internet on classroom computers in groups of 2-3. Instruction becomes inquiry-oriented using the web quest approach.

Students create their documentaries in weeks 3 and 4. At the end of week 4, each movie is burned onto a DVD. Each team shows the movie to 1 or 2 classrooms. Students evaluate their own projects using the rubric and meet with me to compare my ratings with theirs.

Students will utilize these materials throughout this project:

- Science textbook (district provided)
- 1 copy of assorted graphic organizers to use during week 1 and and as needed during week 2, 5 (or more) Apple computers using OS 10.3 or higher with Microsoft Office, iPhoto, iTunes, iMovie, and Safari applications installed, (Note: Computers must have internal microphones to enable voice recordings in iMovie; 1 computer able to burn DVD's.)
- 1 firewire cable to transfer movies from 1 computer to one capable of burning DVD's, Power Point file explaining the web quest project, Microsoft Word file providing websites and questions for the treasure hunt,
- 5 digital cameras with memory cards for field trip,
- A criteria guide for what pictures to take on field trip,
- 1 visual organizer per team to plan out documentaries,
- 10 blank DVD-R,
- DVD player,
- 1 rubric copy per student,
- 30 notebooks to use as research logs,
- 1 writing prompt list, and field trip arrangements.

5. What will you purchase with your classroom award? (Provide item, cost, and quantity, 200 words maximum)

Many of the above materials are already available in my classroom. The following materials will need to be purchased and are essential for this project to happen:

- Classroom Field Trip cost to Los Trancos Earthquake Trail: $260.00 (includes a classroom presentation prior to field trip)
- Approximate cost for 1 bus for transportation: $240.00
- 1 Apple MacBook purchased from CDW for $1300.00 to burn movies onto DVD's
- 1 HP Photosmart E427 Digital Camera, memory card, and case from HP.com for $200

K-12 SO WHAT ARE MY SECRETS TO GRANT WRITING? HERE WE GO!

BY BRYAN FECI

1. **HAVE A STUDENT-CENTERED PROJECT IN MIND!** Grant committees like projects when they improve learning and are innovative. Unique and creative projects that use "out of the box" thinking won't guarantee you'll win, but will certainly help. I have written numerous grants that focus on units that incorporate the use of technology. Word processing might be an important skill, but using voice recordings to narrate a story typed onto Power Point gives that project a whole new look!

2. **STAY POSITIVE!** No one wants to read 1 proposal after another that complains about the lack of funding in schools. That's why you are writing a grant! Negativity does not promote success. Write grants for units of study that you will be excited to teach. Being positive also means being professional. I wish I could teach only what I enjoyed. Unfortunately, I have district and state standards to adhere to. Sometimes the best way to teach that boring topic is to write a grant to generate excitement! That is exactly what I did for teaching about landforms, rocks, and minerals in Science and now I look forward to teaching that unit every year!

3. **BE SELECTIVE IN THE GRANTS YOU CHOOSE TO APPLY FOR!** Only apply for grants you will see yourself excited about carrying out. Some grants are very specific for the types of projects they will fund. I came across a grant opportunity for a gardening project one time while searching online. As nice as it would be to get a few hundred dollars for a garden, I immediately moved on to the next grant listing as I don't have a green thumb. Every time I buy a plant, I forget to water it and you know what happens in just about a week! Some grants are not for everyone!

4. **FOLLOW DIRECTIONS!** Many grant opportunities have strict rules and procedures for applying. The way I see it, that organization is deciding whom to give money to. They receive anywhere from hundreds to thousands of grant applications so the least thing I could do to show my appreciation would be to obey the rules. By adhering to page limit, font size and style, whether or not sample materials are permitted, and due dates, you are showing your commitment in carrying out the grant should it be funded.

5. **ANSWERING QUESTIONS IN ORDER** (especially if requested) can help your application at least be considered instead being tossed aside. Many grant applications are divided up into various questions. Make sure your responses completely answer the questions. Are they clear and concise, or do they still leave too many unanswered questions?

6. **PROOFREAD!** Why should a company or agency fund your grant if you didn't even make the time to check over your writing? As a courtesy to the grant reviewers whom have many proposals to look over, please be nice enough to have your proposal be error free.

7. **AVOID THE WORD "WILL".** That is often difficult since implementing the project requires funding and it may sound petty. As a teacher, I cannot stand it when a student uses the same word constantly. Here is a first example: After our field trip to Mission San Juan Bautista, students will download the pictures onto classroom computers and will create 5-minute movie documentaries to explain about mission life. And now for the second example: After our field trip to the mission, students download the pictures on classroom computers and create 5-minute movie documentaries to explain about mission life. Reviewers know that implementing projects depend on funding. My overall point here is that the little details can make a big difference.

8. AVOID BEING TOO WORDY. Get to the point! Your proposal should show a style of creative writing, but don't waste the grant reviewers time in the process. Over-explaining and taking too much time to explain can turn people off to your proposal. Many times being concise is necessary as some grants require overall word limits, page limits, or word limits on each question.

9. Refer to information provided by the organization on what type of grants they are looking for and the criteria they will use to select winning grants. Think of it as a cheat-sheet. Many grants offer a scoring rubric for how your application will be scored.

10. RESEARCH EXACT COSTS.
Call the location where the materials will be purchased and get a quote. Make sure you have included all costs. You might have selected a new computer for classroom use for example. Is there applicable tax and shipping? What about that extended warranty? The electricity kit sounds like a great learning experience, but you the saying... "batteries not included!"

11. MATERIALS SHOULD RELATE WITH YOUR LEARNING GOALS. I'm a big fan of the latest technology available, but it is very unlikely a grant will be funded if you want something for your classroom just to have. There has to be a learning experience connected to its usage. In one grant proposal for $500, I designed a Social Studies unit where students wrote their own diaries using Power Point and budgeted the money for a laptop storage cabinet in order to maintain the safety and security of technology in the classroom in order to ensure future projects that incorporate computers are possible.

12. WHEN A PROPOSAL IS SELECTED, MAKE AN EFFORT TO MEET ALL DUE DATES IN SUBMITTING REQUIRED FEEDBACK. Make sure feedback is complete and thorough. Many companies enjoy hearing thank you letters from teachers and students. Your thank you letter should describe the project, explain how this project was a unique experience for the students, and sound appreciative. Obtain parent permission if photographs are requested from the grant organization. Make sure students only sign their first names. Names should never be included in photographs that could identify students. The organization may require additional feedback information. Meeting deadlines may often aid in receiving materials in a timely manner or in receiving reimbursement if necessary.

13. PURCHASE MATERIALS WHEN GIVEN THE APPROVAL TO DO SO. This might not be necessary as some organizations such as Donor's Choose buy the materials and mail them to your school. Others send the money to the school that is deposited into your classroom account. Make sure the money is available before spending it! If good faith, spend the money on what you said you would spend it on. Many organizations request receipts and invoices used for reimbursements and for accountability. If a resource is unavailable now, obtain permission before purchasing a similar item. Should you decide to write a grant, please remember that some proposals are processed through a very difficult, competitive process. You might have written a proposal for a terrific project, however, not everyone's proposal can be funded. I always say that it is better to try, because you'll never know otherwise.
Good luck!

K-12

ADC Science, Technology, Engineering, and Mathematics (STEM) Education Grants

MS70, 13625 Technology Drive
Eden Prairie, MN 55344
952.917.0580
Bill Linder-Scholer
http://www.adc.com/aboutadc/adcfoundation/howtoapply/
http://tiny.cc/l0sLd

Description

Grants to organizations whose primary mission impacts K-12 or higher education, for projects where the aim is systemic improvements in the teaching or learning of mathematics and science or enhancements to the "pipeline" for the preparation of students for work in technology-oriented industry.

AlphaGrants Program

Wisconsin Rapids, WI, USA
54495-8036
800-656-6740
http://www.renlearn.com/fundingcenter/grantwriting.aspx
http://tiny.cc/i1Cxd

Description

AlphaSmart's philanthropic program is designed to help K-12 schools implement classroom technology solutions that improve the teaching and learning environment in math, science, and language arts. K-12 schools, including public, non-profit, charter and private institutions, are eligible to apply for an AlphaGrant, as are educators within higher education institutions who are working with a K-12 school. Each year, four U.S. K-12 schools are selected to receive a complete classroom solution based on AlphaSmart's Neo or Dana computer companions.

Recent Awards, Winning Projects & Award Winners

Summerfield Elementary School
Riverview, FL
Environmental Studies Gardening Project
Marcy Ringdahl, Network Administrator & Media Specialist, had used the Neo at a previous school and loved them. "The AlphaSmart Cart was the most sought-after piece of tech equipment at our

site," she said. When she came to Summerfield Elementary, she was disappointed that the school didn't have the same equipment.

But that's changed now that Ringdahl applied and won the AlphaGrant to receive a NEO SmartOption Mobile Lab. "I never dreamed in a million years we would win this grant," she said. "I think it was probably the best day of my professional life, thus far."

Ringdahl applied for the grant to incorporate the NEO into an all-encompassing community project that would enable the school's third and fourth graders to conduct onsite environmental studies in gardens, starting next fall.

"Students will be given the opportunity to make authentic world connections to writing, fostering an understanding of the environment in which they live," Ringdahl wrote in her application. "The classes will experience the benefits of a garden as it relates to reading, science and writing. The students will use the technology to journal data and personal reflection of the project."

Through portability of the NEOs, Summerfield students will be able to record data from the garden onsite where the learning is taking place.

Ringdahl is excited about the possibilities. "This grant will mean access to technology that was previously unavailable. The classroom will become high-tech…aligning itself more to the kind of technology these kids may have in the home," she said. "The AlphaSmart units are the way to create and assess authentic writing and to provide collaboration between teacher and student, and student-to-student. It provides a means of instruction unequal to any other product that I know of."

Iowa School for the Deaf
Council Bluffs, IA
Roots & Shoots Global Environment Project

"Non-auditory technology in any form is beneficial and serves as a lifeline to our language-delayed students, providing them with a tool that serves as a communication link to a hearing world," wrote Sue Purcell, the IEP/Transition Coordinator for The Iowa School for the Deaf in Council Bluffs, Iowa.

So school officials were thrilled to discover that they'd won the AlphaGrant to receive a Neo SmartOption Mobile Lab with 30 NEOs. "We are a small school, so to be chosen as a recipient of one of the two grants was indeed a very pleasant surprise," Purcell said. "It certainly ended our day on a high note!"

Because deaf students are very visual learners, the NEOs offer them the ability to review assignments and critical information with the touch of a finger.

"Hearing loss leaves our students with an inability to learn incidentally, which adversely affects their educational performance," Purcell wrote in her application. "With an average language level of fourth grade, our high school students must learn more at a faster rate than their hearing peers if they are to succeed in their post-secondary lives and live independently in the community."

The 30 NEOs will enable the school's high school students to partake in a learning adventure that will incorporate their language curriculum with Jane Goodall's Roots and Shoots global environmental program. Students will be able to take downloaded information on their Neo with them to their project site, record ideas and take notes onsite while they work on their projects. "As our students grow in their knowledge of the environment and their responsibilities to it, their vocabulary, writing skills and confidence will develop and progress as they experience success," Purcell wrote. "By using the NEOs, students will also have the advantage they need to become motivated to develop their writing skills to make the Roots and Shoots project success, and to become more confident young adults, ready to face the future."

Purcell said that the addition of this technology is exciting, because both the students and the teachers stand to gain from the benefits the Neo will offer. "If the NEOs can help our students become successful in the classroom, this award becomes priceless to all of us."

American Honda Foundation

Torrance, CA 90509-2205
(310) 781-4090
http://corporate.honda.com/america/philanthropy.aspx?id=ahf
http://tiny.cc/umIEo

http://www.cybergrants.com/pls/cybergrants/quiz.display_question?x_gm_id=2587&x_quiz_id=1338&x_order_by=1
http://tiny.cc/FUIsN

Description

The American Honda Foundation reflects the basic tenets, beliefs and philosophies of the Honda companies, which are characterized by the following qualities: imaginative, creative, youthful, forward-thinking, scientific, humanistic, and innovative. The Foundation engages in grantmaking that is consistent with these characteristics.

Grants are provided in the fields of youth education and science education to the following: educational institutions, K-12; accredited higher education institutions (colleges and universities); community colleges and vocational or trade schools; scholarship and fellowship programs at selected colleges and/or universities or through selected non-profit organizations; other scientific and education-related, non-profit, tax-exempt organizations; gifted student programs; media concerning youth education and/or scientific education; private, non-profit scientific and/or youth education projects; other non-profit, tax-exempt, institutions in the fields of youth education and scientific education; and programs pertaining to academic or curriculum development that emphasize innovative educational methods and techniques.

Recent Awards, Winning Projects & Award Winners

Aquatic Adventures Science Education Foundation
SEA (Science, Education and Awareness) Series
San Diego, California
$45,000

http://tiny.cc/f6Vme

The SEA Series program exposes students in grades three through six to marine science involving such activities as dissections, interaction with live animals, microscope work and experiments. Students also participate in a community service project, which provides practical application of knowledge through civic engagement. Teachers also receive professional development and are provided a lending library and additional curricula to utilize in the classroom.

Catholic University of America
Washington, D.C.
$50,000

http://tiny.cc/tpioe

Public elementary school teachers in the District of Columbia will receive summer and fall training sessions in using FOSS (Full Option Science System) in addition to ancillary activities to support the concepts of FOSS. Follow-up support will be provided to the teachers throughout the school year, and tutoring support for students as recommended by the classroom teacher.

Center for Science Teaching and Learning
Young Explorers Science Club
Rockville, New York
$75,000

http://tiny.cc/wBZo5

Through the "Young Explorers Science Club" students in grades three through eight will engage in enjoyable, inquiry-based science experiments with their families. The Club provides a bi-monthly science kit, a bi-monthly newspaper with news and activities, and a membership card entitling kids to reduced admission to zoos, aquariums and science centers throughout the United States.

Chicago Botanic Garden
The Center for Teaching and Learning (CTL)
Chicago, Illinois
$85,000

http://tiny.cc/F7NgF

The Center for Teaching and Learning (CTL) was established to serve as the heart of the Garden's science education programs for youth and educators. Its programs are designed to provide a continuum of learning opportunities for children of all ages and are based on a hands-on, inquiry-based approach that brings science and nature alive for students. Fiscal Year 2007April 1, 2006-March 31, 2007

Cincinnati Zoo and Botanical Garden
Earth Expeditions Program
Cincinnati, Ohio
$85,500

http://tiny.cc/letME

The Earth Expeditions program offers extraordinary opportunities to K-12 teachers by bringing together the world-class wildlife conservation programs of the Cincinnati Zoo & Botanical Garden (CZBG) and the academic expertise of Miami University's Project Dragonfly in inquiry-based learning. CZBG will provide scholarships to enable 3,000 students and 120 teachers to come to the Zoo.

Dallas Concilio of Hispanic Service Organizations
Psyched About Science and Math (PASM)
Dallas, Texas
$20,000
http://tiny.cc/1V5RI

Psyched About Science and Math was created to encourage Hispanic girls to develop an early interest in math and science. Sixth grade girls attend a workshop and engage in hands-on activities facilitated by professional Hispanic women working in math, science, health and technology careers.

Dana-Farber Cancer Institute
School Partnerships Program
Boston, Massachusetts
$20,000
http://tiny.cc/GNEmF

Through the School Partnerships Program, high school students from three Boston public high schools are provided paid summer internships and part-time employment during the academic school year that complement the student's school curriculum. Students are interviewed and placed to work and learn in such areas as Cancer Biology, Nursing, Radiology, the Infusion Clinic, Occupational Health and more.

Eastern Michigan University
Design by Nature
Ypsilanti, Michigan
$85,933
http://tiny.cc/hGU3Q

Design by Nature is an innovative after-school program that introduces middle school students to the cutting-edge field of environmental product design. Through the use of everyday objects, students explore the science of materials use and product lifecycles, design products that minimize pollution and energy use and make a difference in their communities through a service project.

Everybody Wins! DC
Power Lunch and Readers Are Leaders Programs
Washington, D.C.
$80,000
http://tiny.cc/iGJhH

The Power Lunch program partners professionals from the public and private sectors with Title I elementary school students in the Washington, DC metropolitan area. Each week, adult mentors and students share laughs, conversation and good books, one-on-one, over school lunch. Through the Readers Are Leaders program, fourth through sixth grade students are paired with first through third grade students from the same school for one-on-one reading during the school lunch hour. This program was established to serve the schools that are in areas that have no adult readers/ mentors available.

Explorations In Math
Seattle, Washington
$80,000
http://tiny.cc/5JWLk

Explorations In Math was formed to create an engaging math culture, where students, teachers and parents work together to succeed in math. Children are encouraged to explore, question and experience math using games, hands on activities, group projects, chess and technology.

HighTechHigh-Los Angeles
Robotics After-School/Summer Program
Los Angeles, California
$70,680
http://tiny.cc/Kn7Ok

Students will engage in exciting project-based learning through robotics. Teams of four to five students will design and build robots using reusable robot construction kits such as BattleBots, LEGO Mindstorms and Robovation. In addition, some students will participate in a two-week robotics summer camp serving as counselors to 3rd-12th grade students, teaching them LEGO Robotics and Robovation.

Los Angeles Harbor College
Fire Instruction, Recruitment and Education (F.I.R.E.) Academy
Wilmington, California
$50,000
http://tiny.cc/zrZX1

High school students (cadets) from the Los Angeles Unified School District are recruited to receive training in firefighting and emergency services through the Fire Instruction, Recruitment and Education (F.I.R.E.) Academy. Program participants spend four hours for 10 weeks on Saturdays learning and training. With two new modules, the Emergency Medical Services and Emergency Medical Technician, cadets will have the opportunity to earn certification in CPR, defibrillation and first aid and receive training in multi-casualty incidents, such as an earthquake, bus or train crash or other types of disasters.

McHenry County Schools
McHenry County Schools Environmental Education Program (MCSEEP)
Woodstock, Illinois
$50,000
http://tiny.cc/3mFBM

The McHenry County Schools Environmental Education Program (MCSEEP) embodies the belief that environmental education is vital in that it creates a personal connection with the Earth and a commitment to the well-being of all life. Environmental lessons are provided for K through 12 classes with each grade level focusing on a different aspect of reducing, reusing and recycling.

Memphis Academy of Health Sciences
Assessment and Learning in Knowledge Spaces (ALEKS)
Memphis, Tennessee
$74,250
http://tiny.cc/PuJ56

The Memphis Academy of Health Sciences provides high curricula standards and uses the best and most effective research-based instructional practices. It will implement the Assessment and Learning in Knowledge Spaces (ALEKS) program, a web-based computer program that provides an individualized, structured, interactive and self-paced environment in which children can be actively engaged in their learning.

Merrimack College
Lawrence Math and Science Partnership
North Andover, Massachusetts
$41,000
http://tiny.cc/9q2MR

Merrimack students and faculty visit five, well established after-school sites in the city of Lawrence and spend 20 weeks during the school year leading middle school students through activities and experiments focused on STEM (science, technology, engineering, math). In addition, participants have the opportunity to attend a one-week summer camp for further enrichment.

Milwaukee Science Education Consortium
Project Lead the Way
Milwaukee, Wisconsin
$55,380
http://tiny.cc/9FMV1

Project Lead the Way (PLTW) is a research-based national pre-engineering program for middle and high school students. The program is currently being taught to all 7th graders at the Milwaukee Academy of Science and with this grant award, the program will be expanded to all 8th grade students.

New Horizons Family Center
MathWorks, Inc.
Glendale, California
$53,835
http://tiny.cc/FJe0p

MathWorks, Inc. is an innovative and fun math enrichment project that targets 150 elementary and middle school students ages five through 14. Program participants will engage in the following activities: "math tours," to collaborating companies to see real world applications of math; innovative "win-win" math games; team math assignments; quarterly written and oral presentations that will be made to parents and other participants; and math tutoring.

North Carolina Central University
Students Making Another Science Success Story (SMASSS) Program
Durham, North Carolina
$79,993
http://tiny.cc/6MEkU

Students Making Another Science Success Story (SMASSS) is a science and math enhancement program that provides monthly Saturday Academies during the school year followed by a summer science camp. Students from Durham Public Schools begin in the eighth grade and remain with the program through the tenth grade, engaging in activities in life sciences, physical sciences and math/computer sciences. The long-term goal of the program is to increase the number of students who are both interested and competitively prepared to pursue college studies and subsequently enter careers in the science, technology, engineering and math (STEM) fields.

Rhode Island Children's Crusade
Saturday Literacy Program
Providence, Rhode Island
$59,696
http://tiny.cc/I4A9h

The Saturday Literacy program targets fourth and fifth grade students that are not performing at their reading grade level. The core element of the program is Scholastic Inc.'s ReadAbout, an adaptive computerized reading system. In addition students have quiet reading time, as well as group sessions to process and communicate what they have learned and interact with each other in a learning circle. The program is offered over 24 Saturdays during the school year.

Robbinsdale Area School District
"Tools for Tomorrow" Program
Minneapolis, Minnesota
$58,651 for one year
http://tiny.cc/fKf9v

Seventh and 8th grade students take engineering courses involving computer design, modeling, automation and robotics. Students will be selected to form teams called "Tech Crews" and will be trained and held responsible for coordinating the use of "Tech Buggies," which are mobile carts containing hardware and other equipment available for use by the entire school.

Science Buddies
Topic Selection Wizard Tool
Carmel, California
$60,000
http://tiny.cc/wSZeV

The Topic Selection Wizard is an interactive tool that helps students explore different topic areas for their science fair project. The tool offers an array of project ideas in physical science, engineering, life science, behavioral science and earth science and will be expanded to include project ideas focused on sports science, food science, safety engineering, computer engineering and programming and robotics.

United Negro College Fund
Los Angeles, California
$75,000
http://tiny.cc/JexzF

The United Negro College Fund's Los Angeles Branch will provide students from the Los Angeles, Riverside and San Bernardino counties scholarships to attend college at one of the 39 historically black colleges and universities (HBCUs) and major in one of the science, technology, engineering or math (STEM) fields.

Wichita State University Foundation
Switched-On Science Academy
Wichita, Kansas
$38,631
http://tiny.cc/56K9V

The Switched-On Science Academy provides students in grades five through eight with inquiry-based activities in exciting hands-on venues to increase their enjoyment of science, technology, engineering and math. Students commit four hours on Saturday over seven months out of the school year.

Christopher Columbus Awards

105 Terry Drive, Suite 120
Newtown, PA 18940-3425
http://www.christophercolumbusawards.com/
http://tiny.cc/MDgTH

Description

The Christopher Columbus Awards program is a national competition that taps the natural curiosity and creativity of kids to better their communities. The program is designed for sixth through eighth grade students, and they must work in teams of three or four with an adult coach. The team must identify a problem in its community, and devise a solution that requires the team to obtain hands-on experience with the scientific process-exploring, analyzing and drawing conclusions-and learn how to apply it to everyday life.

Recent Awards, Winning Projects & Award Winners:

2007 Gold Medal Award Winner

Entry Title: Energizers
Coach: Lisa Johnson
Whiteface Elementary School
Whiteface, Texas
Problem: Rising fuel prices affecting the cotton farmers.
Solution: Use wind turbines to generate electricity to run water pumps and irrigation systems.

2007 Chairman's Award Winner

Entry Title: Saltwater Marshals

Coach: Michelle Ruthenberg

Ripley's Aquarium

Myrtle Beach, South Carolina

Problem: Disappearance of saltwater marshes because of economical growth, population increases and lack of knowledge.

Solution: Education outreach program to teach the public about the importance of the saltwater marshes along with building a tidal mill to harness the energy from the tides.

Curriculum Associates Partners for Growth Matching Grant Program

CURRICULUM ASSOCIATES®, Inc.

712 Bancroft Road, No. 508

Walnut Creek, CA 94598-1531

U.S.A.

(800) 225-0248, ext. 545

http://www.curriculumassociates.com/educator-resources/grants/default.asp

http://tiny.cc/c8IZ9

http://www.casamples.com/downloads/GrantApplication0507.pdf

http://tiny.cc/4mdh3

Description

Curriculum Associates®, Inc. supports efforts by educators to improve student learning in public schools and non-profit organizations in united states and Canada. We make matching grants to educators in pre-K–12 who demonstrate an innovative approach to teaching with our research-based instructional and assessment materials.

Recent Awards, Winning Projects & Award Winners

Tammy Rankin, Principal

Jackson Avenue Elementary School (Livermore Valley Joint USD)

Project: Benchmark Assessments

Jeff Keller, Principal

Marylin Avenue School (Livermore Valley Joint USD)

Project: Curriculum Associates' Assessments

Candice Flint-Torres, Principal

Altamont Creek Elementary School (Livermore Valley Joint USD)

Project: Content Standards Assessments

Jane E. Ledoux, 3rd Grade Teacher
South Street School, Fitchburg, MA
Project: Mathemagicians—Test Ready Magic

Lynn Johnson, Principal
Van Buren Elementary School, Stockton, CA
Project: Academic Acceleration

Joan Marks, Curriculum Support Teacher
Pioneer Elementary School, Sacramento, CA
Project: Pioneer School Reading Academy

Sharon Apple, Teacher
Encante Elementary School, San Diego, CA
Project: The Writing Club

Susan Chenoweth, Assistant Principal
Rolling Green Elementary School, Boynton Beach, FL
Project: Quotable Quick Quips

Digital Wish Grants

PO Box 1072, Manchester Center, VT 05255
(802)375-6721
Jennifer Sweeney
http://www.digitalwish.com/dw/digitalwish/grant_awards
http://tiny.cc/jlzqB

Description

Digital Wish (http://tiny.cc/Mw7jP) is a public charity designed to help educators locate much-needed funding for technology. Regardless of whether you win one of these grants, your technology wish list will be posted publicly so that donors can make a contribution to your classroom. It's basically a wedding registry for technology products! There's a searchable library of grants (http://tiny.cc/0GR1z) , and a myriad of ideas for fundraising (http://tiny.cc/LJLOO). The entire site is designed to help teachers find funding for technology for the classroom.

Recent Awards, Winning Projects & Award Winners

Nann Thomson, New Britain High School
New Britain, CT
LESSON TITLE: Seeing is Understanding

I am a Family and Consumer Science teacher in an urban high school of 3300+ students. I teach a two-year culinary arts sequence using the National Restaurant Association's ProStart curriculum. The text aptly describes the course content: "Becoming a Restaurant and Foodservice Professional". Therefore my students are not only learning the basics of food preparation, but other topics like nutrition, sanitation and safety, business management, and preparing for a successful career. This diverse curriculum is an ideal platform for using technology to enhance student learning.

Fruit & Vegetable Project*, A Jigsaw

Learning Objectives:

By the end of the project students will:
- be able to effectively operate a digital camera, utilizing the Digital Camera Basics workbooks
- be able to effectively utilize MultiMedia Lab V software to create projects
- understand the characteristics of various vegetables and fruits, including their identification, uses, cost, physical characteristics, descriptions of flavor and integration in typical dishes
- create a poster using a digital camera and Tool Factory Workshop software
- create a slide or slides for integration into a MultiMedia Lab V presentation for the entire class to view and learn

Students will be introduced to the new technology available to our class at the beginning of the school year. In preparation for covering the chapter on Fruits and Vegetables, students will receive an assignment which will require them to hone research and writing skills, and utilize their new or developing skills in the use of technology. Students will visit a large local supermarket (some for the first time) to see the produce display. Through the cooperation of the manager of the local store, our students will be allowed to touch and photograph the produce, thus creating a permanent record of the visit and a visual means of identification of the foods. Students will use Multimedia Lab V to create a presentation, with their photographs illustrating the slides which contain text derived from their research.

The entire "jigsaw" slide presentation will be shared with all students in the class and made available to the other teachers in our department, who study fruits and vegetables in their Foods classes. The presentation can later be duplicated, and by editing out the name of each fruit or vegetable, can be made into a study/review tool for student viewing before their assessment on the material. (Or it can become an assessment tool itself.) Finally, using Tool Factory Workshop, a hard copy of the presentation can be published, which becomes another reference resource for the classroom.

*Please note: this same project outline can be used with other topics that our curriculum covers, such as "herbs and spices", and kitchen equipment, particularly since students who aspire to being successful in the kitchen need to be introduced to many food products/equipment that they are unfamiliar with at the beginning of the course.

Each year a group of students from my classes compete in the Connecticut ProStart Invitational, either cooking (two identical dishes, within one hour, with no electrical appliances) or in a knowledge bowl. If successful, we compete in the national ProStart Invitational. In the culinary piece of this competition students have to prepare a three-course meal under the same conditions. The students are graded, inter alia, on how identical the two dishes (display and judging plates) in each course were prepared and plated. Having a digital camera and attendant software would allow the students to evaluate how well they were meeting this requirement during practices, as well as providing for post-practice discussion regarding the technical aspects of the platings and whether they should make changes to the presentation or garnish.

Having the technology available to my students will also allow them to complete other projects embedded in our curriculum, such as creating a resume (using Tool Factory Workshop). They can also incorporate photographs into their portfolios, which could be maintained digitally. They will be able to complete additional projects to reinforce their learning, such as illustrating appropriate and inappropriate dress for interviewing (using a digital camera and Tool Factory Workshop); creating cleaning schedules, job schedules and tracking food purchases, orders and sales in our kitchen (using Tool Factory Workshop); creating flyers, posters and menus for kitchen sales (using Tool Factory Workshop); and creating "Jeopardy"-like questions and answers for use in chapter reviews in a slide show format (using Tool Factory Workshop /Multimedia Lab V).

In an effort to utilize an authentic assessment of student learning, a two-hour portion of my students' final exam is a food production assignment in the kitchen. A digital camera and attendant software would be invaluable to me as a teacher as assessment tools for recording students' food preparation techniques and ability to mise en place.

I believe that the possible uses for the technology represented by this grant are nearly endless, and all of them would enhance the learning that takes place both inside and outside my classroom and kitchen. For the visual learners and special education students in my classes, they present another way to deliver instruction, which can help them succeed. I thank you for your consideration.

Project Budget:
Bus: $53.00
Carrying Cases (3) @ $19.99, $59.97
P-11 Photo Printer $149.99
2 Print pack (ribbon and paper for 100 4x6 prints) $77.98
CD-R's ~$40.00
CD Burner (external) ~$65.00
256 MB Memory Cards (3); @$90.00

Judges' Comments:

"I enjoyed this idea because the teacher has a clear vision of how to use the cameras and software. It is clear exactly how the students will benefit from the camera and software. "

"Cool project that has real life relevance. Utilizes the digital cameras in a way usually reserved for Art classes (smart!) "

Carmen Beasley, Central High School
Baton Rouge, LA
LESSON TITLE: CSI: Chemistry Student Investigators

Many of today's students are intimidated by chemistry. Sure, they want to get into the lab to learn how to blow things up, but few enter the class with the confidence and courage needed to achieve skills necessary for success. For many chemistry students, chemistry is a massive wall and they feel that they do not possess the stamina needed to scale the wall. This attitude of fear or hopelessness sets a climate of failure for these students' academic year. Throughout my years of teaching, I have witnessed these same fears place a stronghold on students' science scores not only in chemistry, but also on the GEE21 Louisiana state exit test and the Scientific Reasoning portion of the ACT. I know that the more the students work with or manipulate the data that they generate, the more that they will understand data that is presented to them in the future. These fears are present when confidence is lacking. Students can build confidence through experience and experience through role playing in the laboratory. In the words of Bill Cosby's Fat Albert, "If you're not careful, you might just learn something."

The CSI television series (three in all) are very popular across the nation and many careers have been pursued by interest generated through watching the exciting episodes. CSI: Chemistry Student Investigators gives students an answer to "When are we ever going to use this?" and "Why are we doing this?" By embedding chemistry content into scenarios that students must investigate, teachers can bypass the fears and tap into an already present interest.

CSI: Chemistry Student Investigators

Episode 1: Students are grouped into academically heterogeneous groups and don the persona of laboratory investigators. They are informed of the latest case that they will be working on. Student investigators must construct testable hypotheses and design the experiments which they will use in their investigation. These lab investigations will occur throughout the year and will be linked to the chemistry comprehensive curriculum GLEs. Topics will include density, substance identification, stoichiometry, percent composition, solution concentration, titrations of acids and bases, and organic chemistry and be presented to the laboratory investigators in the context of a mystery that they will solve through their experimentation. The student investigators perform their experiments, generate data that is collected with hand held computers, and take DIGITAL PHOTOS and MOVIE CLIPS of their procedures with OLYMPUS DIGITAL CAMERAS. Software is loaded on the hand helds and along with TOOL FACTORY WORKSHOP WORD PROCESSING and MULTIMEDIA LAB V on school computers allows students to graph, make tables, memos, and notations for the next Episode of the project.

Episode 2: The groups of student investigators sync the data, photos, and movie clips generated by their investigations with the aid of TOOL FACTORY WORKSHOP and MULTIMEDIA LAB V software into their computers. They organize the data and create visual representations such as graphs and tables. They then write their lab reports using TOOL FACTORY WORKSHOP WORD PROCESSING in the required format of the lab by which they are employed.

Episode 3: Student investigators compile the separate components of the data from their hand held computers and DIGITAL CAMERAS as they begin construction of their personal laboratory DATABASE or electronic lab journal using MULTIMEDIA LAB V software to log the cases on which they have consulted. Over the school year, the electronic journals demonstrate proof of the investigators' growth in lab experience, and more importantly, their maturation in understanding not only chemistry, but the underlying skills necessary to master scientific inquiry and technology.

Episode 4: Investigators convene to discuss their cases and findings and present their electronic lab reports orally as the result of the MULTIMEDIA LAB V created journals are shown via a projector to their investigator peers.

Timeline: This cyclic project will continue throughout the year with each of the 11 units in chemistry; scientific inquiry skills will be reinforced during each unit. August and September will host investigations based on general technique, density, separating mixtures, and problem solving. October-physical and chemical properties and changes. November-chemical changes and identifying substances. January-reactions and conservation of matter. February hosts percent composition and colligative properties. Unknown concentrations of solutions will be determined in March and in April acid-base titrations will be performed. Energy changes will be observed in April. May will host biochemical investigations and the year end final presentations of the lab journals created using the Olympus digital cameras, Tool Factory Workshop, and Multimedia Lab V software.

One goal of CSI: Chemistry Student Investigators is to remove fear of science from high school students. The project will allow students to replace the reticence that they exhibit with open-minded invigoration and excitement and create a feeling of "I can do this" and "Let me show you!" CSI: Chemistry Student Investigators will turn students onto chemistry and generate pride in their academic work. Students who achieve this goal will exhibit positive attitudes and pride in their work.

The second goal is to provide a bridge over the chasm of chemistry content-specific GLEs and science inquiry GLEs in the chemistry comprehensive curriculum. While the content of the investigations are rooted in the eleven chemistry units, the investigations and roles that the students will assume are based on the scientific inquiry area of the curriculum. The pacing guide does not allow time to focus solely on scientific inquiry although mastery of these GLEs provide the foundation on which all other concepts are understood. The curriculum is packed with eleven units which are also packed with theory, history, and problems to be mastered by each student, and then there is the separate unit which must be addressed throughout each of the other eleven units. The scientific inquiry GLEs are of extreme importance to each unit, but could easily get squeezed out by concentrating on content specific GLEs. Students who achieve this goal will exhibit a growth in understanding how science works including writing testable hypotheses; designing investigations; recording, organizing, and displaying data appropriately; using technology to enhance laboratory investigations; identifying safety procedures to be followed when in the lab; analyzing conclusions from an investigation; choosing appropriate models to explain scientific knowledge.

The third goal is for students' chemistry, GEE21 Science, and ACT Science Reasoning scores to increase as they gain knowledge of science through inquiry and manipulation of data so that understanding scientific processes are more easily achieved. These scores can easily be compared to previous scores of students and individual students' past ACT science reasoning scores.

The three top priorities of our school improvement plan are: thinking and reasoning skills, learning to learn skills, and expanding and integrating knowledge. CSI: Chemistry Student Investigators addresses each of these needs by getting students involved in an active learning role and engaged in the construction of their body of knowledge through scientific inquiry.

The comprehensive curriculum for chemistry hosts a potential chasm between content-specific Grade Level Expectations (GLEs) and the scientific inquiry GLEs which must be covered throughout the year. Although the scientific inquiry GLEs are of utmost importance to the understanding of scientific processes, they could easily get squeezed out of the curriculum because they are presented only once in the curriculum. CSI: Chemistry Student Investigators is designed to address each scientific inquiry GLE many times throughout the year.

Both formative and summative evaluations will be made. Formative evaluations will be made on each student as they work together in the laboratory. Student investigators will be graded by performance rubrics that feature the anticipated results of each activity or question from the labs, graphs, data tables, and oral presentations at the conclusion of each case. Oral lab report presentations will be made to the entire class by academically heterogeneous groups at the conclusion of each lab activity. Electronic Lab Journals will also be graded by a rubric before they are burned onto discs for each student to keep as a record of his year in chemistry.

Summative evaluations will be made at the completion of each unit.

The electronic lab journal will also provide evidence for an improvement in School Improvement Plan's Thinking and Reasoning Skills as one observes the students' products from the beginning of the school year to the end. The School Improvement Plan's Learning to Learn skills will also be evaluated by examining student performance in chemistry, their scores on the science portion of the GEE21, and scores on the science reasoning portion of the ACT. Students scores across the curriculum will be evaluated to determine the progress of the students. Expanding and Integrating Knowledge skills featured in the School Improvement Plan. The electronic journals will also feature an introspective area where students will reflect upon any changes in their perception of their fear of chemistry, their scientific understanding, and how they feel that they have progressed throughout the year.

Project Budget:
1 Olympus FE 230 Digital Camera 199.99
4 1G memory cards 34.99 each
4 Universal AC Power Adaptors 39.99 each
Total: 499.91

Judges' Comments:

"I loved this proposal. I was a student that hated science, mostly because it made no sense to me and was incredibly boring. This teacher is making chemistry interesting and exciting. I think using the cameras and Tool Factory software will make science much more enjoyable."

Sonja Mix, Thomas Dale High School
Chester, VA
LESSON TITLE: Poetry Alive! Interpreting Poetry Using Digital Images

During my teaching career, I can predict my student's responses when I tell them that we will begin a new unit reading, analyzing and discussing poetry. After a few minutes of moaning and the occasional "Oh Ms. Mix, anything but poetry," and the most famous question of them all, "Why do we have to study poetry? What does poetry have to do with my life?" It is easy to conclude that most students do not appreciate poetry. I designed this project with the intentions of making poetry come "alive" by using traditional teaching methods with technology.

Lesson Objectives:
- Understand how different camera images and techniques convey the tone of a poem
- Learn to film using video and still images to convey poem's tone.
- Understand that poetry is a way of expressing one's innermost feelings and be able to express their own feelings through this medium.
- Understand and appreciate how a poet's message is conveyed through the use of various poetic techniques/devices.
- Appreciate how memorization and recitation of poetry can aid in self-expression and self-confidence.
- Understand effective rate, volume, pitch, and tone for the audience and setting,

A team of English students will take the role of a production company and will create a 4-5 minute film using the digital image as a medium for interpreting students' original poems. Three classes will be working together in order to complete this project: Creative Writing, English, and The Actor's Studio.

The Creative Writing students will write original poems using various poetic techniques to convey a specific tone. These tone words include awe, cynical, didactic, jovial, mocking, quizzical, reflective and indignant. The English students will use these poems for their image projects. A team of English students will take the role of a production company and create an original digital film interpreting the poem using the DIGITAL CAMERAS. Each production team will be paired with a student, from the Actor's Studio class, who will recite the poem.

Each team will recite, interpret, and create digital still images and short video clips using various camera shots and techniques. The TOOL FACTORY PAINTER will be used to enhance the images using the various special effects. The students will use these still images and video clips and create their movies in Windows Movie Maker and create MPEGs. At the end of the project, the students will use TOOL FACTORY WORD PROCESSOR and MULTIMEDIA LAB V to create their poetry and film interactive projects on the internet, so other students will be able to view the projects. Each group will give a brief presentation of their films discuss the artistic decisions made after examining the language of the poem.

LESSON SEQUENCE

Stage One: The first stage of this project is for the Creative Writing class to write poems based on specific tone words. The creative writing teacher will give specific instructions on how to work with language and use specific poetic techniques to reflect a specific tone.

Stage Two: While the Creative Writing students are creating their poems, my English students will be given a lesson on how to identify a poem's tone. They will read and analyze several poems and the poetic techniques used to convey the tone of the poem. In the next step of the project, I will show the students examples of how still and moving images can reflect the tone of the poem. In this stage of the project, I show them several soliloquies from Shakespeare's plays as a demonstration of the different ways in which image is used to interpret the soliloquies. I will use scenes from Macbeth, Othello, King Lear, Twelfth Night, Midsummer Night's Dream, and Richard III to show how various film techniques are used. These techniques include lighting, framing, set design, use of color, costume, and camera techniques.

Stage Three: I will divide the students into five groups which will consist of a Producer, Director/ Camera Operator, Storyboard Artist, Set Designer, Film Editor. The Producers will meet with me and we will create each group. The producers are responsible for planning, organizing, and disseminating information to their group members. Also, they will help their group members with their roles. The Producers will use the TOOL FACTORY BANK MANAGER to organize the image bank that the students will create during the course of the project. Before the students begin work, they will choose a poem from the Creative Writing class and discuss the word choice in the poem and how it reflects the tone. Listing these important words will be the foundation of their project. The Director is responsible to document the narrator of the poem as well as the character traits that he or she possesses. Then he or she will decide on the camera shots and techniques that support the tone of the poem. The Set Designer will make the decisions of the setting and costumes to capture the mood of the poem. The Storyboard Artist will document the sequence of events of the images, the set design, and the camera techniques. The editor will use the Storyboard to edit the images and video into the Moviemaker program. The editor will also be responsible for creating the opening image, credits, and closing credits of the film.

Stage Four: Once the group has made its artistic decisions, they will need to choose an actor. The production team will choose an actor from the Actor's Studio class. The group will work together and discuss their artistic decisions.

Stage Five: The groups will start to film using a mixture of still and video images with the DIGITAL CAMERAS. FRESCO will be used to add special effects to the images. Once the images and video clips have been created, the film editor will retrieve the images from the TOOL FACTORY BANK MANAGER to import the images into Microsoft Windows movie maker and create a MPEG movie. After the films have been created, they will use the MULTIMEDIA LAB V to create their own WebPages. On the webpage they will include the text of the poem as well as the film.

Stage Six: Each group will present to all classes, Creative Writing, and Actor's Studio. At this stage, the production teams will present to all the classes involved. They will give a brief presentation of their artistic decisions, as well as answer questions that the other students might have about their films. Every student will have an evaluation sheet and give constructive feedback for each project.

Stage Seven: All the films will be burned on a DVD and given to each student. The films will be posted on the Internet so other teachers will be able to use these projects in their own poetry units. For example, the students from other classes could read the poems and watch the films and write an essay explaining how the film does or does not capture the tone of the poem.

This type of project gives the students a personal and hands on experience dealing with the language of poetry. Using the digital image to aid in their interpretations will help them analyze, discuss and interpret other poems that they will read.

Supplemental Material:
Each student will receive a packet for this project. I will include handouts on Copyright laws, story board design, background music, Introduction to editing, framing, and video titles. These worksheets will help focus and organize students so they can work independently. After each group meeting, the students must complete a Self-Reflecting survey. This survey helps them stay organize, keeps me up to date of the group's progress, and gives me an evaluation tool for each student.

VIRGINIA STANDARDS OF LEARNING:
English
- The student will plan, present, and critique dramatic readings of literary selections (9.1)
- The student will read and analyze a variety of poetry. (10.5)
- The student will use writing to interpret, analyze, and evaluate ideas. (10.10)
- The student will make a 5 to 10 minute formal oral presentation. (12.1)
- The student will evaluate formal presentations. (12.2)
- The student will explain how the choice of words in a poem creates tone and voice. (12.5)

Computer/Technology
- The student will demonstrate proficiency in the use of technology. (C/T 9-12.2)
- The student will demonstrate knowledge of technologies that support collaboration, personal pursuits, and productivity. (C/T 9-12.5)
- Use available technological tools to expand and enhance understanding of ideas and concepts. (C/T 9-12.6)
- Use technology-based options, including distance and distributed education, to collaborate, research, publish, and communicate. (C/T 9-12.9)

Visual Arts
- The student will produce works of art that demonstrate the experimental application of the elements of art and the principles of design. (AI.3)
- The student will recognize and identify technological developments in the visual arts. (AI.4)
- The student will demonstrate the use of technology and electronic media as artistic tools. (AI.5)

- The student will identify and examine symbols in works of art and discuss possible reasons for their use. (AI.18)
- The student will demonstrate in writing the ability to support personal criteria for making visual aesthetic judgments. (AI.28)

Theatre Arts
- The student will understand and apply principles of technical theatre by demonstrating knowledge of the technical components of theatre¾set, properties, lighting, sound, costuming, and makeup (TI.4)
- The student will demonstrate acting skills and techniques, including vocal control, stage movement, script analysis, and rehearsal techniques representing selected styles, by making vocal and physical choices that represent characterization, conflict, and production style; performing a fully rehearsed and memorized role; and, incorporating suggestions from the director.

NOTE: Because of our limited server space and because the students are not allowed to save their projects on the computer's hard drive, it is important that we have an external hard rive to store the projects' images and videos.
- G-Technology G-Drive mini - 100GB Ultra Portable FireWire-800 Bus-Powered Hard Drive - 5400rpm - Titanium $ 248.95
- LaCie d2 DVD+/-RW with LightScribe 16x External FireWire-400 DVD Burner with Toast Titanium 7 $ 169.95
- 100 DVDRs $40.00
- DVD Labels $20.00

Judges' Comments:
"Well thought out, objectives clearly defined, entertaining/creative, students will be engaged- TOOL FACTORY software well utilized."

"Extremely well devised proposal! I appreciated the different roles the students could take in the project. I also was impressed with the different software chosen to assist in the project."

Terry Henry, P.S. 256 - Benjamin Banneker Elementary
Brooklyn NY
LESSON TITLE: The Best of Bedford Stuyvesant

As grant coordinator, Mr. Smith, our technology teacher and I collaborated to submit this grant. Mr. Smith wrote this project for his fourth and fifth grade technology club. We would like to do a documentary about our community- called The" Best of Bedford Stuyvesant- our Community." Our school is in the Bedford Stuyvesant area of Brooklyn, New York and many of our students live in the neighborhood. Too often, our community is depicted in the media as a bad community, filled with all the ills of the world, poor housing, drugs and crime. This is what the children hear and have come to believe. I would like to use this project to help my students learn about the wonderful community they live in.

The students will be immersed in the documentary from beginning to end. They will do research about the blocks they live on. They will work in teams of three. Each team will knock on doors and using tape and digital recorders will talk to people about how things were on their block many years ago. The teams will use the digital cameras to take photographs of the people they interview.

In addition, the teams using the video function of the digital camera will go out into the bedford Stuyvesnat community to do filming. The students will film in two areas of interest. First, they will film historical sites of Bedford Stuyvesant,such as the house where Laurence Fishburne lived. They will film churches that have been in the community for a century or more. The students will film historical parks and landmarks such as the Magnolia Center which few people have heard about. The students will do research on these sites and using Tool Factory Word Processor and the Tool Factory Database they will type and record all the information they collected doing their field trips.

The second area of interest, is the everyday life that makes Bedford Stuyesant come alive. They will document their trips to the corner store and talk about what makes our corner stores unique. They will film the neighborhood on weekends and show how it comes alive as people hang up their work clothes and put on their weekend gear to enjoy the neighborhood.

The project will be put together in the form of a film documentary, "The Best of Bedford Stuyvesant." The students will use Multimedia Lab V along with the Tool Factory Word Processor and Database to prepare the film. When the project is completed, the documentary will be shown to our school and the P.T.A. After, we have received their feedback, we will invite our local community and politicians to come in and see the film. We hope to be able to have it shown throughout our community, at other schools,our local community board and our Community Education Council. In addition, we will put together a web-site using Tool Factory Front page to be able to share our information with other schools and organizations.

"It takes a village to raise a child," a motto that Benjamin Banneker Elementary school stands by whole heartedly. Knowing that our school is part of that village, it is our responsibility to not only educate and inspire a child for life, but our community as well.
We want to give our child the hope they need to be successful. By being able to have our children put together a film about them, they will see and learn that in spite of what they see and hear on the local news, Bedford Stuyvesant is a wonderful place. It has a rich culture and history and they can be proud of the community they live in.

Project Budget:
3 memory cards $90
1 box of Audio cassettes $20
3- tripods $120
2- Black/Color ink cartridges pkg $130
Photo Paper $50
Rechargeable batteries $40
3 camera cases $50
Total $500.00

Judges' Comments:
"Students will engage in real life learning and build a well needed sense of community. This is a project everyone can be proud to be a part of.... "

"I love the concept of it and the pride it will install in the students."

Amber Wagnon, Huntington High School
Huntington, TX
LESSON TITLE: Through Our Eyes

Learning Objectives:

By the completion of this unit and final project my students will:

- Acquire skills which enable them to successfully use technology equipment such as digital cameras.
- Develop the skills and knowledge necessary to develop and create a web-site.
- Further develop their reading and writing skills.
- Further develop their abilities to work in groups.
- Further develop their communication skills.
- Develop a personal understanding of what it means to be a productive citizen.

Through Our Eyes

"The House on Mango Street" by Sandra Cisneros is a novel that addresses many important themes, but none more important that poverty. By simply talking about a world problem does not teach my students as much as a hands-on problem solving project would! Upon completing the novel my students will tackle the final project "Through Our Eyes." Through this three week project my students would complete the following activities:

1   My students design a canned food drive that benefits our local food bank "Second Blessings." This will be accomplished through groups of students from each class period working cooperatively together to accomplish their specific assigned task.

2   My students will use the TOOL FACTORY WORKSHOP to advertise the food drive in the school and community.

3   From the planning stage to the completion of the project my students will document their progress, work and experiences by using the DIGITAL CAMERAS. This will include working in the classroom, the actual food drive and finally delivering the collection to our food bank. The DIGITAL CAMERAS will also be used to document interviews of classmates and community members.

4   Students will develop their writing skills through out this project by using the TOOL FACTORY WORKSHOP'S to write journal entries which detail their experiences of working in groups and giving back to their community. TOOL FACTORY WORKSHOP will also be used to create and edit the interviews complete by students.

5   Upon completing the delivery of the collected food my students will return to the classroom to create their final product, a class web-page created by using TOOL FACTORY HOME PAGE.

6   Students will use the photos taken with the DIGITAL CAMERAS and the personal narratives and interviews written using TOOL FACTORY WORKSHOP to create a web-page that details the results of the canned food drive.

7   The photos used to forever record the experiences of this project will be enhanced by using WHOLE CLASS FRESCO and MULTIMEDIA LAB V.

8 SHOWCASE NIGHT: The community will be invited to the high school campus when the students will reveal their web-page and present first hand speeches on the affects of this project. The DIGITAL CAMERAS video abilities will be used to document this night. The students will edit the video and create a personal DVD for each student.

9 The equipment used for this project will be re-used in future years to ensure that our freshman students are exposed to a unique learning experience that will mold them into industrious students and leaders.

The "Through Our Eyes" project will have a lasting impact on the students who participate as well as our community. My students will develop necessary real world and job skills by learning to use technology to create a final product. They will develop communication skills, have the opportunity to showcase their creativity and use critical thinking to work through obstacles. But most importantly the estimated 130 high school freshman who will participate in this project will come away with a new perspective on what it means to be a productive contributing citizen. Furthermore, our community will be affected greatly. Not only will our local food bank will see an increase in their food supply, but most importantly our community members will be able to see the work of our students through the web-page. I believe that this web-page will shed new light on our students, their goals and abilities, while at the same time inspiring our community to partake in more projects which benefit everyone.

EDS Technology Grants

5400 Legacy Drive
H3-6F-47
Plano, TX 75024
1 972 605 8429
Erika Louis (erika.louis-eds@eds.com)
http://www.eds.com/about/community/grants/guidelines.aspx
http://tiny.cc/641cT

Description

The EDS Technology Grant Program helps teachers of children ages 6 through 18 and school librarians purchase information technology products and services that will improve their students' ability to learn. Each year, EDS offices worldwide sponsor and award $1,500 grants to teachers through a competitive application process. The grants are awarded to teachers and school librarians through their schools, and schools applying for a grant must be located within 50 miles of a sponsoring EDS team.

Recent Awards, Winning Projects & Award Winners

Greenwood School (Putney)

Don Fitz-Roy's students are talented, curious and challenged in their learning. Fitz-Roy has developed a science project designed to allow his students' strengths to shine through despite the dyslexia, ADHD or other learning differences that can interfere with their academic success. These middle school students will travel to nearby bodies of water, including the Connecticut River, Watt Pond and local streams to conduct water quality testing and analysis. Fitz-Roy will use the grant to purchase smart probes that allow students to record and manipulate water quality testing data, including measures such as turbidity, alkalinity and nitrate levels. After learning how to use the technological tools and developing a database, students will create a series of presentations on topics such as the effects of downstream pollution on the Connecticut River watershed and the reclamation of Watt Pond. Fitz-Roy is enthusiastic about the project's ability to engage students who have a variety of learning styles, using an innovative approach to traditional scientific methodology.

New Horizons Educational Program (Lund Family Center, Burlington)

Lund Family Center is a nationally recognized leader in the development of programs for teen mothers. Lund constantly receives requests for consultation and advice both from similar programs and from pregnant teens across the country. New Horizons, Lund's alternative high school for young mothers, will create an online teen-focused forum, empowering its students to become "virtual ambassadors" to young women seeking advice. New Horizons will use its EDS grant to purchase a laptop computer, software, and flashdrives to support the forum. Kris Hoffman, coordinator of educational services at New Horizons, sees the project as a great opportunity for New Horizons students to develop important personal skills such as self-advocacy, as well as mastering the technology involved in the project.

St Albans City School

Aware of the profound role that visual images play in the formation of her middle school students' thought processes, fine arts teacher Melissa Haberman wants her students to develop "visual literacy" – an ability to analyze, understand and produce visual messages. Haberman and guidance counselor Deb McCarthy will use their EDS grant to purchase a multi-media laptop with DVD burner and an I-Pod. Their students will use these tools to produce animations, videos, and other media projects to better understand how visual images in their world influence them. Fellow students will be the target audience for these productions, which will encourage students to make healthy choices. The productions will be posted on the school website.

Middlebury Union Middle School

Science teacher Sherry Lawson and her students have been studying acid rain and want to understand how acid rain directly affects their community. Lawson will use her EDS grant to purchase calculator/probe interface units, pH probes, and a GPS unit. Students will collect rain water samples at their homes and use a pH probe to determine the acidity of each sample. Students will use a GPS unit to determine the exact location of the unit at their homes, and to plot out the locations of all of the samples on a map. The goal will be to study the degree to which samples are acidic, to hypothesize about any differences they discern in the samples and to see what questions emerge from the study. Capitalizing on the students' interest in the subject of acid rain, Lawson is excited to engage her students in authentic research, in which students form a hypothesis, collect and analyze data and draw conclusions.

eProfessional Association Grants

(507) 453-5153
727 489-2660
Mark Kevitt
http://www.eprofessionalassoc.org/dwcenterprise/se3bin/cliente.cgi?siteid=1000220
http://tiny.cc/4VYUI

Description

eProfessional Association is a Non Profit Organization, located in Minnesota, that historically has provided hundreds of Technology Grants to Schools, City Governments, Hospitals, other non-profits, and a limited number of businesses.

The Grants are technology products and service subsidies, not cash grants. eProfessional Association derives NO cash from anything associated with the Grants, and has no membership fees. The products and services can range from Server Administrative costs to websites and web applications.

eProfessional Association has helped to provide Technology Grants to over 500 organizations and is now ramping up to expand its services to another 1,000 organizations in 2008-2010.

Recent Awards, Winning Projects & Award Winners

Education Technology Grants (http://tiny.cc/RXWMl)
La Crosse, WI School District - $16,340
CalallenTX Ind. School District $6,000
Mankato ISD 77 (MN) -$7,696
Southwest Allen County Schools (IN) - $9,600
Winona MN Independent School District - $17,400
Southeast Conference (MN) - $11,600
Breck Schools - $9,000 plus $1200 per year
Big 9 Conference - $5800 plus $1,080 per year
Northwest Suburban Conference (MN) - $16,700
Glencoe-Silver Lake School District (MN) - $4245
Cotter High School (MN) - $1,200
Winona Area Catholic Schools - $3,300
Northshore School Distirct (WA) - $3795
Cochrane Fountain City School District (WI) - $2,400
St. Charles Public Schools (MN) - $2,400
Marble Falls School District (TX) - $2,300
Rochester School District (MN) - $2,000
Burnsville-Eagan-Savage School District 191 (MN) - $6,400 per year
Dakota Hills Middle School (MN) - $500 per year
Eagan High School (MN) - $450 per year
Tri-Metro Conference (MN) $7,440

Government Technology Grants (http://tiny.cc/RXWMl)
City of Winona, MN - $2,400
Winona Area Chamber of Commerce - $4,000
Winona Area CVB - $3,000
Eden Prairie (MN) Chamber of Commerce - $12,000
Galena/Jo Davies County CVB - $5,000
City of Glencoe, MN - $6,000
City of Mazeppa, MN - $7,600

Church and Religious Organization Technology Grants (http://tiny.cc/RXWMl)
Habitat for Humanity - Winona, MN $10,900   International Adventure Center - $4,795
St. Marys Church - Winona, MN - $4,000
St. Thomas Beckett Church & Parish - $6,295
Valley Christian Church, Apple Valley, MN- $8,800
Pleasant Valley Evangelical Fre Church, MN- $7,500

GTECH After School Advantage program

10 Memorial Boulevard
Providence, RI 02903
401-392-7705
Elena Lupinacci
http://www.gtech.com/about_gtech/proposal_guidelines.asp
http://tiny.cc/55tYW

Description

The GTECH After School Advantage program provides non-profit agencies with state-of-the art, Internet ready computer centers. For each After School Advantage program, GTECH donates an average of $15,000 in state-of-the-art computers, online technology, software, and volunteer hours. More than 100 After School Advantage computer centers are already successfully operating across the United States. To find a center near you, visit our photo gallery.

HP Technology for Teaching Grant

20555 SH 249
Houston, TX 77070
(281) 370-0670
http://www.hp.com/hpinfo/grants/us/programs/tech_teaching/index.html
http://tiny.cc/AI2UQ

Description

The HP Technology for Teaching Grant Initiative is designed to support the innovative use of mobile technology in K-16 education, and to help identify K-12 public schools and two- and four-year colleges and universities that HP might support with future grants.

Recent Awards, Winning Projects & Award Winners

J. F. Drake State Technical College, Huntsville
The University of Central Arkansas, Conway
California State University, Monterey Bay, Seaside
National University, La Jolla
Santa Clara University, Santa Clara
The National Hispanic University, San Jose

Intel Community Grants

2200 Mission College Blvd.
Santa Clara, CA 95054-1549
USA
http://www.intel.com/community/grant.htm
http://tiny.cc/MVXrE

Description

Intel Corporation is committed to maintaining and enhancing the quality of life in the communities where the company has a major presence.

Our primary giving focus is education; we Intel has a strong interest in supporting K–12/higher education and community programs that deliver the kind of educational opportunities that all students will need to prepare themselves to succeed in the 21st century. Intel vigorously supports education through grants for programs that advance science, math and technology education, particularly for women and underserved populations.

Intel is also committed to the responsible use of natural resources, and funding for environmental programs will be considered. Within this broad category, Intel continues to give priority to programs with educational and technological components.

Lemelson-MIT Program

30 Memorial Drive
Building E60, Room 215
Cambridge, MA 02142
617-253-3352
Joshua Schuler
http://web.mit.edu/invent/a-main.html
http://tiny.cc/DhuXC

Description

The Lemelson-MIT Program is dedicated to honoring the acclaimed and unsung heroes who have helped improve our lives through invention. We inspire and encourage great inventors through various outreach programs such as Lemelson-MIT InvenTeams, a non-competitive, team-based national grants initiative for high school students. The cornerstone of the Lemelson-MIT Program is a prestigious awards program that includes the $500,000 Lemelson-MIT Prize (http://tiny.cc/mZDsq).

The Program was established in 1994 at the nation's premier technological university, the Massachusetts Institute of Technology, by one of the world's most prolific inventors, Jerome Lemelson (1923-1997), and his wife, Dorothy. It is funded by the Lemelson Foundation (http://tiny.cc/TQjST) and administered by MIT's School of Engineering. The Lemelson-MIT Program recognizes outstanding inventors, encourages sustainable new solutions to real-world problems, and enables and inspires young people to pursue creative lives and careers through invention.

Mathematics Education Trust NCTM grants

1906 Association Drive
Reston, VA 20191-1502
703-620-9840, ext. 2112
http://www.nctm.org/met.aspx?linkidentifier=id&itemid=198
http://tiny.cc/sgINd

Description

Established by the National Council of Teachers of Mathematics, the Mathematics Education Trust (MET) offers opportunities to expand your professional horizons! MET supports the improvement of mathematics teaching and learning at the classroom level through the funding of grants, awards, honors, and other projects by channeling the generosity of contributors into classroom-based efforts that benefit all students.

Recent Awards, Winning Projects & Award Winners

NCTM's Lifetime Achievement Awards for Distinguished Service to Mathematics Education

Awards are designed to honor members of NCTM who have exhibited a lifetime of achievement in mathematics education at the national level. The NCTM Lifetime Achievement Awards are presented annually following a nomination and selection process.

Douglas A. Grouws, Columbia, Missouri

Judith E. Jacobs, West Covina, California

School In-Service Training Grants

Supported by the Clarence Olander Fund and NCTM. Grants of up to $4,000 for support of in-service programs.

Grades K–5: *Westwood Elementary School, San Diego, California.*

Grades 6–8: *Schrop Intermediate School, Akron, Ohio; Frontier Middle School, Moses Lake, Washington.*

Grades 9–12: *Mena High School, Mena, Arkansas.*

Emerging Teacher-Leaders in Elementary School Mathematics Grants (Grades K–5)

Supported by the Irene Etkowicz Eizen Fund and NCTM. Grants of up to $6,000 to develop expertise in specific mathematics content, which is aligned with the NCTM Principles and Standards for School Mathematics. Haley James, Madison Cross Roads School, Toney, Alabama; Dawn Stiegert, César Chávez Elementary School, Madison, Wisconsin.

Teacher Professional Development Grants

Grants of up to $3,000 for full-time teachers currently working at the required grade level to improve their own professional competence as classroom teachers of mathematics.

Grades K–5 (Supported by the Ernest Duncan Fund and NCTM): *Meghan Colasanti, Sixth Avenue Elementary School, Aurora, Colorado.*

Grades 9–12 (Supported by the Mary Dolciani Fund and NCTM): *Christine G. Free, Lassiter High School, Marietta, Georgia.*

Using Music to Teach Mathematics Grants

Supported by the Esther Mendlesohn Fund and NCTM. Grants of up to $3,000 for full-time grades K–2 teachers for projects and activities that use music to teach mathematical skills and concepts. *Julie Dutcher, Poland Central School, Poland, New York; Julie Hinze, Paul Ecke Central School, Encinitas, California.*

Engaging Students in Learning Mathematics Grants

Supported by the Veryl Schult–Ellen Hocking Fund. Grants of up to $3,000 for full-time grades 6-8 teachers to incorporate creative use of materials to actively engage students in tasks and experiences designed to deepen and connect their mathematics content knowledge. *Janice Broyles, Anchorage Public School, Anchorage, Kentucky.*

Improving Students' Understanding of Geometry Grants

Supported by the John & Stacey Wahl Fund. Grants of up to $3,000 for full-time grades K–8 teachers to develop a project or activities that will enable students to better appreciate and understand some aspect of geometry that is consistent with the NCTM Principles and Standards. *Darlene Black, Castleberry Elementary School, Newport, Arkansas; Terry Muscutt, Rock Island Elementary School, Rock Island, Washington.*

Connecting Mathematics to Other Subject Areas Grants

Supported by the Theoni Pappas Fund. Grants of up to $3,000 for full-time grades 9–12 teachers to develop classroom materials or lessons connecting mathematics to other disciplines or careers. *Wendy Groot, Whitinsville Christian School, Whitinsville, Massachusetts; Marisa Laks, Louis D. Brandeis High School, New York, New York.*

Classroom-Based Research Grants (Grades K–12)

Supported by the Edward Begle Fund and NCTM. Grants of up to $8,000 to support collaborative classroom-based research in precollege mathematics education involving college or university mathematics educators. *Christine Gustafson, Virtual Community School of Ohio, Columbus, Ohio, with Bonnie Beach, Ohio Dominican University, Columbus, Ohio.*

Mathematics Graduate Course Work Scholarships

Supported by the Dale Seymour Fund and NCTM. Scholarships of up to $2,000 for full-time classroom teachers working at the required grade level to pursue graduate courses to improve their mathematics content knowledge.

Grades 6–8: *Katherine Richardson, The Grammar School, Putney, Vermont; Greg M. Williamson, Coolidge Intermediate School, Ferndale, Michigan; Melissa Kincaid, Pleasant Run Middle School, Cincinnati, Ohio;*

Grades 9–12: *Sarah Quebec Fuentes, Ridgewood High School, Ridgewood, New Jersey; Elaina Gile, Gordon Tech High School, Chicago, Illinois.*

Prospective Secondary Teacher Course Work Scholarships

Supported by the Texas Instruments Demana-Waits Fund. Scholarships up to $10,000 each to full-time college or university sophomores who are pursuing a career goal of becoming a certified teacher of secondary (grades 7–12) school mathematics. 2006-08: *Kevin McElrath, Michigan Technological University, Houghton, Michigan.* 2007-09: *Marissa Blewitt, Ohio University, Athens, Ohio; Timothy Joseph Fether, Siena Heights University, Adrian, Michigan; Kim Kanaly, Clarke College, Dubuque, Iowa.*

Prospective Teacher NCTM Conference Attendance Awards (Prospective Teacher Grades K–12)

Supported by the Julius H. Hlavaty Fund and NCTM. Grants of up to $1,200 for travel and subsistence expenses to help support attendance at an NCTM annual or regional meeting by full-time undergraduate students who are NCTM student members and are preparing to be precollege mathematics teachers. *Laura E. Cancienne, Louisiana State University and A&M College, Baton Rouge, Louisiana; Jacqueline Henry, Miami University, Oxford, Ohio; Kevin T. Johnson, Salisbury University, Salisbury, Maryland; Lindsay M. Schell, Wright State University, Dayton, Ohio; Erin Staley, Miami University, Oxford, Ohio.*

Future Leaders Initial NCTM Annual Meeting Attendance Awards

Supported by the Edwin I. Stein Fund and NCTM. Grants of up to $1,200 for travel, subsistence expenses, and substitute teacher costs of NCTM members who are full-time mathematics teachers in grades K–12 and have never attended an NCTM annual meeting. *Debra A. Crable, Cornersville High School, Cornersville, Tennessee; Coni Daufeldt, Durant Elementary/Middle School, Durant, Iowa; Melissa Egbert, Cleveland Heights High School, Cleveland Heights, Ohio; Eric Oscar Hernández, Booker T. Washington Senior High School, Miami, Florida; Janet McLain, Three Rivers School, Sunriver, Oregon.*

International Development Fund Grant

A grant with a maximum of $10,000 for persons working directly with teachers in a developing nation to improve the professional competence of the classroom teachers of mathematics in that country. *Joanna O. Masingila, Syracuse University, Syracuse, New York working with 146 teachers in fourteen schools in the Manyatta Zone in Kenya.*

Motorola Innovation Generation Grants

1303 East Algonquin Road
Schaumburg, Illinois 60196
USA
847 576 6200
http://www.motorola.com/content.jsp?globalObjectId=8152
http://tiny.cc/DnZ1c

Description

With an interest in sparking a love for science and inspiring the next generation of inventors, Motorola and the Motorola Foundation help cultivate the next generation of skilled scientists and engineers needed to create tomorrow's breakthrough ideas.

See Full Listing with Recent Winners Under College – University Category.

National Semiconductor Science in Action Awards

Drive Santa Clara, CA 95052-8090
415-296-9177
http://www.nsawards.com/saa/app/index.shtml
http://tiny.cc/YBYN1

Description

Science in Action Awards help teachers turn concepts into classroom experiences with cash grants to the school and personal rewards for teachers. The awards are open to any credentialed K-12 educator who teaches science as part of his or her curriculum in a qualifying school. Previous winners of the Science in Action Awards are not eligible.

Recent Awards, Winning Projects & Award Winners

Wind Power: Yesterday and Today - Grade 5 (http://tiny.cc/nvQ99)
Silver Oak Elementary School, San Jose, California
Jennifer Shirts
Read More (http://tiny.cc/2sXWU)

Solar Power - Grade 8 (http://tiny.cc/VGAkC)
Bath Middle School, Bath, Maine
Monica Wright and Steve Richard
Read More (http://tiny.cc/H5GiZ)

Implementing a Physics Modeling Curriculum - Grades 9-12 (http://tiny.cc/iBgFt)
Carlmont High School, Belmont, California
Casey O'Hara
Read More (http://tiny.cc/R9Y84)

The Egg Drop Challenge - Grade 8 (http://tiny.cc/9lhao)
English (C.T.) Middle School, Los Gatos, California
Michele Ignoffo
Read More (http://tiny.cc/MW4Sx)

Earth Science Extravaganza - Grades K, 4, 6 (http://tiny.cc/eKFin)
Beth Anderson Elementary School, Arlington, Texas
Margaret Minyard, Heidi Bush, D'Ann Haffner, and Nicole Keith
Read More (http://tiny.cc/X99e9)

NFIE Learning & Leadership Grants

1201 Sixteenth Street NW, Suite 416
Washington, DC 20036-3207
202.822.7840
http://www.neafoundation.org/programs/Learning&Leadership_Guidelines.htm
http://tiny.cc/otXqt

Description

Grants support public school teachers, public education support professionals, and/or faculty and staff in public institutions of higher education for one of the following two purposes:

Grants to individuals fund participation in high-quality professional development experiences, such as summer institutes or action research.

Grants to groups fund collegial study, including study groups, action research, lesson study, or mentoring experiences for faculty or staff new to an assignment.

Recent Awards, Winning Projects & Award Winners

Lisa Marie Allen, Orange Beach
Kindergarten to 12th Grade Science Director
Orange Beach Elementary School

Ms. Allen attends an intensive, week-long, graduate-level training program sponsored by the United States Space Foundation. Working with the U.S. Air Force Academy, Air Force Space Command, and partner aerospace companies, Ms. Allen participates in an immersion program that includes weightlessness training, rocketry, and remote sensing with an emphasis on astronomy principles for the classroom. Ms. Allen shares her learning with colleagues at the Sea, Sand, & Stars Science and Nature Center in her school through a series of seminars to help improve curriculum design and instructional strategies.

Leigh Howell, Menominee
10th to 12th Grade Information Technology Teacher
Menominee Area Public Schools
Partner: Brenda M. Quaak

Mr. Howell, Ms. Quaak, and an interdisciplinary team of educators form a study group to obtain a deeper understanding of Web 2.0 technology and develop methods to incorporate these emerging technologies into the district's curriculum. Participants investigate and practice technology skills such as social-book marking, internet telephony, blogging, wikis, and collaborative workspaces and develop individual units or lesson plans utilizing this technology. The group shares their lessons with colleagues through staff meetings, lesson-modeling, and the creation of a group wiki.

John Walsh, Floral Park
6th to 8th Grade Science Teacher
Irwin M. Altman Middle School 172

To enhance a spiral science curriculum and involve students through exploration and inquiry, Mr. Walsh attends the FLINN Scientific Foundation Summer Chemistry Workshop and the Rhode Island School of the Future Robotics Workshop. Through the chemistry workshop, Mr. Walsh expands his repertoire of laboratory demonstrations, acquires skills to introduce new procedures and technology to students, and designs lessons to meet the National Education Standards. Working at the robotics camp, Mr. Walsh advances his understanding of mechanical design, construction, and programming so that he can help increase students' problem solving skills. In addition to refining his curriculum and practice to increase student achievement, Mr. Walsh shares his learning with colleagues during interdisciplinary team meetings and district science workshops.

Eli S. Rosenberg, Montpelier
7th to 8th Grade Science Teacher
Main Street Middle School
Partner: Andrew Scott

Mr. Rosenberg and Mr. Scott establish a collaborative study group focused on using instructional technology to improve student achievement in science. The group generates student data from learning activities using wireless audience response systems and electronic whiteboards and uses this data to adapt their teaching methods and learning materials to better meet pupils' needs. They share their learning with district curriculum coordinators and educational leaders and present their findings at a state technology conference.

Noreen Michele Colannino, Peabody
10th to 12th Grade Chemistry Teacher
Peabody Veterans Memorial High School
Partners: Mark I. Gardner, Howard Murphy, Barbara Osterfield, James Prato

Ms. Colannino and 17 other science teachers create a study group to explore effective ways to integrate laptop computers and Internet resources across the science curriculum. Investigating content-specific project design in chemistry, physics, biology, ecology, environmental science, and astronomy, the study group designs student projects that require Internet research, spreadsheet manipulation, and the use of science and presentation software. The group also tracks the impact of technology integration on students' science and mathematics test scores.

Delta Education/CPO Science Education Award for Excellence in Inquiry-Based Science Teaching

1840 Wilson Boulevard
Arlington, VA 22201-3000
703.243.7100
http://www.nsta.org/about/awards.aspx#delta
http://tiny.cc/INbQd

Description

The Delta Education/Frey-Neo/CPO Science Awards for Excellence in Inquiry-based Science Teaching will recognize and honor three (3) full-time PreK–12 teachers of science who successfully use inquiry-based science to enhance teaching and learning in their classroom.

Recent Awards, Winning Projects & Award Winners

Amy Nicholl
Skyview Elementary School
Windsor, Colorado

Nicholl updated and revised her school's entire K–5 science curriculum. She aligned every unit and every activity to state science standards and provided each teacher with a dynamic inquiry-based science curriculum complete with teacher background content information. She has been instrumental in developing the Poudre Learning Center, a joint effort among four districts that collaborated to create an outdoor site where teachers and students can experience science concepts in action. Nicholl continues to develop curriculum units to support teachers as they visit the center. She also serves as a mentor and guide to preservice teachers and new staff.

Cary M. Seidman
Science Teacher
Ruffing Montessori School
Cleveland Heights, Ohio

Seidman's Middle School Science Course of study lasts for two years, with seventh and eighth graders mixed in classes. He selects topics for each year of the cycle based on criteria that include alignment with national standards, applicability of math techniques to the subject, demonstrated student interest, extensions of science strands introduced in earlier levels of Montessori education, and results of discussions with science teachers at local high schools where his students will continue their learning. Consistent throughout is an activity-based style of student learning that makes use of students' research abilities, math proficiencies, and writing skills. Teachers at local high schools report that Seidman's students come to them extremely well prepared in terms of content and enthusiastic about science.

Edward Wyrembeck
Howards Grove High School
Howards Grove, Wisconsin

Wyrembeck's two main objectives as a "physics coach and mentor" are to seek out exemplary research-based teaching practices that actively promote student investigations of nature and to find the resources necessary to implement these practices into his curriculum each day. His goal is to continually strive to create the best possible learning environment for all of his students by developing a robust curriculum that focuses on student-centered inquiry. His students enjoy innovative activities such as the Interactive Color Quiz, which does not involve pencil and paper: Wyrembeck throws colored tennis balls to them to get them more actively involved in their study of color addition and subtraction. His teaching practices have been featured in science education publications, and he often presents regional workshops to his colleagues.

Oracle ThinkQuest Competition

500 Oracle Parkway 5OP-8
Redwood Shores, CA 94065
1.866.600.HELP (4357)
http://www.thinkquest.org/aug06may07/entrysub.shtml
http://tiny.cc/XdDc1

Description

ThinkQuest inspires students to think, connect, create, and share. Students work in teams to build innovative and educational websites to share with the world. Along the way, they learn research, writing, teamwork, and technology skills and compete for exciting prizes.

Sponsored by the Oracle Education Foundation (http://tiny.cc/kNVM9), the competition offers a unique project-based learning experience to students and teachers across the globe. Everybody wins by having their completed websites published in the ThinkQuest Library (http://tiny.cc/8SV50), a rich online resource visited by millions monthly.

Recent Awards, Winning Projects & Award Winners

19 & Under
Young Blood: Children of War (http://tiny.cc/OQYBl)
Students: David, Krista, Parth, Thomas
Locations: United States
Coaches: John Harrison, Beth Camper

15 & Under
Sustainability (http://tiny.cc/TM8x5)
Students: Ben, David, Joel, Nick, Richard, Taylor
Locations: United States
Coaches: Christina Lee, Mary Winchell

12 & Under
Living on the Brink (http://tiny.cc/pXQZ4)
Students: Dylan, Shruthi, Courtney, Simran, George, Facundo
Locations: Tunisia, India, United States, Australia, Argentina
Coaches: Salwa Kefi, Heeral Desai

19 & Under
The Credibles (http://tiny.cc/9iWGL)
Students: Arif, Dhruv, Gita, Pranav, Sparsh, Vimal
Locations: Singapore, United States, Indonesia, India
Coaches: Amit Das, Devayan Mallick

15 & Under
Internet Safety (http://tiny.cc/L7ti7)
Students: Andrew, Annastasia, Brendon, Kayla, Michelle, Rafael
Locations: United States
Coach: Karen Fredette

12 & Under
Earth Buddies (http://tiny.cc/6nEUI)
Students: Alonzo, Arun, Jacob, Jonah, Meredith, Rosie
Locations: United States, Singapore
Coaches: Jeanne Paulus, Amit Das

IRA Presidential Award for Reading and Technology

International Reading Association
Headquarters Office
800 Barksdale Rd.
PO Box 8139
Newark, DE 19714-8139
USA
1-800-336-READ (1-800-336-7323), U.S. and Canada
+302-731-1600, elsewhere
http://www.reading.org/association/awards/teachers_presidential.html
http://tiny.cc/PzQmS

Description

The Presidential Award for Reading and Technology honors educators in grades K–12 who are making an outstanding and innovative contribution to the use of technology in reading education.

There will be one grand-prize winner, seven U.S. regional winners, one Canadian, and one international winner. All entrants must be educators who work directly with students ages 5–18 for all or part of the working day.

See Full Listing with Recent Winners Under Individuals-Awards-Contests-Competitions-Scholarships-Fellowships Category.

Qwest Foundation Teachers & Technology grants

http://www.qwest.com/about/company/community/teachers_and_technology.html
http://tiny.cc/xoyUk

Description

The Qwest Foundation granted $900,000 to states in the Qwest® service territory. In each state, the company selected a nonprofit organization to run the mini-grant program and be the recipient of the funds. Partner agencies include Departments of Education, state education groups, or nonprofits with a strong profile in education and technology. Qwest works with each educational organization to determine the parameters of a grant program offered to teachers across the state. The grant may reward programs that use technology or the Internet in innovative ways to advance student achievement.

Through this program, Qwest seeks to disburse the grant money directly to teachers and schools. The company seeks to create a statewide signature program, customized locally, that offers a clear opportunity to position Qwest as a strong and visible educational leader. In alignment with the goals of the Qwest Foundation, this program aims to improve K-12 education and continue to demonstrate Qwest's solid commitment to supporting enhanced student learning and engagement by encouraging teachers to be innovative in their classrooms.

Recent Awards, Winning Projects & Award Winners

Winners of Idaho Teacher Technology grants, 2006-2007

Aberdeen: Wayne Millet, Aberdeen High School
Project: Music Composition Recording Technology
Music composition and recording software and equipment

Bliss: Andrea Robbins, Bliss School
Project: Is Our Water Clean?
Water quality testing probes and other equipment

Boise: Paul Olson, West Junior High School
Project: Keyboard/Syntesizer Lab
Keyboards and related software and equipment

Carey: Lee Pace, Carey School
Project: Quizdom Audience Response Units
Hand-held student response system

SMARTerkids Grants

1207 - 11 Avenue SW, Suite 300
Calgary, AB T3C 0M5
CANADA
403.228.8565
http://smarterkids.org/k12/index.asp
http://tiny.cc/ZT7PY

Description

The SMARTer Kids Foundation is a private organization that provides opportunities for students and teachers to learn new skills and grow in self-confidence by placing technology, Grants and programs at their service. The Foundation helps equip classrooms with technology products and generates practical research on the impact and effectiveness of technology in the classroom. The challenges and opportunities that teachers and students face in accessing and using technology drive us to ensure our efforts make a difference in education.

Delaney, Michelle - Woodstown Middle School

Using the SMART Board Interactive Whiteboard to Create a Hands-on Approach to Learning Mathematics
This project investigated the use of a digital whiteboard to teach linear, nonlinear and exponential relationships in five grade-eight math classes. (Summer 2007) ead the Paper (http://tiny.cc/8RQ5W)

Fortuna, Carolyn– Taylor High School

Report on the Use of a SMART Board Interactive Whiteboard to Enhance Literacy in Teens

This study investigated the effect of the interactive whiteboard to help teenagers connect symbolism with texts and enhance overall literacy. (Summer 2007) Read the Paper (http://tiny.cc/blukk)

Huck, Kelly & Schmitz, Doug – Bishop Roborecki School

Report on the Use of the SMART Board Interactive Whiteboard to Enhance Literacy in Children with Learning Disabilities

This study examined how, when embedded in the curriculum, the SMART Board interactive whiteboard can be used to improve students' learning and motivation in the classroom. (Summer 2007) Read the Paper (http://tiny.cc/t06pf)

Technology Teachers Grants

2929 Buffalo Speedway, Suite 213
Houston, Texas 77098
1-866-843-3493
http://www.us-government-grants.net/article_info.php/articles_id/33
http://tiny.cc/SQlSb

Description

Elementary and secondary education teachers, as well as college and university professors learn to write successful technology teachers grants at U.S.G.G. Grant Writing Workshops. Practical tools and reliable resources to apply for and receive technology teachers grants are provided for all participants interested in getting these grants. Technology teachers grants can include technology training grants, curriculum grants, equipment grants, grants for hardware and software, telecommunications grants, professional development grants, and grants for qualified personnel to administer technology grant projects.

The types of organizations that award technology teachers grants are as diverse as the types of projects that are funded with technology teachers grants. The federal government, state, county and city governments, as well as private and corporate foundations award technology teachers grants. Over the past 10 years, more than 70 high-tech technology companies have created foundations that offer grants for technology.

Toshiba Grants Program for 7-12 Science & Math Education

1251 Avenue of the Americas, 41st Floor
New York, NY 10020
212-596-0620
http://www.toshiba.com/tafpub/upload/page/100045/25964_Executive.pdf
http://tiny.cc/dw3hM

Description

TOSHIBA AMERICA FOUNDATION contributes to the quality of science and mathematics education by investing in projects designed by classroom teachers to improve instruction for students in grades K-12.

Recent Awards, Winning Projects & Award Winners

Adlai E. Stevenson High School (Sterling Heights, MI)
$9.820 to teach physics using familiar aspects of the automobile while also introducing students to alternative energy sources such as solar power and fuel cells. Students at this Detroit-area school

will examine the energy needs of common devices, including computers, lamps, mp3 players and car engines. The class will conclude the course by designing and building a solar-powered car.

California Academy of Mathematics and Science (Carson , CA)

$4,340 to promote science and engineering literacy by building a remote-operated vehicle (ROV) for underwater science experiments. Students will be required to design and construct a workable ROV that will enable them to collect water quality samples and perform other tasks related to the study of marine life.

New York Sun Works (New York , NY)

$5,000 for curriculum development for The Science Barge. The Science Barge – currently docked in the Hudson River off West 44th Street --showcases research on water quality and estuarine habitat restoration. The new curriculum will enable New York City public high school students to learn about plant growth, horticulture and hydroponics both on the barge and in their science classroom. Additionally, students will create their own "Hudson River Report Card" and share their data on estuary health with public officials.

Resurrection High School (Chicago , IL)

$4,280 to upgrade a classroom laboratory for more advanced experiments in physics. After exploring several classic experiments in topics like force and motion, students at this all girls high school will use the new equipment to design their own experiments.

West Orange Board of Education (West Orange , NJ)

$4,970 to improve math instruction and learning for middle school students by creating and modeling new inquiry-based curricula using lessons learned at the Silicon Valley Math Coaching Institute.

Toyota TAPESTRY Grants for Science Teachers

http://www.nsta.org/pd/tapestry
http://tiny.cc/C3vgc

http://www.nsta.org/pd/tapestry/guidelines.htm
http://tiny.cc/gJBul

Description

Toyota TAPESTRY recognizes outstanding educators who are making a difference by demonstrating excellence and creativity in science teaching. Since 1991 the program has awarded more than $8 million to 986 teams of teachers for innovative science classroom projects. Thanks to these teachers' tireless efforts to improve their skills and increase their effectiveness, students nationwide are gaining a better understanding of science principles and methodologies. Toyota and

NSTA sincerely hope these grants continue to inspire teachers and serve as a catalyst for lifetime science learning.

A partnership between Toyota Motor Sales, U.S.A., Inc. and the National Science Teachers Association, the Toyota TAPESTRY Grants for Science Teachers program offers grants to K–12 science teachers for innovative projects that enhance science education in the school and/or school district.

Recent Awards, Winning Projects & Award Winners

2007 Mini-Grant Awardees (http://tiny.cc/JhgnW)
Physical Science Applications

What's in My Backyard? Connecting Students to Community Science
Project Director: Ray Barber
Staff: Tom George, Dr. Bev Marcum
Pleasant Valley High School
Chico, California
530-879-5238
rbarber@chicousd.org

Through the use of innovative video webcasting technology, this project will allow students to experience the practical applications of science in our local community. These virtual fieldtrips will involve 8-10 students, equipped with computers and video cameras, traveling to a local scientific facility and conducting a live webcast tour for their classmates back at school. Viewing the webcast on a projector, the students in the classroom will have the opportunity to interact with the traveling group, ask questions of any expert scientist, view equipment and processes, and even assist in data and sample collection. Seven different field trips will cover topics including geology, astronomy, hydroelectric power and water quality, each field trip employing a different group of students conducting the onsite webcast. This rotating model will allow for maximum student participation and exposure to all seven experiences, while each student only misses one day of school. Through a partnership with California State University at Chico, science teacher candidates will participate in the program as mentors and experts-in-residence. Each webcast will be recorded, edited and posted on the director's website for viewing by other science classes.

GPS Autonomous Vehicle
Project Director: Claude Charron
Staff; Shane Smoleny, George Papazickos
Guliver Preparatory Schools, 6575 N. Kendall Drive,
Pinecrest, Florida 33156
305-666-3791
chac@gulliverschools.org

The goal of this project is to develop an autonomous wheelchair that will facilitate the day-to-day activities for individuals with severe physical limitations. This project requires several areas of expertise including the fundamental principles of mechanics, thorough understanding of engineering and technology, and comprehension of computer programming. Students involved in this project will be divided into specific subunits, including design, programming, and construction. Together the groups will corroborate their specialties through extensive communication implementing group meetings, Internet forums and a daily updated website dedicated to the project.

Hydrogen Fuel Cell
Project Director: Bebi Davis
Staff: Dr. Harry Davis
W.R. Farrington High School
Honolulu, Hawaii
808-832-3600
bebi@hawaii.edu

Due to the depletion of our fossil fuel reserves, the world needs to find alternative energy sources. Fuel cells using hydrogen and other sources may be able to provide the world with sustainable electrical power and hopefully replace gasoline as the main source of fuel for vehicles. An electrolyzer separates hydrogen from oxygen by applying an electrical current to water. By generating hydrogen with a renewable system, the hydrogen becomes a storage medium for the energy contained in the captured sunlight or wind. To increase awareness of the need for alternative sources of energy, students will learn how to use solar energy to produce and store hydrogen that can then be used to power model cars and small household appliances, such as a radio, clock, fan, or notebook computer. This integrates science and real-life experiences. This project will increase our knowledge about the methods and equipment used to produce, store and convert the energy stored in hydrogen into electrical power.

Wave Power Generation, A Closer Look at the Production of Electric Power
Project Director: John McDaniel
Nevada Union High School
Grass Valley, California
530-273-4431
jmcdaniel@nuhsd.k12.ca.us

Wave Power Generation: A closer Look at the Production of Electric Power Using Water Waves. Students will design, fabricate and test a wave tank to be used by science classes at Nevada Union High School. The wave tank will then be used for advanced studies in wave power generation. Students will have the opportunity to design, build and test electric power generators that utilize the Nevada Union High School Wave Tank as a source of wave power.

HOPE: Hands On Physics Education
Project Director: Amanda Potter
Staff: Jim Crites, Mike Sizemore
Frenship High School
Wollforth, Texas
806-866-4440
apotter@frenship.us

The goal of the HOPE project is to use science principles to reduce fatalities and serious injuries caused by young drivers in our community. Another goal is to increase student knowledge of Newton's Laws of Motion and their relevance to the everyday lives of our students. Tenth grade students, Texas' beginning drivers, will conduct speed and motion experiments using state of the art equipment to demonstrate how the laws of physics apply to safe driving practices. Students will use model cars, ramps and other equipment to explore the laws of motion apply them to moving vehicles. Next, police investigators will present the students with actual accident scenes. Students will calculate speed, velocity and force using the data presented by the investigator. Then, a new car dealership will be invited to present the latest safety technology to our students. Finally, students will share what they have learned with the community through posters and presentations.

NSTA/Vernier Technology Award

1840 Wilson Boulevard
Arlington, VA 22201-3000
703.243.7100
http://www.vernier.com/grants/nsta.html
http://tiny.cc/ZFsZ0

Description

A partnership of Vernier Software & Technology and the National Science Teachers Association (NSTA), this award recognizes the innovative use, or potential use, of data-collection technology (e.g. probes or sensors) interfacing with a computer, graphing calculator, or handheld in the science classroom. Seven awards will be presented in the following categories: one elementary (grades K–5) award; two middle level (grades 6–8) awards; three high school (grades 9–12) awards; and one college award.

Recent Awards, Winning Projects & Award Winners

Investigating Seasonal Changes
Wendy Smith
3rd Grade Teacher
Klem Road South Elementary School
Webster, NY
Synopsis:
Wendy's 3rd grade curriculum includes learning about cycles and patterns of seasonal change. To meet this standard, Wendy engaged her 3rd grade students as "environmental scientists" in a year-long investigation of the ecosystem around the ponds at nearby North Ponds Park. Wendy created guided inquiry lessons in which students investigated whether shade affects the temperature of a body of water, and whether it is easier for fish to breathe in warm or cold water. Wendy used these activities to show how data-collection technology can be used to investigate scientific phenomena. Her students developed their own questions and took sensors to the park to gather data. The students collected air, water, and soil temperatures around the park, as well as pH and dissolved oxygen levels in the ponds. The students shared their work by creating e-books, pod-casts, and videos, which are available on their school web site. Student response to this activity was amazing. Wendy is pleased with how this project has allowed her students to shine in ways like never before.

Middle School Level (Grades 6 - 8)

Learning Physics at the Ballpark
Michael Breslow
7th Grade Science Teacher, NBCT
Belhaven Middle School
Linwood, NJ

Synopsis:

Mike is always looking for ways to help his students make connections between abstract concepts and the world around them. Teaching physics concepts to 7th grade physical science students can be challenging. Mike's solution was to create Project Surf – a culminating physics lesson the students complete at Sandcastle Stadium, the Atlantic City Surf's minor league baseball stadium. The students determine the velocities of pitched baseballs and explore how the velocity relates to the acceleration of the ball and the force exerted by the pitcher. The fun doesn't end at the ballpark. The students then have to turn this experience into an "Academic" Idol video in which they explain the lesson and what they learned. Mike extends the pop culture connection by reviewing the videos in his Mr. "Trump"-low, the Physics Apprentice, persona. The success of this activity has led to donations of additional technology from the community, and the activity has expanded into a cross-curricular project including baseball history, literature, math, and science.

Biotic Indexing and Stream Water Quality
Thomas Eddy
Science Teacher
Green Lake School District
Green Lake, WI

Synopsis:

Tom's passion for preserving the 55,000+ acre Green Lakes Watershed has led to his involvement in a "Partners in Education" project sponsored by the Green Lake Sanitary District. Tom's students are introduced to the semi-annual activity of monitoring seven streams found in the Green Lake watershed. The students perform a survey of the aquatic organisms that inhabit the water resource, and use a biotic index that relates the presence (or absence) of specific invertebrates to a quantitative measure of the stream's health. In addition, to determine water quality, they use data-collection probeware to measure temperature, pH, flow rate, conductivity, turbidity, and ion levels (nitrate, ammonium, and chloride). The project has motivated students to develop their own studies, some of which have been presented to the Wisconsin Association of Lakes, the Wisconsin Science Congress, and the Green Lake Area Chapter of the Izaak Walton League of America. Tom's use of field work has made a positive impact on his students and has turned a school lesson into a project that benefits the greater community.

High School Level (Grades 9 - 12)

In the Footsteps of Galileo: The James River Pumpkin Drop
Timothy Couillard
Teacher
James River High School
Midlothian, VA

Synopsis:

Tim believes the best way to promote science is to use technology that puts "discovery" back into science classes. Students taking his senior science research course are expected to research, design, conduct, and present a scientific inquiry of their choosing. Tim introduces this methodology by having them participate in a Pumpkin Drop project. This activity combines a replication of Galileo's Tower of Pisa free fall experiment with the excitement of an egg drop competition. Not only are the students required to produce a container that can protect a pumpkin dropped from various heights, they must determine which data-collection option (Motion Detector, Video Analysis, Wireless Sensors, or GPS) will best track the motion of their pumpkin during freefall. Tim credits his desire to provide student-driven inquiry to his physics teacher, Bob Devantery (Winnacunnet High School, NH), who taught him to "find things out for himself," and to Dr. David Hestenes' (Arizona State University) Modeling Instruction in Physics program, which showed him the potential of probeware in a student-centered classroom.

A Flashlight Without Batteries! How Does That Work?
Michael Liebl
Physics/Chemistry/Mathematics Instructor
Mount Michael Benedictine School
Elkhorn, NE

Synopsis:

Michael has found a unique tool to motivate the discussion of energy production, storage, and transfer with his physics students. He uses a "battery-less" LED flashlight as a paradigm for these processes. The investigation begins with discovering how the flashlight generates energy. A voltage probe connected to a resistor in series with a solenoid allows his students to explore Faraday's law of induction and highlights some of the challenges of energy production. The flashlight's ability to remain lit after shaking has stopped leads to an investigation in energy storage. Michael has his students use a light sensor to study the exponential decay of the light intensity as the internal capacitor discharges. A third experiment involves using a spectrometer to investigate the spectra from LED light sources. This investigation leads to a discussion of quantum energy transitions. An appreciation of the challenges of our modern technological society is impossible without a good understanding of energy. Using a "battery-less" flashlight has helped Michael motivate the exploration and discussion of the issues facing our modern society.

Category: College - University

Dept of Labor – ETA Tech Training

Community-Based Job Training Grants
US Department of Labor
Employment and Training Administration
Business Relations Group
200 Constitution Avenue, NW
Room N-4643
Washington, DC 20210
(202) 693-3949
http://www.doleta.gov/business/Community-BasedJobTrainingGrants.cfm
http://tiny.cc/FJggD

http://www.doleta.gov/BRG/CBJTGrants/
http://tiny.cc/n6fUI

Description

Community-Based Job Training Grants seek to strengthen the role of community colleges in promoting the U.S. workforce's full potential. The grants are employer-focused and build on the President's High Growth Job Training Initiative (http://tiny.cc/eKAQv), a national model for demand-driven workforce development implemented by strategic partnerships between the workforce investment system, employers, and community colleges and other training providers. The primary purpose of the CBJTG grants is to build the capacity of community colleges to train workers to develop the skills required to succeed in high growth/high demand industries.

Recent Awards, Winning Projects & Award Winners:
http://www.doleta.gov/sga/awards/awards08.cfm
http://tiny.cc/BdPqB

University of Alaska Fairbanks (http://tiny.cc/Fln8w) Target Industry: Healthcare Grant Amount: $1,858,528.00

The Rural Alaska Health Education and Training (HEAT) Project will build the capacity of the University of Alaska at Fairbanks to train incumbent and entry-level workers living in rural Alaska. Candidates -- primarily Alaska Natives -- will receive training for billing/coding and healthcare assistant jobs. This will be done by increasing the number of articulated allied health courses delivered through distance learning and itinerant clinical instructors who can travel to regional campuses. The program will create pathways to health careers that allow students to earn industry-accepted endorsements and certificates.

Northwest-Shoals Community College (http://tiny.cc/SwgM0) Target Industry: Advanced Manufacturing Grant Amount: $1,911,507.00

Northwest- Shoals Community College will establish an Advanced Manufacturing Training Center (AMTC) to focus on industrial machinist training. The center will expand the college's capacity by upgrading classroom and laboratory facilities and adding additional faculty resources. Additionally, industry input will help to expand and improve curriculum and course delivery methods. Training will result in short term and advanced certificates, an associate's degree in Occupations Technology, and preparation for industry certification. Finally, a manufacturing career ladder and outreach activities will be developed to promote the admission and advancement of rural, minority and other at-risk students.

Northwest-Shoals Community College (http://tiny.cc/XrDlN) Target Industry: Healthcare Grant Amount: $1,929,716.00

The Shoals Nursing Transitions Program will be established to meet the workforce needs of the local healthcare industry. The program will expand capacity to train Certified Nursing Assistants (CNAs), Licensed Practical Nurses (LPNs) and Registered Nurses (RNs) by offering new LPN progression options, upgrading classroom and laboratory facilities, delivering instruction through distance education, adding faculty resources, and adapting curriculum and delivery options. An innovative dual enrollment nursing program will be developed in cooperation with partner high schools. It will include a career ladder component allowing high school students to participate in a pilot program where they will receive academic support, advising, counseling and mentoring.

Phillips Community College of the University of Arkansas (http://tiny.cc/FMu2o) Target Industry: Energy Grant Amount: $1,986,735.00

The Arkansas Delta Renewable Energy Training and Education Initiative will seek to raise the skill level of the workforce through: 1) creating the Center for Excellence for Renewable Energy Technology to create training materials and programs of study, provide region-wide support to the renewable energy industry, and create career pathways in renewable energy technology; 2) creating a pool of funds for tuition and training fees jointly accessed by community colleges and One-Stop Career Centers; 3) creating capacity to train workers in each of the region's five community colleges; and 4) developing partnerships between community colleges and the workforce investment system to facilitate enrollment of participants and tracking of common measures.

Pulaski Technical College (http://tiny.cc/Sl4OW)Target Industry: Aerospace Grant Amount: $1,506,652.00

Pulaski Technical College and its partners will create technical certificates and an associate's degree program in Aircraft Manufacturing Technology. The strategic partnership will work to double enrollment in the current Aircraft Maintenance Technology two-year degree program. An introductory aviation course will be created for secondary students in Pulaski County. Pulaski Tech will purchase equipment and supplies, contract with an instructional designer and hire new faculty to overcome its current capacity constraints.

East Los Angeles College (http://tiny.cc/WlmnG) Target Industry: Healthcare Grant Amount: $1,777,710.00

The Licensed Vocational Nurse (LVN)-RN Bridge Program will enable East Los Angeles College (ELAC) to prepare graduates of the St. Francis Career College LVN program to attain associate's degrees in Nursing and to pass the state RN Licensing Exam. This will be done by raising student awareness of the Nursing Career Advancement Program Lattice; providing a "bridge" session to prepare LVNs for RN coursework; offering academic support services; and providing students with RN exam preparatory activities upon completing their degrees.

DHS Homeland Security Science, Technology, Engineering, and Mathematics (HS-STEM) Career Development Grants

Department of Homeland Security
245 Murray Lane, SW, Bldg 410;
Washington, DC 20528
202-254-6309
Desiree Linson (Program Officer)
Larry Thompkins (Grants Officer)
http://www07.grants.gov/search/search.do?oppId=41255&flag2006=false&mode=VIEW
http://tiny.cc/qZPQY
http://homelandsecurity.psu.edu/news/HS-STEM-CDG.pdf
http://tiny.cc/j5mca

Description

The Department of Homeland Security (DHS) Science and Technology Directorate (S&T) invites proposals from colleges and universities with established homeland security-related science, technology, engineering and mathematics (HS-STEM) curricula in the fields listed below to establish scientific career development awards to students in priority HS-STEM programs of study. DHS intends to establish an HS-STEM Career Development grants program to enable colleges and universities to award scholarships and fellowships to qualified undergraduate and graduate students in HS-STEM disciplines who intend to pursue homeland security professional and scientific careers. Research areas eligible for DHS support for students studying in those areas are: 1. Explosives Detection, Mitigation and Response; 2. Social, Behavioral, and Economic Sciences; 3. Human Factors; 4. Chemical and Biological Threats; 5. Border Security and Immigration Studies; 6. Maritime, Coastal and Port Security; 7. Infrastructure Protection and Geophysical Applications to Natural Disasters; 8.Emergency Preparedness and Response; 9. Communications, Operations and Interoperability; 10. Advanced Data Analysis and Visualization; and 11. HS-STEM Introductory and Survey Courses preparatory to one of the above areas of study. Institutions may submit more than one application from different departments. DHS intends to give preference to institutions included in the existing DHS Centers of Excellence and other DHS S&T affiliated institutions, for a list see (http://www.dhs.gov/xres/programs) because it is both efficient and appropriate to train the next generation of scientists and HS-STEM professionals through research and education programs already funded by DHS to meet its HS-STEM needs. As part of its mission, DHS S&T is responsible for developing scientific research and technology programs to protect the Nation from terrorist threats and the consequences of natural disasters. To ensure homeland security research programs continue into the future, DHS S&T will support grants to qualified undergraduate and graduate students in homeland security-related fields who will use their education and training to become the next generation of scientists and technology leaders. These grants will support the best programs that will train future homeland security-oriented scientists and technologists and ensure their placement in HS-STEM careers.

Motorola Innovation Generation Grants

1303 East Algonquin Road
Schaumburg, Illinois 60196
USA
847 576 6200
http://www.motorola.com/content.jsp?globalObjectId=8152
http://tiny.cc/DnZ1c

Description

With an interest in sparking a love for science and inspiring the next generation of inventors, Motorola and the Motorola Foundation help cultivate the next generation of skilled scientists and engineers needed to create tomorrow's breakthrough ideas.

Recent Awards, Winning Projects & Award Winners

Cesar Chavez Academy / East Palo Alto, Calif. — Students learn in depth about how a computer operates, how to troubleshoot and how to install software.

Ariel Community Academy / Chicago —Through the afterschool Orion's Kingdom program, students will complete virtual and real-life science and math projects.

Arizona State University Foundation / Tempe, Ariz. —The COMPUGIRLS program will introduce girls ages 8–12 to computers, science and technology.

Arrowhead Elementary School /Virginia Beach,Va. —Growing Better Scientists assists struggling elementary school students with science.

Boys & Girls Club of Greater Lowell, Inc. / Lowell, Mass. —ZoomSci provides at-risk students with opportunities to do the things that scientists do — observe, ask questions, make predictions, test ideas, collect data, change one variable and share results.

NCIIA Advanced E-Team Grant

100 Venture Way
Hadley, MA 01035
(413) 587-2172
http://www.nciia.org/grants_eteam.html
http://tiny.cc/7ykrk

Description

Advanced E-Team grants provide E-Teams with the support they need to bring an innovative product or technology from idea to prototype, and eventually to market. Successful E-Team grant proposals demonstrate an idea's technical feasibility, social value, and potential for commercialization. Advanced E-Team grants range in size from $1,000 to $20,000; the grant period is twelve to eighteen months. Annual application deadlines are in December and May. The Principal Investigator will be notified within approximately 90 days of the submission deadline.

Recent Awards, Winning Projects & Award Winners

Ultrasound-Guided Noninvasive Measurement of Central Venous Pressure, View profile (http://tiny.cc/crjNX)
Johns Hopkins University - 2007

Method to Close Laparoscopic Fascial Trocar Sites, View profile (http://tiny.cc/d8yz1
Stanford University - 2007)

Expandable Fusion Cage, View profile (http://tiny.cc/WBZaj)
Johns Hopkins University - 2007

A Dynamic-Response Sling System for the Treatment of Stress Urinary Incontinence, View profile (http://tiny.cc/sEfal)
Stanford University - 2007

Plastic Microneedles for Drug Delivery, View profile (http://tiny.cc/Oo4fb)
Georgia Institute of Technology - 2007

NCIIA Grants

(including Course and Program Grants, Advanced E-Team Grants and Sustainable Vision Grants)
100 Venture Way
Hadley, MA 01035
(413) 587-2172
http://www.nciia.org/grants.html
http://tiny.cc/TTfxL

Description

With support from The Lemelson Foundation, the NCIIA awards grants to its member institutions to support and strengthen invention, innovation, and entrepreneurship education through curricular development and the work of Advanced E-Teams. To check whether your college or university is a member or to renew your membership, please click http://tiny.cc/FBRtl .

We award grants in three major categories:

Course and Program Grants (http://tiny.cc/pl40c) are awarded to faculty and staff at colleges and universities to help improve existing curricular programs or build new programs in invention, innovation, and entrepreneurship. Course and program grants support creative pedagogy that generates E-Teams, bringing real life applications into the classroom setting and beyond. For Course and Program grant application guidelines, please click http://tiny.cc/hEKyS .

Advanced E-Team Grants (http://tiny.cc/mzo2V) support commercial outcomes by moving innovative products or technologies from the idea stage to prototype, as well as helping collegiate innovators secure Intellectual Property. E-Teams' grant proposals must demonstrate an idea's technical feasibility, potential for commercialization and social value. The proposal should also involve students, faculty and outside (industry) advisors. For E-Team grant application guidelines, please click http://tiny.cc/gwDtA .

Sustainable Vision Grants (http://tiny.cc/wlGb7) support innovative educational programs based at U.S. institutions of higher education. These programs move ideas to commercialization while addressing basic human needs such as health, food, security, clean water and affordable energy for people living in poverty in the U.S. or abroad. Grant recipients partner with a non-profit, for-profit educational or governmental organizations to plan and implement precuts or services in an economically sustainable way. For Sustainable Vision grant guidelines, please click http://tiny.cc/MGOqS .

Recent Awards, Winning Projects & Award Winners

Course and Program Grants
Center for Bioengineering Innovation and Design , View profile (http://tiny.cc/KN3ns)
Johns Hopkins University – 2007
Design, Development, and Implementation of a Nanotechnology Entrepreneurship Course Series at PSU, View profile (http://tiny.cc/XwRWv)

Advanced E-Team Grants

Ultrasound-Guided Noninvasive Measurement of Central Venous Pressure, View profile (http://tiny.cc/aQPnZ)
Johns Hopkins University - 2007
Method to Close Laparoscopic Fascial Trocar Sites, View profile (http://tiny.cc/MMdz8)
Stanford University - 2007

Sustainable Vision Grants

Innovations in International Health, View profile (http://tiny.cc/JRBuj)
Massachusetts Institute of Technology - 2007
Improving Drinking Water Quality for Rural Villages in Africa: A Pedagogy for Empowerment , View profile (http://tiny.cc/BeSZ0)
Hope College - 2007

NEH Collaborative Research Grants

Room 318
National Endowment for the Humanities
1100 Pennsylvania Avenue, N.W.
Washington, D.C. 20506
202-606-8200
http://www.neh.gov/grants/guidelines/collaborative.html
http://tiny.cc/dc6Ws

Description

Collaborative Research Grants support original research undertaken by a team of two or more scholars or research coordinated by an individual scholar that, because of its scope or complexity, requires additional staff and resources beyond the individual's salary.

NEH Digital Humanities Start-Up Grants

National Endowment for the Humanities
1100 Pennsylvania Avenue, N.W.
Washington, D.C. 20506
202-606-8401
Brett Bobley (Chief Information Officer)
http://www.neh.gov/grants/guidelines/digitalhumanitiesstartup.html#submit
http://tiny.cc/Jc4wK

Description

The National Endowment for the Humanities (NEH) and the Institute of Museum and Library Services (IMLS) invite applications to the Digital Humanities Start-Up Grants program. This program is designed to encourage innovations in the digital humanities. By awarding relatively low-dollar grants during the planning stages, the goal is to identify projects that are particularly innovative and have the potential to make a positive impact on the humanities.

In an effort to foster new collaborations and advance the role of cultural repositories in online teaching, learning, and research, this program is co-sponsored by the Institute of Museum and Library Services (IMLS). NEH and IMLS encourage library and museum officials as well as scholars, scientists, educational institutions, and other non-profit organizations to apply for these grants and to collaborate when appropriate.

NEH Grants for Teaching and Learning Resources and Curriculum Development

Division of Education Programs
National Endowment for the Humanities
Room 302
1100 Pennsylvania Avenue, NW
Washington, DC 20506
202-606-8380
http://www.neh.gov/news/awards/Teaching&LearningFeb2007.html
http://tiny.cc/LntgP

http://www.grants.gov/search/search.do?oppId=11678&mode=VIEW
http://tiny.cc/IMKZE

Description

Grants for Teaching and Learning Resources and Curriculum Development support projects that improve specific areas of humanities education through the development of new or revised curricula and instructional and learning materials. Projects are intended to serve as national models of excellence in humanities education. They must draw upon scholarship in the humanities and use scholars and teachers as advisers. NEH is especially interested in projects that offer solutions to problems frequently encountered by teachers in a particular field of the humanities.

Preservation and Access: Humanities Collections and Resources

Division of Preservation and Access
Room 411
National Endowment for the Humanities
1100 Pennsylvania Avenue, NW
Washington, DC 20506
202-606-8570
http://www.neh.gov/grants/guidelines/Collections_and_Resources.html
http://tiny.cc/7LHd2

Description

These grants support research and development projects that address major challenges in preserving or providing intellectual access to humanities resources. Applicants should define a specific problem, devise procedures and potential solutions, and evaluate findings. Successful proposals ought to have broad applicability to the humanities. NEH encourages applications that will explore new uses of digital technology in the humanities.

NEH Preserving & Accessing Reference Materials

Division of Preservation and Access
Room 411
National Endowment for the Humanities
1100 Pennsylvania Avenue, NW
Washington, DC 20506
202-606-8570
http://www.neh.gov/GRANTS/guidelines/referencematerials.html
http://tiny.cc/8Ihfc

Description
These grants support projects that create reference works and research tools.

Category: College - University - NSF

NSF Cyber-enabled Discovery and Innovation (CDI) Initiative

4201 Wilson Boulevard, Arlington, Virginia 22230, USA
703-292-8910
Michael Foster
http://www.nsf.gov/funding/pgm_summ.jsp?pims_id=503163

Description

CDI seeks to support ambitious, transformative, multidisciplinary research that, through computational thinking, promises radical, paradigm-changing research findings, within or across the following three thematic areas:

- From Data to Knowledge: enhancing human cognition and generating new knowledge from a wealth of heterogeneous digital data;
- Understanding Complexity in Natural, Built, and Social Systems: deriving fundamental insights on systems comprising multiple interacting elements; and
- Building Virtual Organizations: enhancing discovery and innovation by bringing people and resources together across institutional, geographical and cultural boundaries.

Award Number	Title	NSF Organization	Program(s)	Start Date	Principal Investigator	State	Organization	Awarded Amount to Date
703070	Computer Engineering Technology Security Curriculum Expansion and Enhancement	http://tiny.cc/WIIj9	ADVANCED TECH EDUCATION PROG, S-STEM:SCHLR SCI TECH ENG&MATH	10/1/2007	Yousif, Wael	FL	Valencia Community College	$547,203.00
703163	Viticulture and Enology Science and Technology Alliance (VESTA)	http://tiny.cc/fLttA	ADVANCED TECH EDUCATION PROG, S-STEM:SCHLR SCI TECH ENG&MATH	10/1/2007	Law, Dale	MO	Missouri State University	$1,645,889.00
741911	Exploring Common Ground: Convening NSF-ATE and Philanthropic Organizations	http://tiny.cc/oQr3c	ADVANCED TECH EDUCATION PROG	10/1/2007	Winters, Laura	IL	The Council for Adult and Experiential Learning	$42,926.00

NSF ADVANCE Program

4201 Wilson Boulevard, Arlington, Virginia 22230, USA
(703) 292-5350
Jessie DeAro
http://www.nsf.gov/funding/pgm_summ.jsp?pims_id=5383

Description

The goal of the ADVANCE program is to develop systemic approaches to increase the representation and advancement of women in academic science and engineering careers, thereby contributing to the development of a more diverse science and engineering workforce. Creative strategies to realize this goal are sought from women and men. Members of underrepresented minority groups and individuals with disabilities are especially encouraged to apply. Proposals that address the participation and advancement of women with disabilities and of women from underrepresented minority groups are encouraged.

Award Number	Title	NSF Organization	Program(s)	Start Date	Principal Investigator	State	Organization	Awarded Amount to Date
750230	ADVANCE Leadership Award: Cross-Disciplinary Initiative for Minority Women Faculty (PI Transfer)	http://tiny.cc/VuPF4	ADVANCE	10/1/2007	Barabino, Gilda	GA	GA Tech Research Corporation - GA Institute of Technology	$300,001.00
756277	HRD/ADVANCE Professional, Technical and Administrative Services	http://tiny.cc/qBv24	PROGRAM	9/26/2007	Mitchell, Susan	MD	GUARDIANS OF HONOR	$275,642.00
620083	ADVANCE Partnerships for Adaptation, Implementation, and Dissemination Award - Increasing Junior Faculty's Productivity and Leadership	http://tiny.cc/fIt70	ADVANCE-PAID	6/1/2007	Valian, Virginia	NY	CUNY Hunter College	$499,901.00
618977	ADVANCE Partnerships for Adaptation, Implementation, and Dissemination Award: Gender Equity in STEM at the University of Missouri-Columbia	http://tiny.cc/S4Ebq	ADVANCE-PAID	1/1/2007	Litt, Jacquelyn	MO	University of Missouri-Columbia	$499,993.00
619979	ADVANCE Partnerships for Adaptation, Implementation, and Dissemination Award	http://tiny.cc/N20IK	ADVANCE-PAID	1/1/2007	Sheridan, Jennifer	WI	University of Wisconsin-Madison	$499,991.00

NSF Advanced Technological Education (ATE) Program

4201 Wilson Boulevard, Arlington, Virginia 22230, USA

(703) 292-8670

Elizabeth J. Teles

http://www.nsf.gov/funding/pgm_summ.jsp?pims_id=5464

Description

With an emphasis on two-year colleges, the Advanced Technological Education (ATE) program focuses on the education of technicians for the high-technology fields that drive our nation's economy. The program involves partnerships between academic institutions and employers to promote improvement in the education of science and engineering technicians at the undergraduate and secondary school levels. The ATE program supports curriculum development; professional development of college faculty and secondary school teachers; career pathways to two-year colleges from secondary schools and from two-year colleges to four-year institutions; and other activities. A secondary goal is articulation between two-year and four-year programs for K-12 prospective teachers that focus on technological education. The program also invites proposals focusing on applied research relating to technician education.

Award Number	Title	NSF Organization	Program(s)	Start Date	Principal Investigator	State	Organization	Awarded Amount to Date
703001	Regional Information Systems Security Center (RISSC)	http://tiny.cc/M2Dy2	ADVANCED TECH EDUCATION PROG	10/1/2007	Mehta, Jaishri	CA	Mount San Antonio College	$600,000.00
703002	MEMS, Nanotechnology, and the Silicon Run Series	http://tiny.cc/GLMsN	ADVANCED TECH EDUCATION PROG	10/1/2007	Carranza, Ruth	CA	Film Arts Foundation	$849,783.00
703070	Computer Engineering Technology Security Curriculum Expansion and Enhancement	http://tiny.cc/BZElr	ADVANCED TECH EDUCATION PROG, S-STEM:SCHLR SCI TECH ENG&MATH	10/1/2007	Yousif, Wael	FL	Valencia Community College	$547,203.00
703163	Viticulture and Enology Science and Technology Alliance (VESTA)	http://tiny.cc/Rqul9	ADVANCED TECH EDUCATION PROG, S-STEM:SCHLR SCI TECH ENG&MATH	10/1/2007	Law, Dale	MO	Missouri State University	$1,645,889.00
741911	Exploring Common Ground: Convening NSF-ATE and Philanthropic Organizations	http://tiny.cc/ZoAq0	ADVANCED TECH EDUCATION PROG	10/1/2007	Winters, Laura	IL	The Council for Adult and Experiential Learning	$42,926.00

NSF Broadening Participation in Computing (BPC) Program

4201 Wilson Boulevard, Arlington, Virginia 22230, USA
(703) 292-8489
Janice Cuny
http://www.nsf.gov/funding/pgm_summ.jsp?pims_id=13510

Description

The Broadening Participation in Computing (BPC) program aims to significantly increase the number of U.S. citizens and permanent residents receiving post secondary degrees in the computing disciplines, with an emphasis on students from communities with longstanding underrepresentation in computing: women, persons with disabilities, and minorities. Included minorities are African Americans, Hispanics, American Indians, Alaska Natives, Native Hawaiians, and Pacific Islanders. The BPC program seeks to engage the computing community in developing and implementing innovative methods to improve recruitment and retention of these students at the undergraduate and graduate levels. Because the lack of role models in the professoriate can be a barrier to participation, the BPC program also aims to develop effective strategies for encouraging individuals to pursue academic careers in computing and become these role models.

Award	Title	NSF Organization	Program(s)	Start Date	Principal Investigator	State	Organization	Awarded Amount to Date
739289	Into the Loop: University-K-12 Alliance for Computer Science Education for African-American, Latino/a, and Female Students	http://tiny.cc/six28	ITR-BROADENING	10/1/2007	Margolis, Jane	CA	University of California-Los Angeles	$1,003,168.00
739233	BPC-DP: Broadening Female Participation in Computing: Middle School through Undergraduate Study	http://tiny.cc/dWA9P	ITR-BROADENING	9/15/2007	Moskal, Barbara	CO	Colorado School of Mines	$579,557.00
739020	BPC-DP: CSTEP: Computer Science TransfEr Programs	http://tiny.cc/NNZhv	ITR-BROADENING	9/15/2007	Labrador, Miguel	FL	University of South Florida	$195,677.00
634502	Collaborative Proposal: BPC-DP: Practices Aggregation, Infrastructure, and Retrieval	http://tiny.cc/XsBzU	ITR-BROADENING	4/15/2007	Agogino, Alice	CA	University of California-Berkeley	$213,394.00
634338	Collaborative Research: BPC-DP: Practices Aggregation, Infrastructure, and Retrieval Service for	http://tiny.cc/dsLVU	ITR-BROADENING	4/15/2007	Barker, Lecia	CO	University of Colorado at Boulder	$285,826.00

NSF Cyberinfrastructure Training, Education, Advancement, and Mentoring for Our 21st Century Workforce (CI-TEAM) Program

4201 Wilson Boulevard, Arlington, Virginia 22230, USA

703-292-8276

Diana Rhoten

http://128.150.4.107/funding/pgm_summ.jsp?pims_id=12782&org=OCI&sel_org=OCI&from=fund

Description

The CI-TEAM program supports projects that position the national science and engineering community to engage in integrated research and education activities promoting, leveraging and utilizing cyberinfrastructure systems, tools and services. CI-TEAM awards will:

Prepare current and future generations of scientists, engineers, and educators to design and develop as well as adopt and deploy, cyber-based tools and environments for research and learning, both formal and informal. Expand and enhance participation in cyberinfrastructure science and engineering activities of diverse groups of people and organizations, with particular emphasis on the inclusion of traditionally underrepresented individuals, institutions, and communities as both creators and users of cyberinfrastructure.

Award Number	Title	NSF Organization	Program(s)	Start Date	Principal Investigator	State	Organization	Awarded Amount to Date
730065	PIRE: A Global Living Laboratory for	http://tiny.cc/eoMh9	CI-TEAM,	9/15/2007	Deng, Yi	FL	Florida International University	$353,820.00
749253	Summit to Create a Cyber-Community to Advance Deaf and Hard-of-Hearing Individuals in STEM	http://tiny.cc/pqi3C	CI-TEAM, RES IN DISABILITIES ED	9/1/2007	Clymer, Edward	NY	Rochester Institute of Tech	$95,188.00
736291		http://tiny.cc/zoFKv	EXP PROG TO STIM COMP RES, CI-TEAM, NATIONAL SMETE DIGITAL Libr	6/1/2007	Lathrop, Scott	IL	University of Chicago	$144,151.00
636139	CI-TEAM Implementation Project: Collaborative Research - A National Engineering Dissection Cyber-Collaboratory	http://tiny.cc/HBi4h	CI-TEAM	1/1/2007	Shooter, Steven	PA	Bucknell University	$111,361.00
636151	CI-TEAM Implementation Project: Collaborative Research - A National Engineering Dissection Cyber-Collaboratory	http://tiny.cc/AdAn7	CI-TEAM	1/1/2007	Terpenny, Janis	VA	Virginia Polytechnic Institute and State University	$104,378.00

NSF Centers of Research Excellence in Science and Technology (CREST) Program

4201 Wilson Boulevard, Arlington, Virginia 22230, USA

(703) 292-4988

Patrick Mensah

http://www.nsf.gov/funding/pgm_summ.jsp?pims_id=6668

Description

The Centers of Research Excellence in Science and Technology (CREST) program makes resources available to enhance the research capabilities of minority-serving institutions through the establishment of centers that effectively integrate education and research. CREST promotes the development of new knowledge, enhancements of the research productivity of individual faculty, and an expanded presence of students historically underrepresented in STEM disciplines. Awards are offered as new centers, supplements to existing centers, proposals for the CREST Historically Black Colleges and Universities Research Infrastructure for Science and Engineering (HBCU-RISE) initiative, or supplements to CREST/HBCU-RISE-eligible awardees for diversity collaboration in projects co-funded with NSF's Small Business Innovation Research and Small Business Technology Transfer (SBIR/STTR) programs, which are administered by NSF's Directorate for Engineering.

Award	Title	NSF Organization	Program(s)	Start Date	Principal Investigator	State	Organization	Awarded Amount to Date
734800	Expanding interdisciplinary research at the Center for Gravitational Wave Astronomy	http://tiny.cc/YczKD	CENTERS FOR RSCH EXCELL IN S&T	11/1/2007	Diaz, Mario	TX	University of Texas Brownsville	$991,981.00
734232	Center for	http://tiny.cc/AxGtt	CENTERS FOR RSCH EXCELL IN S&T	10/1/2007	Singh, Shree	AL	Alabama State University	$993,627.00
734645	Development of Collaborative Multidisciplinary Experimental-Computational Approach for Design, Synthesis and Characterization of Novel Compounds with Potential Biological Activitie	http://tiny.cc/Ev6zl	CENTERS FOR RSCH EXCELL IN S&T	10/1/2007	Leszczynski, Jerzy	MS	Jackson State University	$1,005,651.00
734845	HBCU-RISE Advanced Infrastructure Composites (AIC)	http://tiny.cc/rbAtQ	CENTERS FOR RSCH EXCELL IN S&T	10/1/2007	Woldesenbet, Eyassu	LA	Southern University	$996,612.00
734635	Doctoral Research in Multifunctional Optical Nanomaterials (HBCU-RISE)	http://tiny.cc/AwnGe	CENTERS FOR RSCH EXCELL IN S&T	10/1/2007	Seo, JaeTae	VA	Hampton University	$1,000,000.00

NSF CISE Computing Research Infrastructure (CRI) Program

4201 Wilson Boulevard, Arlington, Virginia 22230, USA
(703) 292-8930
Tanya Korelsky
http://www.nsf.gov/funding/pgm_summ.jsp?pims_id=12810

Description

The CISE Computing Research Infrastructure (CRI) program drives discovery and learning in the computing disciplines by supporting the creation, enhancement and operation of world-class computing research infrastructure. Further, through the CRI program CISE seeks to ensure that individuals from a diverse range of academic institutions, including minority-serving and predominantly undergraduate institutions, have access to such infrastructure.

Award	Title	NSF Organization	Program(s)	Start Date	Principal Investigator	State	Organization	Awarded Amount to Date
709430	CRI: CRD: Raising the Standard of Scientific Publishing Through an Experiment Archive	http://tiny.cc/8oAZD	COMPUTING RES	10/1/2007	Lepreau, Jay	UT	University of Utah	$49,834.00
708597	Collaborative Research: CRI: IAD: Electronic Testing Education, Research and Training Infrastructure	http://tiny.cc/4xnid	CISE MINOR INST INFRA (MII) PR, COMPUTING RES	10/1/2007	Narang, Hira	AL	Tuskegee University	$169,083.00
708962	Collaborative Research: CRI: IAD: Electronic Testing Education, Research and Training Infrastructure	http://tiny.cc/uk4oy	COMPUTING RES	10/1/2007	Agrawal, Vishwani	AL	Auburn University	$334,488.00
708945	Collaborative Research: CRI: IAD: Electronic Testing Education, Research and Training Infrastructure	http://tiny.cc/e8S0G	COMPUTING RES	10/1/2007	Gaede, Rhonda	AL	University of Alabama in Huntsville	$157,041.00
708788	CRI: IAD Keeping Pace with Growing Computing Needs: A Strategy for Enhancing Multi-Core Microprocessor Research and Education at Cornell University	http://tiny.cc/xoalu	COMPUTING RES	10/1/2007	Albonesi, David	NY	Cornell University	$93,865.00

NSF Computer Systems Research (CSR) Program

4201 Wilson Boulevard, Arlington, Virginia 22230, USA

(703) 292-8950

David Du

http://www.nsf.gov/funding/pgm_summ.jsp?pims_id=13385

Description

CSR-funded projects will enable significant progress on challenging high-impact problems, as opposed to incremental progress on familiar problems. Collaborative CSR projects that actively involve industry or other academic communities are particularly welcome. For example, to stimulate breakthroughs in human-aware computer and software systems and applications, multi-investigator, multidisciplinary proposals are encouraged. Further, CSR PIs should describe credible plans for demonstrating the utility and potential impact of their proposed work, for example, through empirical prototypes disseminated to and evaluated by the community.

Award	Title	NSF Organization	Program(s)	Start Date	Principal Investigator	State	Organization	Awarded Amount to Date
749508	SGER: A Virtual Target For Next Generation Hardware Accelerated Multi-Core Systems	http://tiny.cc/ED2r9	COMPUTER SYSTEMS	1/1/2008	Givargis, Tony	CA	University of California-Irvine	$200,000.00
703139	Tightly-coupled Heterogeneous Supercomputing	http://tiny.cc/pkEkq	COMPUTER SYSTEMS	11/1/2007	Saltz, Joel	OH	Ohio State University Research Foundation	$30,170.00
713895	Mathematical reliability models for energy-efficient parallel disk systems	http://tiny.cc/cZ6bo	COMPUTER SYSTEMS	10/1/2007	Qin, Xiao	NM	New Mexico Institute of Mining and Technology	$98,649.00
	CSR EHS: Formal Model Based Health and Medical System Composition	http://tiny.cc/psa9S	COMPUTER SYSTEMS	10/1/2007	Sha, Lui	IL	University of Illinois at Urbana-Champaign	$285,411.00
720721	CSR--EHS: Invariants for Continuous and Hybrid Dynamical Systems	http://tiny.cc/Upmvb	COMPUTER SYSTEMS	10/1/2007	Tiwari, Ashish	CA	SRI International	$90,000.00
720841	CSR-CPS: Action Webs Seedling	http://tiny.cc/7fvyV	COMPUTER SYSTEMS	10/1/2007	Lee, Edward	CA	University of California-Berkeley	$129,998.00

NSF Cyber Trust (CT) Program

4201 Wilson Boulevard, Arlington, Virginia 22230, USA
(703) 292-8950
Karl Levitt
http://www.nsf.gov/funding/pgm_summ.jsp?pims_id=6191

Description
The NSF Cyber Trust (CT) program promotes a vision of a society where trust enables technologies to support individual and societal needs without violating confidences and exacerbating public risks. It is a vision of cyber space that is supportive of our basic principles of fairness and safe information access. The goal of the NSF CT program is to develop new insights and fundamental scientific principles that lead to software and hardware technologies on which people can justifiably rely.

Award	Title	NSF Organization	Program(s)	Start Date	Principal Investigator	State	Organization	Awarded Amount to Date
832943	Collaborative Research: Automated and Adaptive Diversity for Improving Computer Systems Security	http://tiny.cc/hvrze	TRUSTED COMPUTING	12/1/2007	Song, Dawn	CA	University of California-Berkeley	$249,290.00
716172	CT-ISG: Collaborative Research: Massive Dataset Algorithmics for Network Security	http://tiny.cc/z8VZo	ITR-CYBERTRUST, CYBER TRUST, COMPUTING RES	10/1/2007	Lee, Insup	PA	University of Pennsylvania	$60,000.00
716208	Collaborative Research: CT-T: TRIESTE: A Trusted Radio Infrastructure for Enforcing Spectrum Etiquettes	http://tiny.cc/SttbK	CYBER TRUST	10/1/2007	Park, Jung-Min	VA	Virginia Polytechnic Institute and State University	$50,000.00
716223	CT-ISG: Collaborative Research: Massive-Dataset Algorithmics for Network Security	http://tiny.cc/1aRs2	ITR-CYBERTRUST, CYBER TRUST	10/1/2007	Feigenbaum, Joan	CT	Yale University	$35,000.00
716400	Collaborative Research: CT-T: TRIESTE: A Trusted Radio Infrastructure for Enforcing Spectrum Etiquettes	http://tiny.cc/PzpOn	CYBER TRUST	10/1/2007	Trappe, Wade	NJ	Rutgers University New Brunswick	$50,000.00

NSF Discovery Research K-12 (DR-K12) Program

4201 Wilson Boulevard, Arlington, Virginia 22230, USA

(703) 292-8620

http://www.nsf.gov/funding/pgm_summ.jsp?pims_id=500047

Description

The Discovery Research K-12 (DR-K12) program seeks to enable significant advances in K-12 student and teacher learning of the STEM disciplines through research about, and development and implementation of, innovative resources, models, and technologies for use by students, teachers, and policy makers. Activities funded under this solicitation begin with a research question or hypothesis about K-12 STEM learning or teaching; develop, adapt, or study innovative resources, models, or technologies; and demonstrate if, how, for whom, and why their implementation affects learning.

Award	Title	NSF Organization	Program(s)	Start Date	Principal Investigator	State	Organization	Awarded Amount to Date
736305	Mathematicians Writing for Teachers Conference, Mt. Holyoke College in early summer 2008.	http://tiny.cc/MPcW6	DISCOVERY RESEARCH K-12	12/15/2007	Russell, Susan Jo	MA	TERC Inc	$98,223.00
736558	Research Agenda Project Conference	http://tiny.cc/xFZSW	DISCOVERY RESEARCH K-12	12/1/2007	Rubillo, James	VA	National Council of Teachers of Mathematics	$99,850.00
620083	ADVANCE Partnerships for Adaptation, Implementation, and Dissemination Award - Increasing Junior Faculty's Productivity and Leadership	http://tiny.cc/flt70	ADVANCE-PAID	6/1/2007	Valian, Virginia	NY	CUNY Hunter College	$499,901.00
618977	ADVANCE Partnerships for Adaptation, Implementation, and Dissemination Award: Gender Equity in STEM at the University of Missouri-Columbia	http://tiny.cc/S4Ebq	ADVANCE-PAID	1/1/2007	Litt, Jacquelyn	MO	University of Missouri-Columbia	$499,993.00
748041	(SGER) Youth-based Program Impact on Education and Career Choices: An Exploration of Issues in Planning and Implementing Longitudinal Research	http://tiny.cc/eJCxh	DISCOVERY RESEARCH K-12	11/1/2007	Tai, Robert	VA	University of Virginia Main Campus	$91,744.00

NSF Emerging Models and Technologies for Computation (EMT) Program

4201 Wilson Boulevard, Arlington, Virginia 22230, USA
(703) 292-8910
Pinaki Mazumder
http://www.nsf.gov/funding/pgm_summ.jsp?pims_id=11176

Description

The EMT program supports cross- and inter-disciplinary research and education projects that explore ideas, theory and experiments which go beyond conventional wisdom and venture into a range of uncharted territories in order to advance computing capabilities, and/or that produce innovative curricula or educational materials to help advance the training of new experts in emerging computing models and technologies. Explicit efforts will be made to support untested theories and approaches that provide plausible but high-risk opportunities. Proposals that are not clearly collaborative and/or interdisciplinary in nature are likely to be less competitive.

Award Number	Title	NSF Organization	Program(s)	Start Date	Principal Investigator	State	Organization	Awarded Amount to Date
728703	EMT: Toward Large Scale Integrated Nucleic Acid Circuits	http://tiny.cc/diQvc	EMERGING MODELS &	9/15/2007	Winfree, Erik	CA	California Institute of Technology	$250,000.00
726648	Collaborative Research: EMT: Novel Operations, Circuit Optimization, and Technology Evaluation for Large-Scale, Fault-Tolerant Quantum Computing	http://tiny.cc/pkjoM	EMERGING MODELS &	9/15/2007	Chuang, Isaac	MA	Massachusetts Institute of Technology	$125,000.00
726554	Collaborative Research: EMT: Novel Operations, Circuit Optimization, and Technology Evaluation for Large-Scale, Fault-Tolerant Quantum Computing	http://tiny.cc/6q9SH	EMERGING MODELS &	9/15/2007	Chong, Frederic	CA	University of California-Santa Barbara	$125,000.00
726378	Collaborative Research: EMT - Programmable Molecular Movements	http://tiny.cc/v7nXX	EMERGING MODELS &	9/15/2007	Seeman, Nadrian	NY	New York University	$150,000.00
745366	WORKSHOP: Workshop on Biological Communication Technology	http://tiny.cc/Ufu0Y	INFORMATION TECHNOLOGY RESEARC	9/1/2007	Nakano, Tadashi	CA	University of California-Irvine	$69,998.00

NSF Research on Gender in Science and Engineering FY2008 (GSE) Program

4201 Wilson Boulevard, Arlington, Virginia 22230, USA

(703) 292-4684

Tayana Casseus

http://www.nsf.gov/funding/pgm_summ.jsp?pims_id=5475

Description

The program seeks to broaden the participation of girls and women in all fields of science, technology, engineering, and mathematics (STEM) education by supporting research, the diffusion of research-based innovations, and extension services in education that will lead to a larger and more diverse domestic science and engineering workforce. Typical projects will contribute to the knowledge base addressing gender-related differences in learning and in the educational experiences that affect student interest, performance, and choice of careers; how pedagogical approaches and teaching styles, curriculum, student services, and institutional culture contribute to causing or closing gender gaps that persist in certain fields. Projects will communicate and apply findings, evaluation results, and proven good practices and products to a wider community.

Award	Title	NSF Organization	Program(s)	Start Date	Principal Investigator	State	Organization	Awarded Amount to Date
734004	GSE/COM: Telling STEM Stories through Content Clips	http://tiny.cc/aA1Gy	RES ON GENDER IN SCI & ENGINE	11/1/2007	McLean, Lois	CA	McLean Media	$198,880.00
734072	GSE/COM: Increasing Assessment Capacity in Engineering Outreach (SWE AWE)	http://tiny.cc/4Xc57	RES ON GENDER IN SCI & ENGINE	10/1/2007	Bogue, Barbara	PA	Pennsylvania State Univ University Park	$200,000.00
734056	GSE/EXT - STEM Equity Pipeline	http://tiny.cc/nFUOD	RES ON GENDER IN SCI & ENGINE	10/1/2007	Lufkin, Mimi	PA	National Alliance for Partnerships in Equity Education Foundatio	$499,885.00
734100	GSE:Extension Services in Engineering: Improving Climate, Instruction and Community to Recruit and Retain Undergraduate Women	http://tiny.cc/ZPkef	RES ON GENDER IN SCI & ENGINE	9/1/2007	Matt, C. Diane	CO	Wepan Inc	$156,878.00
735000	GSE/COM: Girls Understand, Imagine and Dream Engineering	http://tiny.cc/BsUu8	RES ON GENDER IN SCI & ENGINE	9/1/2007	Cippoletti, Susan	NY	Girl Scouts of the USA	$93,713.00

Civil Infrastructure Systems (NSF CIS)

4201 Wilson Boulevard, Arlington, Virginia 22230, USA
(703) 292-8606
Dennis Wenger
http://www.nsf.gov/funding/pgm_summ.jsp?pims_id=13352

Description

The CIS program supports research leading to the intelligent engineering of distributed infrastructure systems. Areas of interest include intra- and inter-dependencies in infrastructure design and operation for resilience and sustainability, infrastructure protection, and advanced information technologies for health monitoring, condition assessment, deterioration and asset management. Special emphasis is on risk analysis, life-cycle frameworks, cyber-enabled simulation, and technologies for design, construction and operation of resilient and sustainable infrastructure networks.

Award	Title	NSF Organization	Program(s)	Start Date	Principal Investigator	State	Organization	Awarded Amount to Date
741374	SGER: Development of Human Poses for the Determination of on-site Construction Productivity in Real Time	http://tiny.cc/oVKt4	CIVIL	10/1/2007	Bai, Yong	KS	University of Kansas Center for Research Inc	$10,000.00
742211	SGER: A Virtual Community of Construction Scholars and Practitioners	http://tiny.cc/Thbk5	CIVIL	10/1/2007	Rojas, Eddy	WA	University of Washington	$40,001.00
751285	Support for a Workshop Titled Toward Sustainable Critical Infrastructure Systems	http://tiny.cc/msISq	CIVIL	10/1/2007	Stanley, Lynda	DC	National Academy of Sciences	$50,000.00
700492	Skill Development and Transfer from Virtual Training Systems	http://tiny.cc/YN8QN	CIVIL	9/15/2007	Dunston, Phillip	IN	Purdue University	$130,000.00
738613	GOALI-Enhancing Critical Infrastructure Recovery Through Communication Network Visualization	http://tiny.cc/JPTte	CIVIL	9/15/2007	Chinowsky, Paul	CO	University of Colorado at Boulder	$35,000.00

NSF Innovative Technology Experiences for Students and Teachers (ITEST) Program

4201 Wilson Boulevard, Arlington, Virginia 22230, USA

(703) 292-5119

Julia V. Clark

http://nsf.gov/funding/pgm_summ.jsp?pims_id=5467&org=NSF

Description

The program responds to current concerns and projections about shortages of STEM professionals and information technology workers in the United States and seeks solutions to help ensure the breadth and depth of the STEM workforce. ITEST supports the development, implementation, testing and scale-up of models, as well as research studies to address these questions and to find solutions. There are a variety of possible approaches to improving the STEM workforce and to building students' capacity to participate in it. NSF seeks to expand the existing ITEST portfolio by addressing students at any age for grades kindergarten through high school and by including all areas of the STEM workforce, while retaining an emphasis on technology-related areas.

Award	Title	NSF Organization	Program(s)	Start Date	Principal Investigator	State	Organization	Awarded Amount to Date
737683	PROFIT: Pictures Represent Opportunities For Inspiration in Technology	http://tiny.cc/J4H9U	ITEST	12/1/2007	da Vitoria Lobo, Niels	FL	University of Central Florida	$1,200,000.00
737649	Rhode Island Information Technology Experiences for Students and Teachers (RI-ITEST)	http://tiny.cc/cIXBv	ITEST	11/1/2007	Damelin, Daniel	MA	Concord Consortium	$1,199,955.00
737583	IDEAS: Inquiry-based Dynamic Earth Applications of	http://tiny.cc/WOlti	ITEST	10/1/2007	Segee, Bruce	ME	University of Maine	$1,185,460.00
737631	Extreme Experience Lab	http://tiny.cc/42Xwy	ITEST	10/1/2007	Johnson, David	CA	The National Hispanic University	$898,827.00
737638	ITEST Learning Resource Center	http://tiny.cc/tzOIi	ITEST	10/1/2007	Malyn-Smith, Joyce	MA	Education Development Center	$2,766,662.00

NSF Nanotechnology Undergraduate Education (NUE) in Engineering Program

4201 Wilson Boulevard, Arlington, Virginia 22230, USA

(703) 292-5357

Mary Poats

http://128.150.4.107/funding/pgm_summ.jsp?pims_id=13656&org=SBE&from=home

Description

NSF Nanotechnology Undergraduate Education (NUE) in Engineering program aims at introducing nanoscale science, engineering, and technology through a variety of interdisciplinary approaches into undergraduate engineering education.

Award Number	Title	NSF Organization	Program(s)	Start Date	Principal Investigator	State	Organization	Awarded Amount to Date
706194	Studies of Magnetic Domain Wall Injection and Manipulation in a Magnetic Nanowire using Micromagnetic Simulation	http://tiny.cc/hGAXW	CONDENSED MATTER & MAT THEORY	12/15/2007	Kunz, Andrew	WI	Marquette University	$72,000.00
741536	NUE:	http://tiny.cc/TW2oD		11/1/2007	Pourkamali Anaraki, Siavash	CO	University of Denver	$198,657.00
725630	High-performance Hetero-nanocrystal Memories	http://tiny.cc/6yyK3	ELECT, PHOTONICS, & DEVICE TEC	10/1/2007	Liu, Jianlin	CA	University of California-Riverside	$240,000.00
706654	Cooperative Effects Of Impurities On Electron Transport In Low-Dimensional Nanostructures	http://tiny.cc/OyqMN	CONDENSED MATTER & MAT THEORY	9/15/2007	Fogler, Michael	CA	University of California-San Diego	$158,716.00
730465	GOALI: Separation of Oil and Other Organics from Water Using Inverse Fluidization of Hydrophobic Aerogels	http://tiny.cc/0N0QS	GRANT OPP FOR ACAD LIA W/INDUS, SEPAR & PURIFICATION PROCESSES	9/15/2007	Lin, Jerry Y.S.	AZ	Arizona State University	$85,968.00

NSF Science & Engineering Visualization Challenge

4201 Wilson Boulevard, Arlington, Virginia 22230, USA

(703) 292-5111

http://www.nsf.gov/news/special_reports/scivis/index.jsp?id=challenge

http://www.nsf.gov/news/special_reports/scivis/index.jsp?id=eligible

http://www.nsf.gov/news/special_reports/scivis/index.jsp?id=win2007

Description

The National Science Foundation (NSF) and Science created the Science and Engineering Visualization Challenge to celebrate that grand tradition—and to encourage its continued growth. In a world where science literacy is dismayingly rare, illustrations provide the most immediate and influential connection between scientists and other citizens, and the best hope for nurturing popular interest. Indeed, they are now a necessity for public understanding of research developments: In an increasingly graphics-oriented culture, where people acquire the majority of their news from TV and the World Wide Web, a story without a vivid and intriguing image is often no story at all.

Recent Awards, Winning Projects & Award Winners

Photography

First Place (tie)

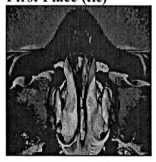

What Lies Behind our Nose?

Credit: Kai-hung Fung, Pamela Youde Nethersole Eastern Hospital
Human anatomy it may be, but the airways that riddle the space behind our noses take on an alien aspect in this unearthly rendering created by Kai-hung Fung, a radiologist at the Pamela Youde Nethersole Eastern Hospital in Hong Kong. A computed tomography (CT) scan from a 33-year-old Chinese woman being examined for thyroid disease provided the raw data for Fung's rendering. He stacked together 182 thin CT "slices" to create a 3D image looking upward at the sinuses from underneath the head. Normally, CT renderings meld slices together into smooth surfaces, but, in

what he terms the "Rainbow Technique," Fung instead broke them apart, creating a topographical map of the airspaces described by the contour lines of individual slices, and colored according to the density of the tissues that border them.

First Place (tie)

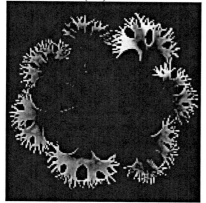

Irish Moss, Chondrus crispus

Credit: Andrea Ottesen, University of Maryland

The slimy, glistening mass of seaweed washed up on a sandy beach seems light-years distant from this feathery, dendritic image of Irish moss (Chondrus crispus) created by Andrea Ottesen, a botanist and molecular ecologist at the University of Maryland, College Park. "If you pull Chondrus out of the ocean, it's folded on itself—really curled up," she says. It wasn't until after she had "pressed every one of those little ends down with sea stones" and left it to dry for 2 days that the seaweed's beautiful, simple shape was revealed. Besides being one of the most common seaweed species on the Atlantic coast, says Ottesen, Irish moss and algae like it are sources of natural thickeners and stabilizers called carrageenans, which are widely used in processed foods as diverse as lunch meat and ice cream.

Informational Graphics

First Place

Modeling the Flight of a Bat

Credit: Kenneth S. Breuer, David J. Willis, Mykhaylo Kostandov, Daniel K. Riskin, Jaime Peraire David H. Laidlaw, Sharon M. Swartz

Most short-nosed fruit bats (Cynopterus brachyotis) spend their nights flitting about in the jungles of Southeast Asia. However, some of the tiny creatures, which weigh less than 50 grams fully grown, lead an altogether different existence: flitting about in wind tunnels under the watchful eyes of aerodynamics researchers. Interested in the tiny mammals' flight dynamics, Brown University engineer Kenneth Breuer used lasers and a sophisticated multicamera motion-tracking system to record how their wings and the air around them distorted as the animals flapped against the wind. Based on the experiments, aeronautical engineer David Willis, who has a joint appointment at Brown and MIT, Brown computer scientist Mykhaylo Kostandov, and their colleagues created a computer model of bat flight--visually conveyed in this poster. "When viewed in slow motion," says Willis, "bat flight is beautiful and complex. The goal of this illustration is to capture that beauty while also adding scientific merit."

Interactive Media (screen shots)

First Place

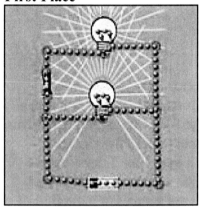

Physics Education Technology (PhET) Project

Credit: Sarah McKagan, Carl Wieman, Kathy Perkins, Wendy Adams, Michael Dubson, Noah Finkelstein, Linda Koch, Patricia Loeblein, Chris Keller, Danielle Harlow, Noah Podolefsky, Sam Reid, Chris Malley, John de Goes, Ron LeMaster, Mindy Gratny, Linda Wellmann

Nobel laureate Carl Wieman was looking for a way to explain his research into Bose-Einstein condensates—strange assemblies of supercold atoms that lose their individuality and form "superatoms"--to both physicists and schoolchildren. He began creating computer simulations, but he swiftly realized their wider potential for teaching physics of all types and initiated the Physics Education Technology (PhET) project at his then-home of the University of Colorado, Boulder, and began churning out simulations. Today, the PhET Web site lists 65 simulations available for free download, illustrating everything from quantum tunneling to projectile motion.

Honorable Mention

Breast Cancer Virtual Anatomy

Credit: CCG Metamedia, Steve Rothman, Cathryn Tune, Nicola Landucci, Joseph Speiser, Samantha Belmont

A visit to the doctor's office can be a scary, confusing experience, particularly when the subject under discussion is chemotherapy's failure to eradicate breast cancer. Cathryn Tune, Samantha Belmont, and their team at CCG Metamedia, a medical education company based in New York City, created this interactive tool to help doctors explain to their patients the anatomy and progression of their cancers in a clear, easy-to-understand manner. The interface allows doctors to select tumor size and level of metastasis and displays the part of the patient's anatomy that cancer is attacking while suggesting treatment options.

NSF Science, Technology, and Society (STS)

4201 Wilson Boulevard, Arlington, Virginia 22230, USA
(703) 292-7283
Frederick Kronz
http://www.nsf.gov/funding/pgm_summ.jsp?pims_id=5324

Description

STS considers proposals that examine historical, philosophical, and sociological questions that arise in connection with science, engineering, and technology, and their respective interactions with society. STS has four components:

- Ethics and Values in Science, Engineering and Technology (EVS),
- History and Philosophy of Science, Engineering and Technology (HPS),
- Social Studies of Science, Engineering and Technology (SSS),
- Studies of Policy, Science, Engineering and Technology (SPS).

Award	Title	NSF Organization	Program(s)	Start Date	Principal Investigator	State	Organization	Awarded Amount to Date
724474	Scholar's Award: Scanning the Globe: Magnetic Resonance Imaging (MRI) Research and Development in the United Kingdom, India and the United States	http://tiny.cc/nLzaB	SCIENCE & SOCIETY PROGRAM, GEN	12/15/2007	Prasad, Amit	MO	University of Missouri-Columbia	$73,550.00
723809	Biology and Ethics: Evaluating the Claim that Biotechnologies Pose a Threat to Human Dignity	http://tiny.cc/F408r	SCIENCE & SOCIETY PROGRAM, GEN	9/15/2007	de Melo-Martin, Inmaculada	NY	Joan and Sanford I. Weill Medical College of Cornell University	$149,839.00
724608	Citizen Science and Sea Turtle Conservation: Critical Perspectives from Social Studies of Science	http://tiny.cc/Zmavm	SCIENCE & SOCIETY PROGRAM, GEN	9/15/2007	Campbell, Lisa	NC	Duke University	$83,944.00
645884	From Ecological Diversity to Biodiversity: Conceptual Changes in the Emergence of Conservation Biology	http://tiny.cc/2tclr	SCIENCE & SOCIETY PROGRAM, GEN, Hist & Philosophy of SET	7/1/2007	Sarkar, Sahotra	TX	University of Texas at Austin	$69,554.00
646807	Scientific and Native Community Collaboration for Sustainability: Process Research and Facilitation	http://tiny.cc/g2CgV	Ethics & Values of SET, SCIENCE & SOCIETY PROGRAM, GEN	6/1/2007	James, Keith	OR	Portland State University	$225,000.00

NSF Funding Science of Science and Innovation Policy

4201 Wilson Boulevard, Arlington, Virginia 22230, USA
(703)292-5145
Julia Lane
http://www.nsf.gov/funding/pgm_summ.jsp?pims_id=501084

Description

The Directorate for Social, Behavioral and Economic Sciences (SBE) at the National Science Foundation (NSF) aims to foster the development of the knowledge, theories, data, tools, and human capital needed to cultivate a new Science of Science and Innovation Policy (SciSIP). The SciSIP program underwrites fundamental research that creates new explanatory models, analytic tools and datasets designed to inform the nation's public and private sectors about the processes through which investments in science and engineering (S&E) research are transformed into social and economic outcomes. SciSIP's goals are to understand the contexts, structures and processes of S&E research, to evaluate reliably the tangible and intangible returns from investments in research and development (R&D), and to predict the likely returns from future R&D investments within tolerable margins of error and with attention to the full spectrum of potential consequences. Specifically, the research, data collection and community development components of SciSIP's activities will: (1) develop usable knowledge and theories of creative processes and their transformation into social and economic outcomes; (2) develop, improve and expand models and analytical tools that can be applied in the science policy decision making process; (3) improve and expand science metrics, datasets and analytical tools; and (4) develop a community of experts across academic institutions and disciplines focused on SciSIP. For purposes of this solicitation, the term "science metrics" refers to quantitative measures or indicators that provide summary information on the size, scope, quality, and impact of science and engineering activities, with particular focus on inputs and outputs of the science, technology and innovation system. Characterizing the dynamics of discovery and innovation is important for developing valid metrics, for predicting future returns on investments, for constructing fruitful policies, and for developing new forms of workforce education and training.

Award	Title	NSF Organization	Program(s)	Start Date	Principal Investigator	State	Organization	Awarded Amount to Date
738142	MOD: Estimating the Effect of Exposure to Superstar Scientists: Evidence from Academia and the	http://tiny.cc/j8DAQ	SCIENCE OF SCIENCE POLICY	12/1/2007	Graff Zivin, Joshua	MA	National Bureau of Economic Research Inc	$398,532.00
738347	Collaborative Research MOD: Contributions of Foreign Students to Knowledge Creation and Diffusion	http://tiny.cc/cGj4p	SCIENCE OF SCIENCE POLICY	12/1/2007	Ginther, Donna	KS	University of Kansas Center for Research Inc	$294,280.00
738371	Collaborative Research MOD: Contributions of Foreign Students to Knowledge Creation and Diffusion	http://tiny.cc/kJx5B	SCIENCE OF SCIENCE POLICY	12/1/2007	Kahn, Shulamit	MA	Trustees of Boston University	$533,875.00
738394	TLS: Assessing the Impact of Science Policy on the Rate and Direction of Scientific Progress: Frontier Tools & Applications	http://tiny.cc/uTc3w	SCIENCE OF SCIENCE POLICY	11/1/2007	Furman, Jeffrey	MA	National Bureau of Economic Research Inc	$398,655.00
738130	State Science Policies: Modeling Their Origins, Nature, Fit, and Effects on Local Universities	http://tiny.cc/92QJX	SCIENCE OF SCIENCE POLICY	10/1/2007	Hearn, James	GA	University of Georgia Research Foundation Inc	$399,739.00

NSF Scholarship for Service (SFS) Program

4201 Wilson Boulevard, Arlington, Virginia 22230, USA

(703) 292-5141

Timothy V. Fossum

http://www.nsf.gov/funding/pgm_summ.jsp?pims_id=5228

Description

The Federal Cyber Service: Scholarship for Service (SFS) program seeks to increase the number of qualified students entering the fields of information assurance and computer security and to increase the capacity of the United States higher education enterprise to continue to produce professionals in these fields to meet the needs of our increasingly technological society.

Award	Title	NSF Organization	Program(s)	Start Date	Principal Investigator	State	Organization	Awarded Amount to Date
723794	A Collaborative Proposal for the Building of Information Security Expertise and Capacity	http://tiny.cc/btUBE	FED CYBER SERV: SCHLAR FOR SER, S-STEM:SCHLR SCI TECH ENG&MATH	10/1/2007	Willis, Robert	VA	Hampton University	$249,917.00
723927	A Collaborative Proposal: For the Building of Information Security Expertise and Capacity	http://tiny.cc/llxtg	FED CYBER SERV: SCHLAR FOR SER, S-STEM:SCHLR SCI TECH ENG&MATH	10/1/2007	Strickland, Albert	ID	Idaho State University	$250,000.00
723763	SFS (Capacity Building Track): Faculty Development to Promote Computer Forensics in the IA Curriculum	http://tiny.cc/nSOHe	FED CYBER SERV: SCHLAR FOR SER, S-STEM:SCHLR SCI TECH ENG&MATH	9/15/2007	Upadhyaya, Shambhu	NY	SUNY at Buffalo	$150,000.00
723368	A Second Generation Faculty Development Program	http://tiny.cc/gRyVc	FED CYBER SERV: SCHLAR FOR SER, S-STEM:SCHLR SCI TECH ENG&MATH	9/1/2007	O'Leary, Mike	MD	Towson University	$299,963.00
723491	Collaborative Project: Focused Faculty Development Workshop on Cyber Games and Interactive Simulations	http://tiny.cc/cFSfg	FED CYBER SERV: SCHLAR FOR SER, S-STEM:SCHLR SCI TECH ENG&MATH	9/1/2007	Yu, Huiming Anna	NC	North Carolina Agricultural & Technical State University	$226,994.00

NSF Scholarships in Science, Technology, Engineering, and Mathematics (S-STEM) Program

4201 Wilson Boulevard, Arlington, Virginia 22230, USA
(703) 292-4630
Duncan E. McBride
http://www.nsf.gov/funding/pgm_summ.jsp?pims_id=5257

Description

This program makes grants to institutions of higher education to support scholarships for academically talented, financially needy students, enabling them to enter the workforce following completion of an associate, baccalaureate, or graduate level degree in science and engineering disciplines. Grantee institutions are responsible for selecting scholarship recipients, reporting demographic information about student scholars, and managing the S-STEM project at the institution.

Award	Title	NSF Organization	Program(s)	Start Date	Principal Investigator	State	Organization	Awarded Amount to Date
717492	A New Approach to Analytical Chemistry: The Development of Process Oriented Guided Inquiry Learning Materials	http://tiny.cc/PdwTO	CCLI-Phase 2 (Expansion), S-STEM:SCHLR SCI TECH ENG&MATH	12/1/2007	Lantz, Juliette	NJ	Drew University	$498,825.00
737030	IONiC: A Cyber-Enabled Community of Practice for Improving Inorganic Chemical Education	http://tiny.cc/2I76b	CCLI-Phase 1 (Exploratory), S-STEM:SCHLR SCI TECH ENG&MATH	12/1/2007	Eppley, Hilary	IN	DePauw University	$149,374.00
737203	Incorporating Mass Spectrometry-Based Protein Identification into Biochemistry Laboratory	http://tiny.cc/sxr8O	CCLI-Phase 1 (Exploratory), S-STEM:SCHLR SCI TECH ENG&MATH	12/1/2007	Wilson, Karl	NY	SUNY at Binghamton	$139,585.00
737474	Science Collaboratory: Open Participatory Learning Infrastructure for Education (SCOPE)	http://tiny.cc/Evafn	CCLI-Phase 1 (Exploratory), S-STEM:SCHLR SCI TECH ENG&MATH	12/1/2007	Donovan, Samuel	WI	Beloit College	$149,975.00
737533	Preparing Students for Citizenship: Fostering Critical Thinking and Problem-solving Skills through Quantitative Reasoning and Scientific Literacy	http://tiny.cc/pOfvy	CCLI-Phase 1 (Exploratory), S-STEM:SCHLR SCI TECH ENG&MATH	12/1/2007	Myers, James	WY	University of Wyoming	$140,495.00

NSF Science and Technology Centers (STC) Integrative Partnerships Program

Room 1270 4201 Wilson Boulevard Arlington, VA 22230
703-292-8040
http://www.nsf.gov/funding/pgm_summ.jsp?pims_id=5541

Description

The Science and Technology Centers (STC): Integrative Partnerships program enables innovative research and education projects of national importance that require a Center mode of support to achieve the research, education, and knowledge-transfer goals shared by the partners. STCs conduct world-class research in partnerships among academic institutions, national laboratories, industrial organizations, and/or other public/private entities to create new and meaningful knowledge of significant benefit to society.

Award	Title	NSF Organization	Program(s)	Start Date	Principal Investigator	State	Organization	Awarded Amount to Date
751515	Student Transitional Alliance (STARS)	http://tiny.cc/uKNf2	SCI & TECH CTRS (INTEG PTRS)	9/15/2007	McHenry, William	MS	Jackson State University	$713,551.00
707707	5th NRCEN Workshop: Creating Positive Influence: Innovative Approaches to Research-based Education and Outreach	http://tiny.cc/itqrB	ENG DIVERSITY ACTIVITIES, NEES RESEARCH, ENGINEERING RESEARCH CENTERS, SCI & TECH CTRS (INTEG PTRS), OFFICE OF	4/1/2007	Molinaro, Marco	MI	University of Michigan Ann Arbor	$99,893.00

NSF Strategic Technologies for Cyberinfrastructure Program (STCI)

4201 Wilson Boulevard, Arlington, Virginia 22230, USA

(703) 292-8970

Abani Patra

http://www.nsf.gov/funding/pgm_summ.jsp?pims_id=500066

Description

The primary purpose of the Strategic Technologies for Cyberinfrastructure Program (STCI) is to support work leading to the development and/or demonstration of innovative cyberinfrastructure services for science and engineering research and education that fill gaps left by more targeted funding opportunities. In addition, it will consider highly innovative cyberinfrastructure education, outreach and training proposals that lie outside the scope of targeted solicitations.

Award	Title	NSF Organization	Program(s)	Start Date	Principal Investigator	State	Organization	Awarded Amount to Date
754077	Workshop on Large-Scale Inverse Problems and Quantification of Uncertainty	http://tiny.cc/DnJnD	STRATEGIC	9/15/2007	Ghattas, Omar	TX	University of Texas at Austin	$10,000.00
726012	The NMI Build and Test Laboratory at the University of Wisconsin-Madison	http://tiny.cc/LxL1b	STRATEGIC	9/1/2007	Livny, Miron	WI	University of Wisconsin-Madison	$1,000,000.00
726077	Network Startup Resource Center (NSRC): Collaboration for Education, Outreach and Training	http://tiny.cc/HQeH5	STRATEGIC	9/1/2007	Smith, Dale	OR	University of Oregon Eugene	$850,000.00

CPSIA information can be obtained at www.ICGtesting.com
Printed in the USA
LVOW081330060713

341391LV00001B/85/P